Panting for Glory

Number 151
Williams-Ford
Texas A&M University
Military History Series

Richard Bruce Winders

Panting for Glory

The Mississippi Rifles in the Mexican War

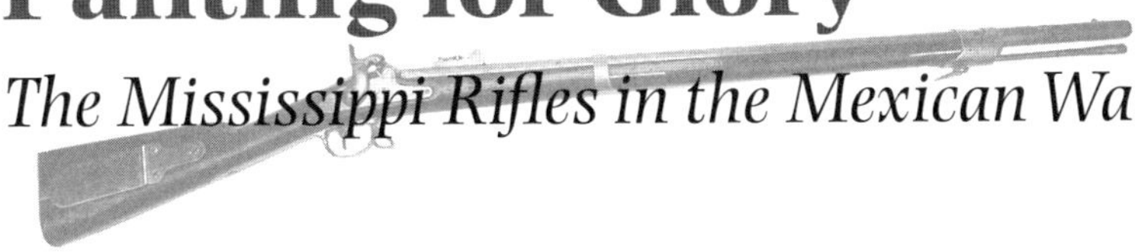

Texas A&M University Press
College Station

First edition

This paper meets the requirements of
ANSI/NISO Z39.48–1992 (Permanence of Paper).
Binding materials have been chosen
for durability.

Manufactured in the
United States of America

Library of Congress
Cataloging-in-Publication Data

Name: Winders, Richard Bruce, 1953– author.

Title: Panting for glory : the Mississippi Rifles in the Mexican War / Richard Bruce Winders

Other titles: Williams-Ford Texas A&M University military history series ; no. 151

Description: First edition. | College Station : Texas A&M University Press, [2016] | Series: Williams-Ford Texas A&M University military history series ; number 151 | Includes bibliographical references and index.

Identifiers: LCCN 2016004930 | ISBN 9781623494162 (book/cloth : alk. paper) | ISBN 9781623494179 (e-book)

Subjects LCSH: United States. Army. Mississippi Infantry Regiment, 1st (1846–1848)—History. | United States. Army. Mississippi Infantry Regiment, 2nd (1846–1848)—History. | Mexican War, 1846–1848—Regimental histories—Mississippi. | Mexican War, 1846–1848—Campaigns, Mexico.

Classification: LCC E409.5.M56 W56 2016 | DDC 973.6/2—dc23 LC record available at http://lccn.loc.gov/2016004930

CONTENTS

ACKNOWLEDGMENTS

Panting for Glory: The Mississippi Rifles in the Mexican War is a book that was 25 years in the making. Like most students of American military history, I was familiar with the red-shirted heroes of Buena Vista and their commander, Col. Jefferson Davis. Thus, as someone working on his master's thesis in the mid-1980s at the University of Texas at Arlington, I was delighted to find a collection of letters from Lt. Andrew Jackson Trussell. As I read his letters, I found that although a member of the Mississippi Rifles, he belonged to the regiment commanded by Rueben Davis, not Jefferson Davis. The experience of the two regiments—the 1st Mississippi Rifles and the 2nd Mississippi Rifles—could not have been more different: fame and glory for one and disappointment and heartbreak for the other. The study of these two regiments became my 1990 MA thesis, *The Role of the Mississippi Volunteers in Northern Mexico*.

I had intended to publish my manuscript, but fate intervened. I went on to work on my doctorate at Texas Christian University under the direction of Dr. Grady McWhiney. My work on Mcxican War soldiers expanded to cover all troops, both volunteers and regulars. My dissertation formed the basis of my first book, *Mr. Polk's Army: The American Military Experience in the Mexican War*. Shortly after graduating from TCU, an incredible opportunity came my way. Offered the position of Historian and Curator at the Alamo, I moved to San Antonio and shifted my focus to the Texas Revolution and its earlier conflicts with Mexico. Two other books followed: *Crisis in the Southwest: The United States, Mexico and the Struggle over Texas* and *Sacrificed at the Alamo: Tragedy and Triumph in the Texas Revolution*. Nevertheless, my work on the Mississippi Rifles was always at the back of my mind.

Unknown to me at the time I produced my thesis, others were also writing on the topic of the Mississippi Rifles. I ascribe my ignorance to the arrogance often inherent in the youthful scholar. One person who would publish two books on the Mississippi Rifles was Dr. Joseph E. Chance, a former professor of mathematics who happens to be an excellent Mexican War historian. One volume was on Jefferson Davis and the 1st Mississippi Rifles, and the other was an edited diary of Mississippi

Lt. Franklin Smith. Another scholar, William C. Davis, was completing his biography on Jefferson Davis. During this same time Grady Howell Jr., a tireless researcher, was collecting information for his reference works on Mississippi Volunteers. Howell was soon to edit and publish the wartime diary of Thomas N. Love, the surgeon of the 2nd Mississippi Rifles. Access to their work, combined with an opportunity to mature as a historian, has allowed me to produce a more meaningful study than my original thesis. Life has shown me that things happen for a reason.

The field of Mexican War studies has undergone a maturation period as well. Several authors have produced insightful and valuable studies since the publication of *Mr. Polk's Army*. These authors include Timothy D. Johnson, Amy S. Greenberg, Paul Foos, David Clary, Steven E. Woodworth, Joseph Wheelen, John Pinheiro, Irving Levinson, Brian Delay, Robert W. Merry, Tom Reilly, Manley Witten, Chris Dishman, and Doug Murphy. Not only have these authors produced new overviews of the war, but several have explored specific campaigns and battles, the Mexican War press, Polk and his contemporaries, and even Native Americans. These later works are important because they demonstrate that scholars—no longer satisfied with the well-worn memes of "stolen territory" and "Civil War rehearsal"—are beginning to look deeper into the conflict, its causes, conflicts, and ramifications.

I would like to acknowledge those who have helped in in my work. Dr. Douglas W. Richmond, Dr. Gerald Saxon, and Dr. Stephen Maizlish were the members of my thesis committee at UTA. Dr. Grady McWhiney, who passed away several years ago, was my mentor at TCU. He was a true scholar who set an example for all his students to follow. Joe Chance, who I now count as a friend, still amazes me with his high volume of output. Like "Doc" McWhiney, independent scholar Jack Davis has set the standard high for academic yet readable history. Special thanks go to David Jackson, The Sommerfield Roberts Foundation, West Point Museum, and the San Jacito Museum of History for making available artwork that appears in the book. Thanks, too, to those who read the manuscript and offered their advice. Dr. Donald S. Frazier generously provided the maps that appear in this volume. Special thanks to my wife, Sharon, without whose support none of this would have been possible.

Preface
Glory

"The hero pants for glory in the field."

Splendor; magnificence; Praise ascribed in adoration; honor; Honor; praise; fame; renown; celebrity; Distinguished honor or ornament; that which honors or makes renowned; that of which one may boast; To boast; to be proud of.—Definitions of "glory" from *Webster's Dictionary* (1828 edition)

The Song of Death
Thou strik'st the dull peasant—he sinks in the dark,
Nor saves *e'en* the wreck of a name;
Thou strik'st the young hero—a glorious mark;
He falls in the blaze of his fame!
In the field of proud honour—our swords in our hands,
Our King and our country to save;
While victory shines on Life's last ebbing sands,
O! who would not die with the brave!
—Robert Burns

The quest for personal, state, and national glory was a powerful motive in the Mexican War. The possibility of achieving it was thought worth the risk of one's life. Those who found it returned home heroes, lauded by their families, friends, neighbors, and even strangers. Those who failed in their quest quietly returned home with their sacrifices and hardships unrecognized. Attaining glory made for reputation, honor, and a bright future. The lack of it left a soldier with his hope for fame unfilled—a peasant among heroes.

What follows is a tale of two regiments. The 1st Mississippi Rifles returned home arguably the most famous volunteer regiment of the Mexican War. To their fellow Mississippians, Col. Jefferson Davis and his men represented the best their state had to offer. They were tested in battle and excelled. Their fame and glory spread to the national stage, making them America's heroes too. As the *Woodville Republican* explained, in the future it would be "sufficient to mark a man for distinction and honor for him to say, 'I was one of the 1st Mississippi Regiment.'"

The 2nd Mississippi Rifles returned home unheralded. The parades and feasts held for their predecessors failed to materialize. The regiment had experienced hardships unequalled by other volunteer regiments.[1] But unlike the 1st Mississippi Rifles, the war offered them no battlefields such as Monterrey or Buena Vista upon which they could cover themselves in glory. The connection between glory and fame was well recognized by these men. Garrison duty, although necessary, did not make heroes. Wrote one disappointed member of the regiment, Lt. Andrew Jackson Trussell, "If we could get in one hard battle and I could come out safe, we could then return home with some honor." Another member of the regiment, Everand Dowsing, stated the situation even more clearly: "I sometimes think of resigning when I reflect upon the dull and cheerless prospect before us. . . . We fancy that we are as brave as the first Regt. and pant for an opportunity to show it."

These two regiments, the 1st and 2nd Mississippi Rifles, offer the perfect opportunity to examine two sides of war: glory gained and glory denied. The experiences of both regiments, although very different, present a complete picture of volunteers at war. It also highlights the role that opportunity or chance plays in shaping a regiment's wartime record. Without the opportunity, there is no battle. Without a battle, there is no glory. Without glory there are no heroes but only those who sink in the darkness with no one to speak their name. This book speaks the names of both regiments—the famous and the forgotten.

Panting for Glory

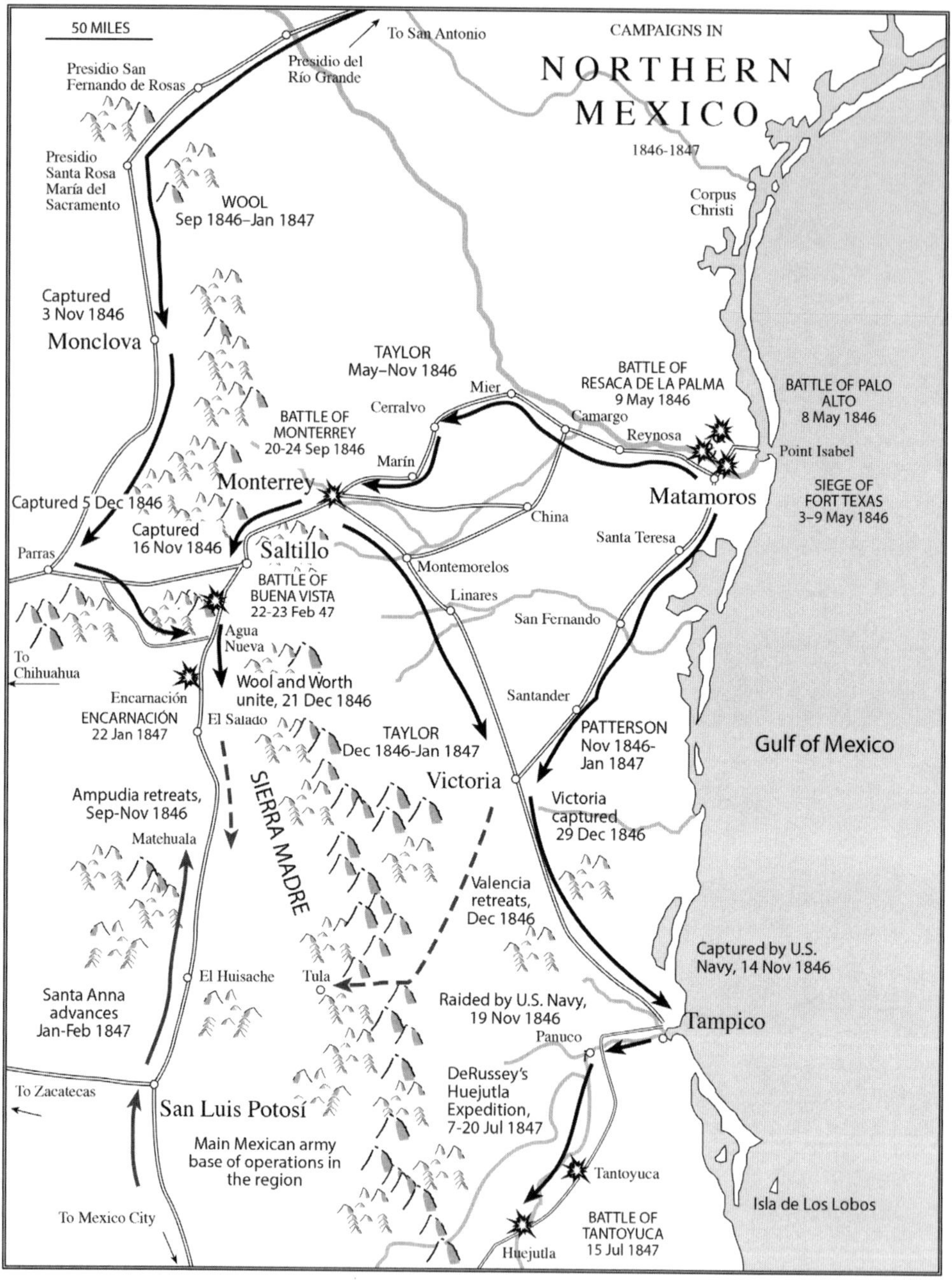

CAMPAIGNS IN
NORTHERN MEXICO
1846-1847
50 MILES
To San Antonio
Presidio San Fernando de Rosas
Presidio del Río Grande
Presidio Santa Rosa María del Sacramento
WOOL
Sep 1846–Jan 1847
Corpus Christi
Captured 3 Nov 1846
Monclova
TAYLOR
May–Nov 1846
BATTLE OF RESACA DE LA PALMA
9 May 1846
BATTLE OF PALO ALTO
8 May 1846
Mier
Cerralvo
Camargo
Reynosa
Point Isabel
BATTLE OF MONTERREY
20-24 Sep 1846
Marín
Monterrey
Matamoros
SIEGE OF FORT TEXAS
3–9 May 1846
China
Captured 5 Dec 1846
Captured 16 Nov 1846
Saltillo
Santa Teresa
Parras
BATTLE OF BUENA VISTA
22-23 Feb 47
Montemorelos
Linares
San Fernando
Agua Nueva
To Chihuahua
Wool and Worth unite, 21 Dec 1846
Encarnación
ENCARNACIÓN
22 Jan 1847
El Salado
Santander
TAYLOR
Dec 1846-Jan 1847
PATTERSON
Nov 1846-Jan 1847
Gulf of Mexico
Victoria
Ampudia retreats, Sep-Nov 1846
Victoria captured
29 Dec 1846
Matehuala
SIERRA MADRE
Valencia retreats, Dec 1846
Captured by U.S. Navy, 14 Nov 1846
El Huisache
Tula
Santa Anna advances
Jan-Feb 1847
Raided by U.S. Navy, 19 Nov 1846
Tampico
Panuco
To Zacatecas
DeRussey's Huejutla Expedition, 7-20 Jul 1847
San Luis Potosí
Main Mexican army base of operations in the region
Tantoyuca
Isla de Los Lobos
To Mexico City
BATTLE OF TANTOYUCA
15 Jul 1847
Huejutla

Introduction
Mississippi on the Eve of War

TO ARMS-TO ARMS!!! Your country now demands your services.
—Yazoo City Whig

THE STATE OF MISSISSIPPI WAS STILL in the process of shedding its frontier character when the United States went to war with Mexico in 1846. Admitted into the Union in 1817, Mississippi had only been a state for twenty-nine of the nation's seventy years. Formed out of the Old Southwest Territory, Mississippi's native population included the Natchez, Chickasaw, and Choctaw Indians.[1] The treaties of Doak's Stand, Dancing Rabbit Creek, and Pontotoc Creek helped open the way for the settlement of Mississippi. Searching for cheap virgin lands, new arrivals from older states quickly filled the areas ceded by these tribes. Settlers flooded into Mississippi, bringing American culture with them to the young frontier state. In the decade of the 1830s, the state's population increased from 136,806 to 239,030. Between 1833 and 1836, thirty new counties were formed. By 1840, Mississippi could boast of a population of 375,651 inhabitants.[2]

Mississippi's towns varied in size and civility. Natchez, the state's largest settlement, had 4,826 inhabitants. Located on the east bank of the Mississippi River 300 miles above New Orleans, Natchez had been the state's first capital and was its center of culture. Vicksburg, 100 miles upstream from Natchez, was steadily growing in influence and was fast becoming the state's major transportation hub. Nearly 4,000 Mississippians made Vicksburg their home. Jackson was 54 miles due east of Vicksburg and situated on the Pearl River. A recently completed rail line linked Jackson and Vicksburg. Jackson had fallen heir to the capital when legislators voted to move the seat of government to a more central location. Resenting the blow to the prestige of their community occasioned by the move, the citizens of Natchez looked down on the small backwoods town of only 1,500 inhabitants. On the state's eastern side, Columbus on the Tombigbee River was a center of transportation, communication, and commerce. Countless small villages and hamlets dotted the Mississippi countryside, home to the majority of antebellum Mississippians.[3]

The geography of the state varied, with pine-covered hills in the north, fertile plains in the center, and lowlands along the coast. Spanning five degrees of latitude, the state measures roughly 300 miles long and 150 miles wide. Bordered on the west by the winding Mississippi River, Mississippians looked to the waterway as a lifeline to the world. Snags and rafts blocked some of the state's other important rivers and progressive-minded Mississippians worked for legislation that would fund improved navigation on the Pearl, Pascagoula, Yazoo, Black, and Tennessee. The first settlers to the state had grown tobacco and indigo, but cotton thrived in Mississippi's soil and had become the big cash crop. Cotton production was centered along the east bank of the Mississippi River, from Vicksburg southward—the area that would later be famous as the Mississippi Delta. Planters raised small amounts of sugar cane along Mississippi's gulf coast. By 1840, Mississippians owned 195,211 slaves, with blacks outnumbering whites in the state by nearly 15,000. While many white Mississippians were small farmers, much like the rest of their fellow Americans throughout the nation, a significant planter class made its presence felt in the economy, society, and in politics.[4]

Many Mississippians admired Andrew Jackson and the democratic ideas for which he stood. The state's 1832 constitution eliminated property ownership as a qualification for voting and holding public office. The famous namesake of the state's capital had been responsible for the 1820 Treaty of Doak's Stand that turned many acres of Indian land over to new settlers. As president of the United States, Jackson continued to affect the development of the state. The policy of Indian removal that he so vigorously pursued opened the way for even more settlement of Mississippi's rich lands. President Jackson's fight with the Second National Bank created flush times in Mississippi as pet banks began to dole out money to fuel the fires of land speculation. In 1837, however, Jackson's Specie Circular dried up the flow of money necessary for the purchase of land. As a result of this action, many Mississippians were caught in the panic that followed, and a number left the state to seek better opportunities in Texas.[5]

Like most other Americans of their time, Mississippians believed in the republican ideals associated with the American Revolution. They welcomed Mexico's break with Spain and its adoption of the federal constitution of 1824. Dismay replaced joy, however, as Mexico entered a long period of political unrest that pitted backward-looking Centralists against forward-looking Federalists. In 1836 Mississippians sympathized with the American colonists living in Texas, then in revolt against the Mexican government headed by Antonio López de Santa Anna. Abandoning the Federalists, Santa Anna joined with the Centralists in their plan to discard the federal constitution. The move stripped all Mexican states of their own legislatures and concentrated political power in Mexico City. Reared on stories of British tyranny, Mississippians eagerly offered money and supplies to aid the republican rebellion in Texas. One Mississippian claimed that he could raise 10,000 men from the western states for the purpose of invading Mexico and capturing Mexico City. Another wrote to Mississippi Congressman Henry S. Foote that "I can raise 1000 to 2000 men here in Mississippi."[6]

Although the large numbers boasted by these men did not go to the rebels' aid, several prominent Mississippians lent their support to the cause of Texas independence. Felix H. Huston and Henry S. Foote raised funds to purchase weapons and other supplies for the rebels. Not satisfied with merely fundraising, Huston went to Texas where he rose to the rank of brigadier general in the new republic's army before returning to Mississippi. Another Mississippian, Natchez's John Anthony Quitman, led a band of seventy Mississippians to Texas to fight against Santa Anna's forces. Unfortunately for Quitman and his men, they reached Gen. Sam Houston's small army two days after the battle of San Jacinto, too late to see any action. Nonetheless, Mississippi could count its sons among the slain of both San Antonio de Béxar and Goliad. Clearly, Texas and her affairs had been a concern of Mississippians a full decade before the outbreak of the war in 1846.[7]

Geography helped determine political affiliation in Mississippi. Democrats dominated the poorer hill-covered land to the east while the cotton-producing west was inhabited by Whigs who favored that party's emphasis on economic growth. Nevertheless, the Mississippi government was firmly in the hands of the state's Democrats in the years directly preceding the Mexican War. In the hard-fought presidential election of 1844, the Whigs made a strong showing, with 19,206 ballots cast for Henry Clay. Democrat James Knox Polk, however, received 25,126 votes, making him the winner in Mississippi. Polk's promise to push for the reannexation of Texas strongly appealed to many Mississippians. Important Mississippi politicians had campaigned hard for their candidate, both within and outside their state, and they expected Polk to keep his campaign promises.[8]

Texans had hoped to join the United States shortly after the Texas Revolution, but many Americans feared that bringing in another slave state would upset the delicate balance of power between the slave and free states that existed at the time. Another deterrent to Texas statehood was Mexico's refusal to recognize the independence of her rebellious territory. Allowing Texas to enter the Union might touch off a war with that country. But by the 1840s, support for Texas statehood had grown until opposition to the move was overcome.[9] Mississippi proponents of statehood for Texas included Gov. Albert G. Brown, Sen. Henry S. Foote, Gen. Felix Huston, John A. Quitman, US Secretary of the Treasury Robert Walker, and newly elected US Representative Jefferson Davis.[10] A proposed 1844 treaty between the United States and the Republic of Texas that would have granted statehood failed to pass the US Senate. The issue, however, was not dead. With John Tyler's urging, Congressional leaders maneuvered through Congress a joint resolution calling for the annexation of Texas to the United States. By February 28, 1845, both houses had passed the resolution to annex Texas to the United States.[11] Although Congress had admitted Texas to the Union with a stroke of a pen, it was up to the incoming president, James K. Polk, to make the action a reality. Mexico contested the annexation, warning that such an act on the part of the United States would result in a war between the two nations. Polk tried unsuccessfully to soothe Mexico's ruffled national pride by sending an emissary to offer money in exchange for Mexican concessions on their land.[12] In both countries, talk of the inevitability of war increased. By the year's end, even the previously anti-expansionist *Yazoo City Whig* announced "War is just if we must."[13]

On December 29, 1845, Texas officially became the twenty-eighth state of the Union. The newly acquired state needed protection, prompting a buildup of US troops at Fort Jessup located near the border between Louisiana and Texas. In June 1845, Polk ordered Bvt. Gen. Zachary Taylor and 1,200 US regulars to advance into Texas. For the next eight months, the general and his men camped near the mouth of the Nueces River at Kinney's Ranch, the location of the future city of Corpus Christi. Arriving reinforcements brought Taylor's strength up to nearly 3,000—about half of the total US Army. In March 1846, Taylor followed Polk's instructions to advance south to the Rio Grande. Taylor established positions at the mouth of the river (Point Isabel/Brazos Santiago) and directly across from the inland port of Matamoros (Fort Texas). The Mexican government perceived Taylor's move to the Rio Grande as a provocation and amassed its own troops along the river. A clash of arms was inevitable. On April 26, 1846, Mexican troops crossed the river and ambushed a detachment of 60 US Dragoons, killing eleven, wounding six, and capturing the rest. Having bloodied Taylor's forces, the Mexicans seized the initiative and launched a major offensive. To their chagrin, Taylor's well-trained army of regulars bested them in the ensuing battles along the Rio Grande.

When President Polk learned of the attack on the American dragoons, he immediately notified the US Congress of Mexico's actions. In his message, Polk announced that a state of war existed between Mexico and the United States and asked Congress to approve a bill allowing for the swift prosecution of the conflict. On May 13, 1846, while in a state of patriotic frenzy, Congress complied with President Polk's request and authorized the raising of 50,000 volunteers to supplement the US Army. All Mississippi Congressmen present showed their support for the president and voted "yea" on the war measure. It passed overwhelmingly.[14]

Mississippi and the nation prepared for war with Mexico. As in the Texas revolt 10 short years before, Americans were eager to defend their honor and carry their republican ideals onto Mexican soil. *The Yazoo City Whig* now shouted out the call, "TO ARMS-TO ARMS!!! Your country now demands your services."[15]

Mississippians heeded the call. During the war, 2,423 Mississippians volunteered to fight for their country. Many more wanted to serve but were denied the opportunity. Mississippians made up over 3 percent of the total number of 72,932 Mexican War volunteers. The state ranked eleventh in order of the number of men who came forward to volunteer. Mississippi supplied three units for the American war effort: one twelve-month regiment, one regiment for the duration of the war, and one five-company battalion for the duration of the war. Although some states provided greater numbers of volunteers, few if any played as great of a role as Mississippi during the Mexican War.[16]

I
Mobilizing Mississippi for War

Our people are in a state of the highest excitement. Old and young, rich and poor, democrats and whigs, are ready to volunteer.
—Gen. John A. Quitman

WAR FEVER RAN HIGH IN MISSISSIPPI in the spring of 1846, and many of her young men had been stricken. Citing the "warlike attitude on the Texas frontier," the owner of Russell's Clothing Depot of Jackson proudly notified his customers that he had taken the precaution of stocking up on ready-made clothing for volunteers who wished to go to Mexico. Confident of the coming conflict, Russell placed the ad several weeks before fighting on the distant Rio Grande actually began. Once hostilities commenced, John A. Quitman, a leading light of the Mississippi militia, urged speedy action. Wrote Quitman, "Our people are in a state of the highest excitement. Old and young, rich and poor, democrats and whigs, are ready to volunteer." Noted the editors of *The Southron*, "Our volunteers are rapidly equipping themselves. They are a noble set of fellows, and we never look at one of them but with emotions of the most gratifying kinds."[1]

Mississippians had their fighting spirit up, and no one wanted to be left behind. Companies from all over the state responded quickly to President Polk's call for volunteers in the war against Mexico. Congress specified that 20,000 of the 50,000 required volunteers were to be provided by the western and southwestern states. Many Mississippians were disappointed—even outraged—to learn that their state had been asked to provide only one regiment. This caused a great dilemma for Gov. Albert G. Brown and the state's militia officials who together faced the chore of overseeing the selection and mustering in of the state's volunteers. Only ten companies—just under 1,000 men—would be allowed to serve even though enough men to fill more than twenty-two companies volunteered. No matter who was chosen to represent the honor of the state, many unhappy constituents would be left at home when the 1st Mississippi Rifles set off for Mexico.[2] The US government missed a golden opportunity when it did not find a way to use this pool of eager volunteers; at no other time in the war would the enthusiasm to volunteer for service in Mexico be so strong. Subsequent units from Mississippi would later struggle to fill their ranks.

As in the case of other volunteers, the Mississippi companies destined for Mexico formed around units that already existed within the state's militia system. Mississippi was divided into five militia divisions, with each division commanded by a major general: 1st Division, Maj. Gen. William L. Brandon; 2nd Division, Maj. Gen. Arthur Fox; 3rd Division, John M. Duffield; 4th Division, Maj. Gen. C. F. Hemingway; and 5th Division, John C. Bradford (John A. Quitman had been the major general of the 2nd Division). These divisions were further subdivided into two brigades. In theory, each one of Mississippi's sixty-eight counties could provide a regiment of ten companies composed of citizens from its towns and rural areas. All five divisions were under the command of the governor.[3]

Governor Brown encountered several problems following the president's call for volunteers. First, Maj. Gen. William L. Brandon of the 1st Division and Maj. Gen. John M. Duffield of the 3rd Division both laid claim to the right to select and muster in the volunteers. Brown angered Brandon's supporters by siding with Duffield. Next, in a situation guaranteed to create political enemies, Governor Brown and General Duffield had to decide which of the twenty-two companies that applied would be accepted. Third, Brown received the wrath of most of the state's citizens and all of the aspiring volunteers when he delayed issuing the call for volunteers nearly three weeks while waiting on the War Department to provide funds needed to raise the new regiment.[4] His tardiness meant other states' volunteers would reach the front before the Mississippians. Brown explained the lack of alacrity, saying "that he had neither the power nor the pecuniary means to meet their wishes: that war was declared: that fifty thousand soldiers and ten millions of money were at the disposal of the President: that it would require time for the President to plan the campaign, to concentrate, and dispose of such an immense force." He advised his constituents that "So soon as ten companies are organized, they will be rendezvoused at Vicksburg or Jackson, and mustered into the service of the U. States." Brown cautioned, though, "There will doubtlessly be many, very many more, to tender their services than can be accepted."[5]

General Edmund P. Gaines, the ranking US officer in the southwest, complicated matters for Governor Brown even further. Monitoring events from his headquarters in New Orleans, Gaines had anticipated Taylor's needs and issued his own call for volunteers for Mexico. Brown was led to believe by Gaines that as many as twenty-eight companies might be accepted by the federal government. In fact, Congress did not recognize the impromptu call for volunteers made by General Gaines. Some of the regiments raised under Gaines's call arrived at the mouth of the Rio Grande only to be rejected and sent home.[6]

The process of raising volunteer companies began on the local level in Mississippi soon after the news of the battles of May 8 and 9 at Palo Alto and Resaca de la Palma appeared in their newspapers. The citizens of Marion, in Lauderdale County, met to discuss raising a company of volunteers. The meeting produced a resolution to "cheerfully respond to the call, and by that means be immediately taken to raise one Company of Volunteer Riflemen." They were encouraged to join up by William J. Daniels, himself a volunteer to Texas in 1842.[7] Members and supporters of two established militia companies, the State Fencibles and the Jackson Dragoons, attended a rally at Jackson reported to be the largest gathering the state's capital had ever seen.[8]

Speed seemed to be the utmost concern and only added to the confusion that already existed. C. W. Clifton, former captain of the State Fencibles, chose not to wait for the state's call and accepted an appointment from Gaines to raise a regiment under the general's unauthorized call.[9] By the end of May, though, the situation was stabilizing and the following companies reported that they were ready to be called on to perform their duty: Natchez Guards, Carroll County Volunteers, Columbus Riflemen, Marshall Guards, Attala Guards, Monroe Troops, Yazoo Volunteers, Raymond Volunteers, Wilkinson Volunteers, Southrons, Piney-woods Dragoons, State Fencibles, and Jackson Cavalry. The popular cry "For the Halls of the Montezumas!" summed up the war-like mood of the state. One Jackson mercantile establishment, Richardson & Fearn's, used the slogan in an advertisement for horse tack to urge the volunteers on, as well as to drum up business for the store.[10]

Toward the end of May, details concerning the regiment from Mississippi called for by Congress began to appear in area newspapers. Secretary of War William L. Marcy notified Governor Brown in a letter dated May 16 that his state was to supply one regiment of infantry or riflemen—the state could choose which it preferred. The regiment was to consist of ten companies of eighty privates each. In addition, each company was to have two musicians, four corporals, four sergeants, one 2nd lieutenant, one 1st lieutenant, and one captain. This brought the strength of each company to ninety-three officers and enlisted men. The regimental staff was to consist of two principal musicians and one each of the following: quartermaster sergeant, sergeant major, adjutant, major, lieutenant colonel, and colonel. Brown designated Vicksburg as the place of rendezvous for the state's volunteers. Companies were to be accepted on a first-come basis, a policy that invoked much criticism from the governor's detractors.[11]

When the governor finally announced the regiment's formation, many Mississippians were still angry that their state had been asked to supply such a small number of volunteers. In an attempt to appease his constituents, Governor Brown suggested to Marcy that Mississippians be allowed to fill the quotas of other states so more of his state's citizens could serve. Quitman complained, "Our people are proud and spirited. They will not volunteer while subject to the mortification of having their services rejected." Moreover, he claimed, Mississippi was entitled to the opportunity because "from the blood and treasure she has poured out in the cause of Texas, when dangers, not laurels were to be reaped." Even the designation as foot troops troubled some of the would-be volunteers. Mounted companies, such as the Jackson Dragoons and the Jefferson Troops, were excluded from the call. The captain of one mounted company, the Pontotoc Dragoons, wrote to Congressman Jefferson Davis to express their disappointment and to ask for his assistance. Davis passed the letter along to the War Department. He was soon to be concerned with the affairs of the Mississippi volunteers in a much more personal way.[12]

In Carrollton, the home of the Carroll County Volunteers, the editors of *The Mississippi Democrat* pondered why men such as these were so eager to leave their friends and families and the comforts of home to endure the dangers and hardships of the field. They stated that they were "actuated by no other feeling than devotion to their country." The departing volunteers were the pride of their families and were being sent off by their fathers, mothers, sisters, and sweethearts with admonitions to prove worthy "of the high name of an American citizen-soldier" and "to incur no dishonor." The editors toasted the volunteers, saying, "Health and good fortune attend our gallant friends!"[13] Words and sentiments like this were repeated across the state as young Mississippians marched off to war.

The companies used the most expedient methods of travel available to bring them from their region of the state to the rendezvous at Vicksburg. Some came by rail. Some marched. Others steamed up or down the rivers. Most arrived without mishap. Samuel Woods of the Wilkinson County Volunteers, though, fell, from the steamer *Cora*; the cause of the fall remained undetermined by authorities.[14] In an effort to expedite the formation of the regiment, Governor Brown authorized the captains of companies to receive loans and give receipts for the cost of subsistence and transportation they incurred for their companies in route to Vicksburg. The governor still had received no funds from the War Department.[15]

Many volunteers and their supporters were upset with Governor Brown and General Duffield at the method employed in the selection of companies for the regiment. Complaints against the policy of "first to come, first to serve" appeared in local newspapers, which claimed that it gave an unfair advantage and preference to those companies near Vicksburg, the spot selected for the rendezvous.[16] There was merit to these accusations: two of the ten companies finally accepted were raised within the city of Vicksburg. The citizens of Natchez, disappointed at not having been chosen as the site of the rendezvous, felt further insulted when they read that General Duffield had rejected the Natchez Fencibles for reporting to the muster with only ninety-two men, one short of the required number of ninety-three. The absent man had reportedly gone for a drink of water and Duffield refused to wait for his return, rejecting the company in favor of another. "[T]he deep and bitter mortification they express makes the blood run warm in sympathy for their unfortunate rejection," proclaimed a gathering of Natchez residents. Some would even claim that Governor Brown colluded with Jefferson Davis to keep the Natchez company out of the new regiment in favor of his neighbors.[17]

On June 3, 1846, the Vicksburg Southrons became the first company of the Mississippi regiment to be accepted and mustered into service. Others soon arrived and went through the process of being brought into the federal service. The volunteers were first sent to an empty warehouse in the city that served as temporary barracks, which the men found hot and uncomfortable. Officials relocated the regiment to Camp Independence, a camping ground located about one mile south of town in a grove under the Vicksburg bluffs. By June 10, the remaining companies had been selected and mustered in to service.[18] The ten companies and their captains who composed the 1st Mississippi Rifles at its organization at Vicksburg were

Company A: Yazoo Rifles	Capt. John M. Sharp
Company B: Wilkinson Volunteers	Capt. Douglas H. Cooper
Company C: Vicksburg Southrons	Capt. John Willis
Company D: Carroll County Volunteers	Capt. Bainbridge D. Howard
Company E: State Fencibles	Capt. John L. McManus
Company F: Lafayette Volunteers	Capt. William Delay
Company G: Raymond Fencibles	Capt. Rueben Downing
Company H: Vicksburg Volunteers	Capt. George Crump
Company I: Marshall Guards	Capt. James H. R. Taylor
Company K: Tombigbee Volunteers	Capt. Alexander K. McClung

The regiment seemed blessed with experienced company commanders, as most had captained militia companies. The list of militia captains included Sharp (Yazoo Mounted Infantry), Cooper (Wilkinson County Volunteers), Willis (Light Artillery Corps, Vicksburg Southrons), McManus (State Fencibles), Delay (Lafayette Volunteers), and Downing (Raymond Fencibles). Although the men banded together in this regiment did not know it at the time, they were destined to win fame and glory at battles yet to be fought.[19]

The volunteers under the bluff at Vicksburg continued to voice complaints, both to each other and to their newspaper editors back home. While some officers tried to make use of idle time to turn the young men under their care into something resembling soldiers, *The Vicksburg Sentinel* boasted that Mississippians could fight well enough without being drilled by officers who behaved like martinets. The article's author boasted, "The best fighting ever done in the world has been done by men who had no knowledge whatsoever of these technicalities. The men who won San Jacinto, and the brave volunteers that sent back Wellington's regulars discomforted and dismayed from the plains of Chalmette, were under no martinets and petty formalists; but in their own known way permitted to pick to whites of the eyes of their enemies."[20] The knowledge that the regiments from Kentucky and Tennessee were already on their way to join General Taylor on the Rio Grande added to their misery as the Mississippians sat sweltering in their camp under the bluffs battling fierce mosquitoes. To add fuel to the already incendiary editorials, a stream of sick recruits was already starting to trickle out of Vicksburg and back to their homes. One member of the Lafayette Guards (Company F) even died at Camp Independence.[21] Mississippians were incensed that their sons' lives were being wasted while there was a war to be fought. Little did they realize that this was only the prelude to the events of the next two years. Still, one Carroll County Volunteer (Company D), Leon Trousdale, believed, "We have been remarkably healthy in camp, when we consider the great and sudden change in our mode of living, climate, water, &c."[22]

The next step in the formation of the regiment was the selection of a major, lieutenant colonel, and colonel. It had long been the custom under the militia system for all company and field officers to be elected by the men of the regiment. Elections to fill the positions of captains, lieutenants, sergeants, and corporals had been taking place throughout the state of Mississippi during the month of May.[23] Now that the companies were together at Vicksburg, it was time to elect the regimental field officers.

Several names already had been proposed for the position of colonel, and it promised to be a hotly contested race. Supporters of John A. Quitman, John M. Duffield, and William L. Brandon lobbied for their respective candidate. Each was a former or current major general of the state's militia.[24] But another name was offered for consideration—Jefferson Davis. Davis was currently serving his state in the US House of Representatives in Washington, DC. When the election for colonel was held on June 18, 1846, Alexander B. Bradford received 350 to Davis's 300 votes. But Bradford—a veteran of the War of 1812 and the Seminole War and former captain of the Marshall Guards—declined the office because he felt he did not have a sufficient majority to assume the post. He called for another ballot. This time Davis was the clear winner by a margin of 147 votes.[25] By the end of June, news of his election had reached Davis in Washington, DC. Davis replied to Governor Brown: "I have the honor to acknowledge and accept the commission of Colonel in the 1st Regiment of Mississippi Volunteers."[26]

The regiment filled the post of lieutenant colonel on the same day it elected Davis as colonel. Several men aspired for the position as second-in-command. Captain Alexander K. McClung (Company K, Tombigbee Volunteers) defeated Major General Duffield and Capt. Reuben E. Downing (Company G, Raymond Fencibles), both unsuccessful contenders in the race of colonel. (Company K elected William P. Rogers to fill the position just vacated by McClung.)[27] McClung had built a reputation in the South as a man who let no insult go unpunished. A noted duelist, McClung's sense of honor and daring made him a natural leader the Mississippians would gladly follow into battle. Alexander B. Bradford, another loser in the race for colonel, was elected the regiment's major the next day.[28] Although Bradford often remained in the background during the regiment's year of service, he performed the task well and commanded the 1st Mississippi for a time in the absence of both Davis and McClung. The editor of *The Republican* expressed his disappointment in the fact that Woodville's local favorites had been passed by but still applauded the elections: "Though our fellow citizens, Gen. Brandon and Col. Cooper have not been elected to either of the offices of the Mississippi regiment of volunteers, and foul play was used to defeat the latter, yet as good men and true have been put in command, there is no objection, but much can be said in their praises."[29]

One leading citizen who would be linked to a second mid-war regiment composed of Mississippians later recalled the officers and men of the 1st Mississippi Rifles. Rueben Davis claimed, "No new troops were better officered, and the regiment went to the field as gayly as if they had been called to a dance. The field officers were already widely known. The company officers and privates were citizens drawn from the various vocations of a prosperous people." Jefferson Davis "had graduated from West Point, and had seen some service in the West during the Black Hawk War." In addition to being courageous and gentlemanly, Rueben Davis reminded people that McClung "belonged to the most intellectual families of Kentucky, the Marshalls, Breckenridges, etc." As for Bradford, not only was he brave but "All the pomp and circumstances of war gave him the purest enjoyment."[30] Who would not want to be commanded by men such as these?

In June 1846 other Mississippians sought appointments in the US Army. Upon the recommendation of Jefferson Davis, the War Department awarded positions to these men whose careers would in some way be linked to the 1st Mississippi Rifles: William Babbit, brigade quartermaster of commissary; Franklin Smith, assistant quartermaster; and Kemp S. Holland (Company A, Yazoo Volunteers), assistant commissary of subsistence. Two doctors who had enlisted in the regiment as privates received positions that would make better use of their much-needed skills. Seymour Halsey (Company C, Vicksburg Southrons) was appointed surgeon while John

Thompson (Company F: Lafayette Volunteers) received the lesser rank of assistant surgeon.[31]

Jefferson Davis's election as colonel of the Mississippi regiment proved to be very fortunate for the volunteers from his state. Largely responsible for the regiment's successes in Mexico, Davis made two significant contributions to the 1st Mississippi Rifles: his military training and his political connections. An 1828 graduate of West Point, Davis had participated in the Black Hawk War in 1832. He transferred soon after to a newly created dragoon regiment and saw limited action against the Plains Indians. Davis resigned from the army in 1835 in order to marry Sarah Knox Taylor, the daughter of then Colonel Zachary Taylor. In an act uncharacteristic for the time and people of their rank in society, the couple supposedly wed against Taylor's wishes. Davis returned to Mississippi with his new bride, who tragically died a short time later. The grieving widower tended his plantation, mourning his loss for nearly a decade before reentering society. In 1843, the 35-year-old Davis met a new love, Varina Banks Howell. Although 18 years his junior, she and Davis were married in 1845. That same year, Davis left Mississippi for Washington, DC, to take possession of his recently won seat in the US House of Representatives. As a Democratic Congressman, Davis helped marshal votes for the administration's tariff bill before leaving Washington to join his regiment. As a reward for his support on the measure, President Polk instructed the War Department to honor Davis's request for enough new pattern percussion rifles to arm his entire regiment. Davis requested this new firearm to help make his regiment distinctive as well as more effective. So while the volunteer regiments from other states would carry conventional flintlock muskets into the field, Mississippians proudly shouldered the excellent Model 1841 Rifle made by the Whitney Arms Company of New Haven, Connecticut, a weapon that came to be known as the "Mississippi Rifle." Although promised the weapon by Polk, Davis had to overcome the opposition of the Commanding General of the US Army, Winfield Scott. After learning of Davis's request, Scott asked that the Mississippian visit him at his office, where he "expressed a doubt as to the propriety of [arming] a whole Regiment with percussion arms and positively insisted that at least six of the Companies should be armed with Muskets, instead of rifles. I knew the confidence the Men I was expecting to lead had in rifles, and their distrust of the musket then in use and therefore notwithstanding my reluctance to oppose the General insisted upon the thousands rifles and claimed from the Secretary [of War] the fulfillment of the President's promise to me." Thus Davis exerted influence on his regiment even before he was united with the men he would command.[32]

Before he left Congress to take charge of his regiment of volunteers, Davis had the opportunity to discuss his belief in and support of West Point and the value of those like himself it had educated. He ascribed Taylor's ability to defeat a superior force to the professionally trained officers—graduates of West Point—serving with his army now on the Rio Grande. He stated that these victories were "the triumph of American courage, professional skill, and the patriotic pride which blooms in the breast of our educated soldier."[33] An even clearer picture of Davis's military philosophy emerged when he advised a young Mississippian seeking an appointment to West Point. Wrote the future hero of Monterrey and Buena Vista: "a superior mind may learn the professions of arms by the experience of service, but the process is slow and toilsome, and the knowledge never sits upon the possessor like a garmen[t] made for the wearer. An officer of Infantry has little opportunity to learn those things which pertain to artillery, still less those great lessons of Engineering the ignorance of which must always cause the useless expenditure of blood, if it does not bring defeat. The commander who is familiar with principles of fortification reconnoitres an enemy's position, sees a part, and knows the whole; without this knowledge he would probably attempt to avoid the salient which he saw, and fall upon the curtain, where both salients would throw a converging fire upon his troops. Still more in defence than in attack are the resources of the Science of War put in requisition."[34] Colonel Jefferson Davis would put his faith in his training on the fields of Mexico and expect the 1st Mississippi Rifles to rise to his high standard. He was determined to make his volunteers perform as well as any regulars.

2
Off to War

The Mississippi Regiment is under the immediate command of "Old Rough and Ready."
—*The Southron*

THINGS BEGAN TO MOVE QUICKLY for the members of the 1st Mississippi Rifles and their commander. Col. and Mrs. Jefferson Davis left Washington, DC, on the Fourth of July, 1846. Varina had confided to her mother that her husband had promised her he would not volunteer but that he "could not help" answering the call to arms. Lamenting his decision, she wrote, "I can bear it but God only knows how bitter it is to me." The couple traveled overland by stage to the Ohio River where Davis arranged passage westward down the waterway to its junction with the Mississippi and then south to New Orleans. Appropriately named, the steamer *Star Spangled Banner* carried the future hero on his journey to assume command of the 1st Mississippi Rifles. Davis, eager to join his regiment, took time to address crowds of citizens that gathered around the boat at stops along the river. Varina Davis, much less enthusiastic about his deployment, had secretly hoped her husband's regiment would not be accepted and that he could remain at home with her, safe and out of danger.[1]

Strategically located near the mouth of the Mississippi River, New Orleans had long been recognized as one of the nation's most important trade and transportation centers. With the outbreak of hostilities between the United States and Mexico, the city became vital to the United States' effort to move troops and supplies to the front. The summer of 1846 brought a flood of volunteers, including Jefferson Davis's Mississippians, through New Orleans on their way to Mexico.[2] Maj. Roger S. Dix of the Pay Department and Lt. Irvin McDowell, an aide to Gen. John E. Wool, had delivered an order from the War Department for the 1st Mississippi Rifles to depart Vicksburg and proceed to New Orleans without Davis.[3] Secretary of War Marcy had given Wool the responsibility of mustering in and transporting volunteers raised in the Mississippi Valley to the seat of war. Before leaving for New Orleans, Major Dix advanced the Mississippians six months' clothing allowance, a sum of $21 each. In the early stages of the war, the government provided money for the volunteers to buy their clothing rather than issue uniforms from its meager stores.[4] This measure led to a wide range of colors and styles worn by the American volunteer regiments in Mexico. It is not clear what uniform, if any, the 1st Mississippi Rifles adopted at the beginning of the war. It was not uncommon for each company in a volunteer regiment to select a different uniform. These companies were from towns and counties that took fierce pride in their volunteers. The volunteers saw themselves as representatives of their communities and tried hard not to bring dishonor to their families, friends, and neighbors at home. Wives, mothers, and sisters gathered together to sew coats, shirts, trousers, and even flags for the men who were to represent their town and country.[5] The confusion created by this custom brought about a call from one Mississippian to end this awkward system that practically allowed every man to choose his own uniform.[6] There had been no shortage of businesses prepared to sell ready-made clothing to the volunteers from Mississippi.[7] Tailors were sometimes contracted to make sets of uniforms for entire companies. Although one witness later claimed that the Mississippi regiment was clothed in the later stage of its career in red overshirts, white pants, and black slouch hats, it is not likely that this was the original uniform the Mississippians wore to Mexico.[8]

On Saturday, July 11, Lieutenant Colonel McClung ordered the men of the 1st Mississippi Rifles to break camp at Vicksburg and board the steamers *Cora*, *M.B. Hamer*, and *Talma*. The Mississippians arrived in New Orleans the following Tuesday. The regiment had made a brief halt at the US arsenal at Baton Rouge to receive its arms and other equipment.[9] Ordnance officers were reluctant to arm an entire regiment with rifles because the custom of the day was for only the left and right flank companies to be so equipped. Only Companies A (Yazoo Volunteers) and I (Marshall Guards) received the promised rifles while the remaining companies were issued the old pattern flintlock muskets. These eight companies carried these flintlock muskets into Mexico where they later exchanged them for the new rifles. Once in New Orleans, the regiment camped on the site of Gen. Andrew Jackson's famous victory over the British in 1815.[10] The Mississippians were not the only regiment of volunteers in New Orleans at that time. They shared the campground on the old Chalmette battlefield with the 2nd and 3rd Indiana and the 2nd Ohio, all awaiting transportation to Mexico. They also shared it with clouds of mosquitoes that thrived along the river and the adjacent lowlands and bayous.[11]

Colonel Davis caught up with his regiment in the Crescent City on July 18, 1846. He found that some of his men had become ill from exposure, which they had endured since leaving their Mississippi homes. Davis arranged to have the sick moved to sheds at the edge of the battleground to lessen their suffering. Even so, the colonel discharged several volunteers from the regiment who were in poor health. Company A (Yazoo Volunteers) lost 1st Lt. Philip J. Burris, who resigned his commission at New Orleans.[12] The regiment, which numbered an aggregate of 941 officers and enlisted men at its muster, was losing men even before leaving the United States.[13]

Lieutenant Colonel Thomas F. Hunt, the deputy quartermaster general in New Orleans, arranged transportation for the 1st Mississippi Rifles to Mexico. The regiment set sail from New Orleans on July 22 and 23, 1846. Companies F (Lafayette Volunteers), G (Raymond Fencibles), and I (Marshall Guards) sailed on the *New York* under the command of Lieutenant Colonel McClung. Major Bradford accompanied Companies A (Yazoo Volunteers), D (Carroll County Volunteers), E (State Fencibles), and K (Tombigbee Volunteers) aboard the *Massachusetts*. Davis traveled with Companies B (Wilkinson Volunteers), C (Vicksburg Southrons), and H (Vicksburg Volunteers) on the *Alabama*. The steamers arrived at the mouth of the Rio Grande on July 26 and 27.[14] One tired volunteer compared the unpleasant trip across the Gulf of Mexico to that of convicts on a prison ship. On the *Massachusetts*, 18-year-old Private Marcellus Foute of Company E (State Fencibles) fell into the hold from the ship's deck. Though gravely injured, Foute continued on with his regiment.[15]

Volunteers on their way to the Rio Grande first disembarked at Brazos de Santiago, sometimes called Brazos Santiago or Brazos Island, a low island at the southern tip of Padre Island near the river's mouth. Brazos Island blocked the entrance to Laguna Madre, the bay that lay to the west of the barrier islands. The harbor behind Brazos Island and Padre Island was too shallow for oceangoing vessels. Men and supplies were unloaded on Brazos Island first and then reloaded onto light draft craft for the short trip to the mainland. The offloading of men and supplies greatly increased the work of the Quartermaster Department.[16]

The hulks of ships wrecked on the gulf side of Brazos Island greeted the volunteers and added to the desolate look of the place. A swamp lay in the center of the island, but the land gradually rose to the west, forming low sand hills. At its southern tip, the mainland was only about 80 yards away, and the water was shallow enough to wade across. Volunteers who crossed the shallow stretch of water, called Boca Chica, marched a short distance inland to one of the several camps established by Taylor for the purpose of marshalling troops and supplies. The largest of the camps was located at Point Isabel.[17]

On August 3, 1846, after spending a week on Brazos Island, the 1st Mississippi Rifles moved 9 or 10 miles inland. After establishing his camp on the Rio Grande, Davis contacted his former father-in-law, Gen. Zachary Taylor, to notify him of the arrival of the Mississippi regiment and to ask for instructions. In a short note to Davis, Taylor welcomed him and his "excellent Regt. of Mississippi Volunteers, & very much regret I cannot at once order you with your Comd. to Camargo." Taylor further wrote, "I can assure you that I am more than anxious to take you by the hand, & to have you and your command with or near me." Taylor showed no sign of hostility to the man who as a young officer had eloped with his daughter. Historians believe that a chance meeting in 1845 between the two men had resulted in a reconciliation between the general and Davis.[18]

Taylor intended to move his army inland to the town of Camargo using both the Rio Grande and the road that paralleled it. Taylor issued General Order No. 93 on July 30, 1846, from Matamoros, setting his troops in motion. "The Louisville Legion (1st Kentucky), Baltimore Battalion, and two regiments of Ohio Volunteers will send heavy baggage by water, with four companies of each regiment and two of the Baltimore Battalion. . . . The Tennessee, Mississippi, Alabama, and Georgia regiments will move forward by water as rapidly as possible."[19] From his new base at Camargo, he could then secure the two major roads that led to Monterrey, a city of 12,000 to 15,000 inhabitants and the capital of Nuevo Leon. In the wake of Gen. Don Mariano Arista's earlier defeats along the Rio Grande by Taylor, Gen. Don Pedro de Ampudia had retreated to Monterrey with the Mexican Army. Situated at the foot of the Sierra Madres, Monterrey offered a defensible position from which Ampudia could block Taylor's advance. It was there that both sides knew the war's next battle would be fought.[20]

The 1st Mississippi Rifles spent much of its time at the mouth of the Rio Grande bickering over leadership. Back home, local newspaper editors printed letters expressing dissatisfaction with Jefferson Davis's command of the regiment. Disgruntled volunteers claimed the staff of the regiment had been filled by Davis's Vicksburg neighbors. Complained Francis M. Robinson of the State Fencibles, "You may possible attribute this language to the natural dissatisfaction which undrilled volunteers feel at anything like military discipline; but a few of the facts will suffice to show you that this is no case of ordinary grumbling. Imprimis, the regimental staff has been entirely taken from the two Vicksburg companies, and when any post of honor or profit is to be filled temporarily, a Vicksburgian is appointed to fill it: When a regimental officer of the 'Southrons' resigns his station, (as occurred the other day,) a '*Vicksburg* Volunteer' is appointed in his stead; in a word, the Colonel's gross partiality towards the companies from his immediate neighborhood has become a byword among us, and officers and men agree in dubbing this 'The *Vicksburg* Regiment.'" The fact that two of the regiment's ten companies came from Vicksburg gave their argument weight. Davis, a West Point graduate and mindful of the duties required of a man in his position, even drew complaints for running his unit like a regiment of US regulars. The same correspondent lamented that Davis "is the only colonel of volunteers who has kept a guard during the day at or near this point [camp near the mouth of the Rio Grande], exposed to the overpowering heat of the hottest sun imaginable; in fact, a thousand instances of his severity, even in the short period we have been under his command."[21] James C. Browning expressed the feelings of a new volunteer, noting "nothing of interest has occurred to day only a scarcity of provisions has caused Great discontent though stinted in provisions we have had to preform Regular duty, drilling and standing guard." In reality, the volunteers had not yet become accustomed to military life and considered Davis's attention to duty as heavy-handedness on his part. Even so, distrust within the regiment still existed, prompting Capt. William P. Rogers to observe, "Col. Davis and Lieut-Col A. K. McClung I do not think are my friends." Rogers had replaced McClung as the captain of the Tombigbee Volunteers (Company K) after the latter was elected lieutenant colonel.[22]

Others besides members of the regiment expressed dissatisfaction with Davis and McClung. Letters reached Mississippi that claimed the two men were abusive toward their men. *The Mississippi Democrat* exclaimed, "The Mississippi Volunteers seem to have been particularly unfortunate in the selection of officer," saying that "Murmurings at these officers come in almost every letter" sent from Mexico. It cautioned that the complaints may be seen as coming from volunteers yet unaccustomed to military service. If found to be true, though, "those [officers] who have abused the 'little brief authority' with which they are invested, will receive merited, universal censure."[23] This was the risk that unpopular volunteers faced: although temporarily in a situation of superiority over their peers, equality and justice awaited them at the end of their service.

The Mississippians, many of whom had never ventured outside of their own county, took note of their new surroundings. Animals, such as horned toads and other reptiles, drew their share of attention, but one of the most interesting animals they encountered was the "hairless dog." At least one Mississippian was quick to point out that some of the Mexicans were as dark complexioned as slaves. In a comment typical of a person reared within the institution of slavery, he joked that the men should have brought cowhide whips for catching the Mexicans instead of muskets for shooting them. The Mississippians wrote home the scandalous news that the Mexican women regularly bathed nude along the banks of the Rio Grande. Such displays of female flesh were unheard of back home.[24]

One member of Company C (Vicksburg Southrons), Howard Morris, wrote his brother and sister to tell them what life was like in the camp near the mouth of the Rio Grande. "The country around this place reminds me of the sandy deserts of Arabia, here is not a bush or tree within sight; in fact I have not seen a shrub two feet high since I left the battleground below New Orleans." Furthermore, "[T]he face of the earth is covered with flies and mosquitoes." The bright sun, hot sand, and constant breezes of the gulf made the days uncomfortable. The wind drifted the sand like snow. In the evening, said Morris, "[W]e lie down in the sand, roll ourselves up in our blankets and in the morning find ourselves completely buried." He even asked his relatives to "Excuse this excuse for a letter. I have no place to write but the sand." Another volunteer, though, Leonidas Trousdale of the Carroll Country Volunteers (Company D), expressed thanks for the "glorious, delicious sea breezes," saying without them "we would literally suffocate."[25]

The volunteers found time for diversion while waiting to travel inland. Morris wrote that the Palo Alto battlefield was only 7 miles from their camp. He revealed there "still lay the carcasses of fifty unburried Mexicans, broken spears, lancets, swords, guns, cannon carriages, &c." Morris also told his relatives that "one of our boys" caught a "Sea Turtle weighing 325 pounds." Wanting a change from army rations, Morris said, "I gave six bits for one of its legs and made a pot of soup my 'mess.'" A person could find all the seashells he wanted in just one walk along the shoreline, he noted. Morris placed his letter home in the care of a small party of Mississippians already returning home, too ill to continue on with the army.[26]

The volunteers complained about their army diet that consisted mainly of hard bread and salt pork. They augmented the fare with items purchased from local venders who visited the camps. The Rio Grande was the main source of drinking water for the inexperienced soldiers camped along its banks. Dysentery disabled and killed volunteers fresh from the United States at an alarming rate. The Mississippians, not immune to the effects of heat, dust, bad food, and dirty water, suffered in the unfamiliar surroundings.[27] James C. Browning noted that a number of Mississippians had already been discharged for "bad health" and that there existed a "great many cases of sickness to day in camps."[28] They shared their misery with volunteers from Kentucky, Indiana, Tennessee, Ohio, Georgia, Missouri, Louisiana, Maryland, and the District of Columbia, all whose camps lined the Rio Grande. Unlike the men from some other states, the Mississippians seemed to behave themselves relatively well while camped along the river.[29] Davis, whom experience had taught the need for discipline, deserves credit for his men's good conduct. The letters back home complaining of his "unnecessary rigor" stemmed from his effort to ready his regiment for the hard service they were about to face.[30]

Needing to prepare his regiment for service, Davis addressed the matter of the missing rifles. Eager to obtain these weapons for his regiment, he fretted that they would not arrive before his men marched into the interior. He sent Capt. Franklin Smith, a Mississippi assistant quartermaster, to the depot at Brazos Santiago to inquire into the missing weapons' whereabouts. After making several hot, uncomfortable trips to the island, Smith reported to Davis that fifty-two boxes containing the new rifles had finally arrived. By August 21, the Mississippians had the promised rifles in their hands. The captain of Company K (Tombigbee Volunteers), Rogers, noted the exchange, writing in his diary, "I have been very busy today distributing rifles to my company. We were armed three weeks ago with muskets—They have been replaced and we have rifles." Smith also delivered swords and pistols for the regiment's officers and drums and new accouterments for the men. His job, though, was not yet done. He boxed up the old muskets and returned them to the depot, necessitating another trip through the sun and sand.[31] James C. Browning expressed delight at the fruit of Smith's efforts, writing that "we delivered up our Muskets and drew the finest quality of Rifles with percussion Locks an article not surpassed by any ever used in the United States Service."[32]

General Taylor had more pressing problems to solve than the whereabouts of a few boxes of missing rifles. Volunteers had been arriving by the thousands at Brazos Santiago. More had come than he could use, and they were draining the supplies he was collecting for his army. In addition to the volunteers called by Congress, the extra, unauthorized regiments formed at General Gaines's request began to arrive in June and continued to pour in throughout July and August. The volunteers who answered Gaines's call expected to serve for only three months. The process of organizing and transporting these units to Texas had already used up a great portion of their time. When Taylor informed these volunteers that he could not use them unless they consented to extend their enlistments to twelve months, most of the disappointed three-month volunteers chose to return to the United States. Thus Taylor sent thousands of volunteers home before he even started on his march to Monterrey. Although General Gaines had acted in what he thought was the best interest of the country when he issued his call for volunteers, the government relieved him of command of his military district and replaced him with Gen. George M. Brooke.[33]

Several Mississippians found themselves in curious arrangements at the mouth of the Rio Grande. These men had either been too impatient to wait for the organization of Davis's regiment or were not accepted once it was formed. One group, raised in Natchez during the first week of May, called themselves the Sparrow Volunteers. These men crossed the Mississippi River to Louisiana and were accepted as Company E of the 4th Louisiana Infantry. A three-month regiment, it was mustered out of service in August. At least one of the disbanded Mississippians, Lt. Ezra R. Price, would later march on his own to Monterrey.[34] Another company of Mississippians, the Claiborne Volunteers commanded by Capt. William R. Shivors, traveled to Mexico on their own after they could not find a spot in the 1st Mississippi Rifles. They were assigned to serve with Col. Albert S. Johnston's 1st Texas Infantry, another of the three-month regiments. When Johnston's regiment was disbanded, about fifty of Shivors's old company voted to reenlist and stay in Mexico. Discharged Texans filled out the company's ranks. Shivors's new company was attached to the 4th US Infantry in Gen. David E. Twiggs's division and served with distinction at the Battle of Monterrey.[35]

On August 18, 1846, as the regulars and volunteers prepared to march, Taylor announced the reorganization of his army. He divided the army into four divisions: Brig. Gen. David E. Twiggs's 1st Division, Brig. Gen. William J. Worth's 2nd Division, Maj. Gen. William O. Butler's 3rd Division, and Maj. Gen. J. Pinckney Henderson's Texas division. The 1st Mississippi Rifles were placed in Butler's division, which consisted entirely of volunteer regiments. It was designated the field division to distinguish it from the other volunteers in Mexico who were not to accompany Taylor on his campaign against Monterrey. Butler's division was divided into two brigades. The 1st Brigade was composed of the 1st Kentucky and the 1st Ohio and was commanded by Gen. Thomas L. Hamer. The 2nd Brigade contained the 1st Tennessee and the 1st Mississippi and was under the command of a fellow Mississippian, Brig. Gen. John A. Quitman from Natchez.[36]

Quitman, who earlier sang the praises of his fellow Mississippians, had not wished to be left behind with the nation at war. Writing to his future biographer, he revealed that he had been "plunged in the deepest grief for the loss of our second daughter." Nevertheless, "The stirring events on the Rio Grande have roused me from my lethargy. I feel anxious to take part in the conflict, . . . I have served actively in the militia over twenty years, and have some knowledge of tactics and discipline, and a turn for military life. It would be a proud day for me to lead the gallant sons of Mississippi to victory." On July 2, 1846, Quitman had learned that he had been nominated by Polk and commissioned by Congress as one of the five brigadier generals of volunteers to lead the new troops in Mexico. He quickly wrapped up his affairs and joined Taylor, Davis, and the 1st Mississippi Rifles on the Rio Grande.[37]

Nearly 4,000 of the approximately 6,700 troops Taylor took to Monterrey were raw recruits who had never seen action. He ordered General Worth's division, veterans of Palo Alto and Resaca de la Palma, to be ready to march on August 18. The Mississippians were not to leave their camp near the mouth of the Rio Grande for another week.[38] Taylor may have been apprehensive about the large number of volunteers in his ranks, but the men of the 1st Mississippi Rifles were eager to move forward and prove their merit in the coming battle. They relished the opportunity fate had given them, prompting one member to exclaim, "The Mississippi Regiment is under the immediate command of 'Old Rough and Ready.' God save the brave!"[39]

3
The March to Monterrey

Their merits place the Mississippi Regiment in front.
—Col. Jefferson Davis

THE 1ST MISSISSIPPI RIFLES PREPARED to move once General Taylor ordered his army to advance up the Rio Grande. Colonel Davis boarded the *Virginia* on August 24, 1846, with Companies A (Yazoo Volunteers), E (State Fencibles), H (Vicksburg Volunteers), and portions of B (Wilkinson Volunteers) and C (Vicksburg Southrons). Lieutenant Colonel McClung had gone to Point Isabel and left the remainder of the regiment to load tents, pots, kettles, and equipment onto the *Colonel Cross* for the journey up the river. The rest of the Mississippians, about 400 in number, set off at sunrise on the morning of August 26 on board the *Colonel Cross*. The Mississippians at first believed themselves luckier than other regiments that had to march the 130 miles to Camargo. Many would change their minds in the days to come, although at least one member of the regiment traveling on the *Virginia* thought otherwise, stating that even though the boat was overcrowded, "we enjoyed the trip, and were very comfortable, in leaving the *very uncomfortable* position in which we had so long been placed at the mouth of the 'Grande Riviore."[1]

The trip on the *Colonel Cross* was punctuated by a series of mishaps. The water of the Rio Grande ran swift and deep, and its currents repeatedly pushed the *Colonel Cross* into the bank. At one of these unscheduled stops, McClung ordered a grave dug for a Mississippian who had died during the night. The dead man's comrades wrapped his body in a blanket and buried him without any ceremony. Captain Franklin Smith noted that, even in this early stage of the war, already "Men had grown familiar with death."[2] Smith learned that the vessel's captain had placed his own cargo on board. In addition to causing the boat to be dangerously overloaded, the captain had violated established rules for carriers of government goods. When the *Colonel Cross* reached Matamoros on the night of August 27, the quartermaster in charge of the town confiscated the unauthorized merchandise, dismissed Captain Birmingham, and placed Captain Pratt in command of the vessel. Captain Bainbridge D. Howard of Company D (Carroll County Volunteers) and six men were left at Matamoros because they were too ill to go any further. A horse belonging to McClung was taken aboard. While attempting to leave Matamoros on the night of August 28, the river's current forced the *Colonel Cross* into a flooded cornfield at the water's edge. The impact of the collision broke one of the ship's paddle wheels. When daybreak came, mechanics in the regiment's ranks labored alongside the ship's crew to repair the damaged wheel. That evening, another boat stopped and towed the *Colonel Cross* to a dry landing. While at the landing, the steamer *Rough and Ready* accidentally struck a blow to the *Colonel Cross* and damaged the boat's rudder. The broken paddle wheel had been fixed, but the crew and volunteers had to spend an additional five hours repairing the damage done to the rudder resulting from the second accident. Leaving the landing that evening, Captain Pratt tried to make up for lost time by running the river at night. He decided to tie up until daylight after the boat again struck the bank, this time losing part of the pilot house to a low-hanging tree limb.[3]

Davis and his detachment on board the *Virginia* arrived at Camargo on August 31, but those on board the *Colonel Cross* suffered for several days longer. Lieutenant Colonel McClung angered the men by ordering a member of Company I (Marshall Guards) left behind on the banks of the river. The man had gone ashore when the vessel stopped to take on wood and failed to return by the time the boat was ready to leave. Another boat picked up the volunteer who later rejoined his regiment unharmed. After this incident, McClung posted a guard whenever the *Colonel Cross* docked and forbade the men to leave the boat. On one occasion McClung even armed himself with a brace of pistols and threatened to shoot several volunteers attempting to leave the vessel to find some food suitable for their sick friends on board. His reputation as a duelist made it unlikely anyone took up his challenge. Officers, on the other hand, could come and go freely. The sight of them and their servants going ashore at stops to buy food from the local inhabitants angered the enlisted men. Even worse, no enlisted man could enter the steamer's cabins unless he was accompanied by an officer. Many were shocked to see the sick placed on the deck with only an awning stretched over them as protection against the sun's rays while their officers enjoyed themselves drinking and eating in the cabin and staterooms. One member of the Carroll County Volunteers (Company D), identified only as "N," condemned McClung, writing, "He is the most heartless man I ever saw." Smith likely captured the general feeling on the *Colonel Cross* when he wrote "everybody dissatisfied unhappy the boat stinking and fetid."[4]

After eight horrible days on the river, the *Colonel Cross* finally reached Camargo on September 3, three days behind the *Virginia*. The Mississippians camped next to Twiggs's division of US regulars. Many of the men felt the effects of dysentery, the result of the poor diet and river water on which they had been living. By the end of August, Davis had discharged 108 men due to illness. In addition, seventy more were listed as present but were too sick to perform their duties. At Camargo, each of the regiment's ten companies carried twenty-five to forty-five men on the sick list each day.[5]

The volunteers tried to make the best of their stay at Camargo. They bought local food to supplement their army rations. The connection between eating strange food and contracting diarrhea was not made by the men. One volunteer reported that the prices they had to pay were as low as those in New Orleans. Items such as milk and wheat cakes were a welcome change from pork and hard crackers. A whole sheep could be bought for 40 cents while beef cost only 3 or 4 cents per pound. Rows of tasseled corn lined the river bank indicating the region's agricultural potential. Although the days at Camargo were warm, nights were cool enough to cause the men to wake up wet from the heavy dews.[6]

Captain Franklin Smith carried on with his duties as quartermaster. His first assignment at Camargo was to track down an allotment of missing government oats. He discovered that Maj. Gen. Robert Patterson's servant had taken the oats to feed the general's horse. Patterson had been a passenger on the *Colonel Cross* and had shared the Mississippians' misadventures but from the relative comfort of a cabin and not the boat's deck. After extracting a promise from the general to replace the oats, Smith returned to the boat to find that his trunks had been put ashore without a guard. A fellow Mississippian, Capt. Kemp S. Holland, offered to store the trunks in his tent until Smith could make other arrangements. Holland, a newly appointed assistant commissary of subsistence, had been Smith's traveling companion on the *Colonel Cross*. Captain Smith was extremely disheartened to find that he had orders to stay at Camargo and would not be allowed to accompany the regiment on the march to Monterrey. Some officers counseled Smith to resign his commission in protest, but Maj. Abraham Van Buren—the eldest son of the former president,—told him "no captain don't think a moment of resignation. The first duty of a soldier is to obey . . . you can't resign here in the heart of the enemy's country." Smith reluctantly decided to stay and perform the duties required of him as quartermaster at Camargo. Another Mississippian, Dr. Alfred Patton, had been ordered to leave the regiment and return to Matamoros to help tend to the army's rapidly increasing number of sick who were piling up there. Patton had enlisted as a private in the Raymond Fencibles (Company G) but since then had received an appointment as surgeon. Like Smith, he too resented being separated from the regiment.[7]

Taylor was soon ready to resume his advance and on September 6 began to break his camp at Camargo. His next objective, the town of Cerralvo, was located nearly midway between Camargo and Monterrey. Worth's division had been sent forward on August 18. Taylor was leaving more than 3,000 troops in his rear, in camps stretched out along the Rio Grande from Camargo to the river's mouth. Seven hundred men alone were left in hospitals at Matamoros. Taylor blamed his inability to take more troops to Monterrey on the Quartermaster Department. The general claimed that the department failed to provide him with adequate transportation to carry all the men and supplies that he needed.[8]

The situation at Camargo was hectic and confused as the Mississippians prepared to leave for Cerralvo. Taylor left General Patterson in charge of the nearly 2,000 troops who were to remain at Camargo. This number included ten members of the Carroll County Volunteers who were too sick to travel. Not more than fifty members of most companies were fit enough to carry their rifles and knapsacks. Two new officers were elected to fill vacancies that existed within the regiment: 1st Lt. Ferdinand Bostick, Company A (Wilkinson Volunteers) and 2nd Lt. Thomas J. Kyle, Company D (Carroll County Volunteers). The 1st Mississippi Rifles broke their camp and marched from Camargo on September 7, 1846.[9]

Jefferson Davis had to fend off accusations that his special relationship with Zachary Taylor had led to his regiment being included in the troops designated for Monterrey. The charges came from the commanders and volunteers of other states' regiments that had been in Mexico longer. Forced to respond, Davis left no doubt he believed the assignment had not been the result of favoritism. He explained, "We spent the time of our delays in the discipline that was to fit us for the front position we intended to claim. And without arrogating undue credit, let me say this time was not fruitlessly wasted, as the result soon showed. We became known as the best drilled Regiment in the volunteer army . . . [When] it was asked how we came to be put in this advanced position in the preference of others who had moved before us, I answered, irritatingly, but truthful—*Their merits place the Mississippi Regiment in front*."[10]

Historians have debated which tactics manual Davis used to train his regiment. Some have even suggested that he wrote his own. This would not have been necessary. Although the standard military long arm of the day was the flintlock musket, manuals already existed for training riflemen. Winfield Scott's 1835 three-volume set contained a section on skirmishers, the traditional role of light infantry and riflemen. It is more likely, however, that Davis relied on one of Scott's earlier manuals written for the militia, which has a section devoted to the conduct of riflemen. In particular, Scott's 1830 *Abstract of Militia Tactics* appears to be the manual that Davis most likely used. His challenge was in employing tactics that were intended for one or two companies to an entire regiment. An examination of after action reports made by the colonel and the regiment's officers support this contention as many of the specific commands mentioned correspond to this manual.[11]

Even though Davis claimed that the regiment was well disciplined, the departing volunteers left chaos in their wake in the rush to leave Camargo. The lack of transportation limited the amount of baggage that the army could take to Monterrey. Lieutenant Colonel McClung and Capt. James H. R. Taylor, Company I (Marshall Guards) asked Franklin Smith to look after their personal trunks that had to be left behind. Smith went to the camp recently vacated by the Mississippians to retrieve the trunks and was astonished by what he found there. Government and personal property littered the ground. Tents, kettles, and even newly issued rifles had been left behind unguarded by their fellow Mississippians. Captain Taylor's trunk could not be located. Smith found ailing Lieutenant Bostick had been left by himself to care for nearly 100 sick men without any arrangements made for their provisions. Smith informed his superior, Capt. George H. Crosman, of the abandoned government's goods as well as the deplorable plight of Bostick and his wards. Crosman arranged for the men of the Quartermaster Department to pick up the scattered equipment and provide rations for Bostick's men. Crosman even sent a detail to bury two dead Mississippians who had been left behind by their companions. One of the deceased was James Boyd, said to have been a former mayor of Jackson. Smith thought a man such as Boyd (Company G, State Fencibles) would have received better treatment from his friends and neighbors.[12]

Captain Smith had to come to the aid of yet another band of stranded Mississippians. These were men who had started on the march to Cerralvo with their regiment but had become too ill to continue. The Tombigbee Volunteers' captain (Company K), William P. Rogers, had been ordered by Davis to escort about twenty of these volunteers back to Camargo. The task completed, Rogers returned to the regiment. The volunteers he had escorted back attached themselves to Capt. George W. McCowen's company of the 2nd Tennessee Volunteers. When Smith encountered them, the Mississippians had been living off rations given to them by McCowen's men. They lacked clothing and other necessary items, but Mr. Phelps, the sutler for the Mississippians, would not advance them credit because they were detached from their regiment. Smith introduced the group's leader to Gen. Gideon J. Pillow, who then took charge of the situation.[13]

The Mississippians headed to Monterrey spent their first night away from Camargo at the historic town of Mier. The buildings still showed signs of the 1842 battle between the Texans and the Mexican Army. After passing through the towns of Chicharrón and Punta Aguada, the Mississippians arrived at Cerralvo on the evening of September 13. The 2nd Division, Worth's regulars, had resumed its march toward Monterrey earlier in the day. The general had been waiting for more troops to come forward before advancing from Cerralvo. Captain Rogers was pleased with the town, writing, "Seralio is a handsome town built of stone." He further stated that the town usually had a population numbering somewhere between two thousand to three thousand, but most had left since the Americans arrived.[14]

Taylor prepared his small army for the battle he knew was drawing near. He instructed the commissary to provide eight days' rations for each man. The soldiers also were issued forty rounds of ammunition apiece. All extra arms, sets of accouterments, and other spare equipment were ordered turned over to the quartermaster at Cerralvo. In paring down his army for battle, Taylor forbade men on the sick list to accompany the advancing troops any further. The Americans took possession of an old convent and moved roughly 200 ailing men into the building that was converted into a hospital by the Medical Department. Most of the ill were suffering from dysentery and diarrhea. After personally helping many of the sick to their new quarters, General Quitman received a promise from the town's *alcalde* that food would be provided for those who had to be left behind.[15]

One of the invalids Quitman assisted was Pvt. Marcellus Foute, the young member of Company E (State Fencibles) who had been injured in a fall aboard the *Massachusetts*. Foute wanted to stay with the regiment but said that his friends "told me it would be perfect madness to proceed." Quitman offered to buy him a horse so he could travel on to Monterrey. In a letter to the young volunteer's father, Col. J. F. Foute, the general wrote that Marcellus insisted on going forward and eventually made it to Monterrey. Once there, though, "his friends consider[ed] his condition such as to require the repose of home to effect a cure."[16]

While at Cerralvo, Foute took note of his surroundings: "Our fort is an old Nunnery; . . . it is interesting to see the stone cross on the centre of the ramparts, which for ages ruled with despotic sway, now supporting and sustaining the American flag-staff; and 'the star spangled banner' floating proudly above it. The fort is manned by about 200 men, who by the aid of the wall surrounding the court, will be able to repel the attack of a thousand from without."[17]

Taylor ordered two companies of the 1st Mississippi Rifles to remain at Cerralvo to garrison the town. Captain John M. Sharp's Company A (Wilkinson Volunteers) and Capt. William Delay's Company F (Lafayette Volunteers) reluctantly agreed to stay behind as their comrades marched away to take part in the upcoming battle. While stationed at Cerralvo, one member of Company F was murdered. Friends of the victim found his half-hidden body in some chaparral by the side of the road. The key to solving the case was a lasso that was tied around the dead man's neck. The Mississippians traced the rope to a notorious inhabitant of the town who recently had been seen gambling with the volunteer. When confronted with the evidence, the Mexican confessed to the crime. With a twist of irony, the volunteers hanged the culprit with the same lasso that he used to murder their friend.[18]

The Mississippians left at Cerralvo had the opportunity to experience a pleasant change in diet that reminded them of the comforts of home. The commissary substituted corn for their usual bread ration of hard crackers. The kernels presented a problem at first, but, using hand mills begrudgingly loaned to them by the quartermaster, the hungry Mississippians soon filled the air with the sounds of grinding corn. The Southerners much preferred cornbread to the army's hard crackers.[19]

News of Mexican forces in the area caused the troops of Taylor's vanguard to be on the alert.[20] Butler's field division, which included the eight remaining companies of the 1st Mississippi Rifles, advanced from Cerralvo on September 15.[21] Captain Ben McCulloch's Mounted Texas Volunteers had skirmished with 200 of Anastasio Torrejón's cavalry the day before.[22] Worth's division spent the night of August 16 at the town of Marin waiting for Twiggs' and Butler's divisions to close the gap that separated them before advancing further. Although Monterrey was still 25 miles away, the city could be seen from the church tower at Marin.[23]

On September 18, advance elements of Taylor's army reached the town of San Francisco, only nine miles from Monterrey. That evening, General Henderson's Brigade of Mounted Texas Volunteers joined Taylor. The next day, Taylor's army moved to within three miles of the city and camped in a 6-mile-long grove of pecan trees called Walnut Springs by the Americans. On September 20, the troops, anticipating a fight at any moment, hastily formed in line of battle as a body of mounted men rapidly approached from the direction of Monterrey. According to Quitman's biographer, the volunteers "believed that the hour of battle had come, and in a few moments the column was in close order, and ready for the assault. Even the invalids of Quitman's brigade sprung from the wagons, seized their arms, and filed in with their comrades. Such was the ardor of men who had never been in battle, and who only served for honor and the glory of their country!"

Furthermore, asserted the same writer, "Gen. Quitman, sharing the enthusiasm of his troops, addressed them as follows: 'Volunteers, we are now in the vicinity of the enemy, and may, in an hour, be called to encounter them in battle. Your spirit inspires me. I know your metal, your impetuosity, and your recklessness of danger. There is no coward in my command. I shall never have to urge you on, but I must impress on you the necessity of preserving your ranks under all circumstances. Repress your personal impetuosity. Confide in your officers, and preserve your discipline in the excitement of the conflict. The eyes of the veteran officers of the army and the whole of the regulars will be fixed upon you. They know your gallantry, but they doubt your coolness. Prove to them, to your country, and to the world, that American volunteers are as admirable for their discipline and self-restraint as for their courage.'" The scare proved to be a false alarm as it was only a group of Texas volunteers returning from their reconnaissance of the city's defenses and not the Mexican Army after all.[24] The disappointed Mississippians would have to wait a little longer for the battle they so eagerly sought.

The 1st Mississippi Rifles had been much reduced in its march toward Monterrey. The regiment, which was 941 strong when mustered in at Vicksburg, now numbered only about 500. Of the men no longer with the regiment, fourteen had died. The rest either had been discharged because of illness or occupied beds in army hospitals along the Rio Grande.[25] Two determined Mississippians overcame extreme obstacles to arrive at Walnut Springs on the eve of the battle. Captain Ezra R. Price and Lt. Stokes A. Smith of the disbanded Sparrow Volunteers had walked all the way from Camargo by themselves to catch up with their countrymen. Their odyssey had taken six days, but the two Mississippians had been determined to be with Taylor's army when it fought the Mexicans at Monterrey.[26] They, along with their fellow Mississippians, were eager to prove that their place at the front was merited.

4
The 1st Mississippi Regiment at Monterrey

These "Rifle Charging" Mississippians Were Led on by the Gallant Davis
—Joseph Davis Howell

MONTERREY SITS AT THE MOUTH of the mountain pass that leads to the heart of Mexico by way of Saltillo. A mountainous landscape forms a backdrop to the city and gives it an aura of invincibility. The Americans hoped that capturing this fortified city would force the Mexican government to abandon its struggle and sue for peace. General Taylor had brought his army to Monterrey to accomplish the task, but it would not be easy. Opposing him was a veteran soldier, General Pedro de Ampudia, and an estimated force of nearly 10,000 Mexican regulars and irregulars.

Monterrey had been laid out in a narrow stretch along the north bank of the Santa Catrina River, coursing west to east at the base of the mountains. The houses and public buildings, as in all Mexican towns, were each built like a small fortress. Walls of adobe brick could be several feet thick. Flat roofs, surrounded by two- to three-foot-high parapets, gave Ampudia's troops defending the city a clear view of the streets that Taylor's men would have to enter. Furthermore, the Mexican military engineers had ringed the town with a series of small forts intended to block the obvious entry points. Hilltop fortifications on Independence Hill and Federation Hill overlooked the town as well as guarded that western approach to Monterrey. Guns from the Bishop's Palace commanded the town's eastern and northern flanks. Even the town's *Compo Santo* (cemetery) had been converted into a bastion with holes knocked into its surrounding walls for the placement of cannon. Located on the northern outskirts of Monterrey was a large structure known to the Americans as the "Black Fort" or the Citadel. A volunteer writing to *The Mississippi Democrat* attempted to give readers back home an idea of its strength, writing that "the principal and strongest fortress of the town, ominously called by the b-hoys 'the black fort'—and the boys are right, for its name bears not half so black and threatening an aspect as the fortification itself."[1]

Once outside the approach to Monterrey, Taylor divided his army into two wings. He sent Worth's division to the southwest edge of the city to close the road that ran through the pass to Saltillo to prevent the Mexican Army from either retreating or receiving reinforcements. Once that task

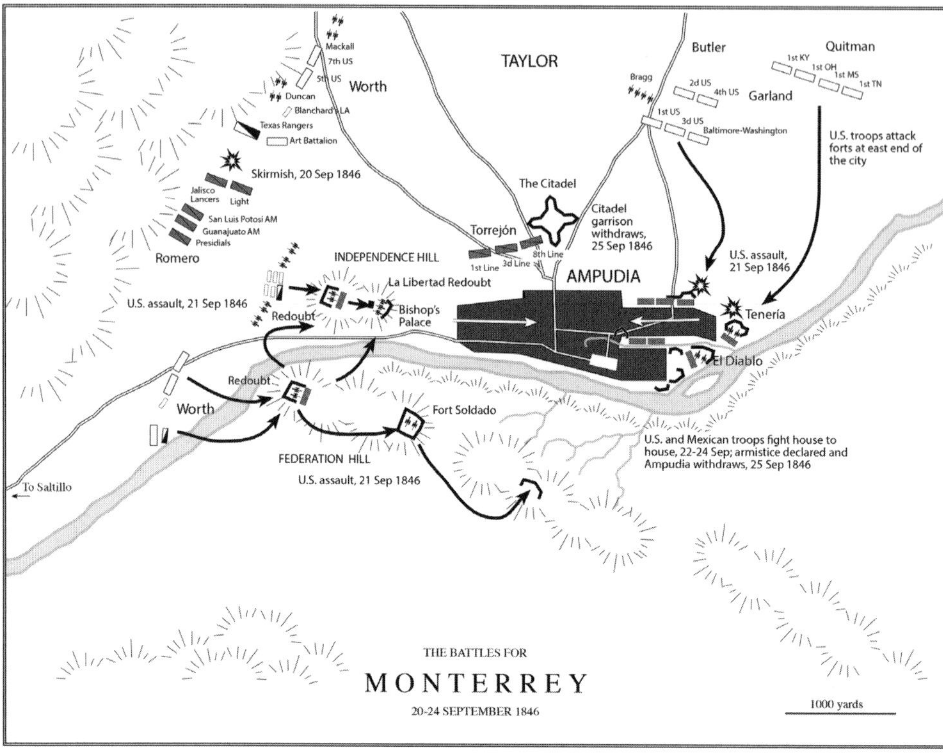

was completed, Taylor intended for Worth's men to seize the Mexican forts overlooking the city from the line of hills that formed the boundary to the city's southern limits. Taylor planned to use the troops under his immediate command as a diversion by assaulting the city's eastern edge so as to keep the enemy from massing its forces against Worth.[2]

General Worth's division included the following units of regulars and volunteers:

Lt. Col. Thomas Staniford's 1st Brigade
Capt. James Duncan's Battery
Maj. Thomas Child's Artillery Battalion (acting as Infantry)
8th Infantry under Capt. Richard B. Screven
Col. Persifor F. Smith's 2nd Brigade
Lt. William W. Mackall's Battery
5th US Infantry under Maj. Martin Scott
7th US Infantry under Capt. Dixon S. Miles
Capt. Albert G. Blanchard's Company of Louisiana Volunteers

Taylor augmented Worth's force by attaching additional units to his division. These were

Gov. T. Pinckney Henderson's Texas Division
1st Texas Mounted Volunteers under Col. John C. Hays
2nd Texas Mounted Volunteers under George T. Wood
Capt. Charles May's 2nd US Dragoons

Worth commenced his march toward the city's west side at 2 p.m. on the afternoon of Sunday, September 20. Four hours later, Worth's troops had reached a position from which they could block the road to Saltillo. The general's men slept on their arms that night while they waited for the assault on the city scheduled for the next morning.[3]

At about 6 A.M. on the morning of September 21, the light companies of the 1st Brigade, under Capt. Charles Ferguson Smith, joined Hays's Mounted Texas Volunteers and advanced toward the Saltillo road. An enemy force of infantry and cavalry commanded by Col. Don Juan N. Najera blocked their way. Duncan and Mackall's artillery batteries moved forward and engaged them, throwing the Mexicans back. By noon, Worth's troops had prepared to assault the fortified hill positions called Fort Federation and Fort Soldada. A quick charge conducted by Captain Smith leading a force of 300 regulars and Texans placed the fort on Federation Hill in the Americans' hands. Worth ordered Captain Miles and the 7th US Infantry to advance to aid Smith in his attack. The spirits of the American soldiers were high and in their enthusiasm to win the day, the 5th US Infantry and Blanchard's Louisiana Volunteers joined Capt. Charles Ferguson Smith's assault force. A race ensued to see who would be the first to reach Fort Soldada, and this second important enemy work quickly fell to the American rush.[4]

On the eastern sector of the city, Taylor heard the sounds of firing announcing Worth's attack and began his diversion. Unfortunately, Taylor brought along no artillery capable of reducing Monterrey by siege. He ordered Capts. George D. Ramsey and Lucien Bonaparte Webster to deploy a 10-inch mortar and two 24-pounder howitzers on the city's northeast edge near the junction of the road leading to Marin. The guns merely annoyed the entrenched enemy while exposing the gunners to unnecessary risks. Taylor ordered Twiggs's division to assault the northeast section of the city. Twiggs, however, was unable to lead his men into battle that morning. As a precaution, the general had taken a laxative the night before, believing that "a bullet striking the belly when the bowels are loose might pass through the intestines without cutting them." He would eventually join his division around noon.[5]

Lieutenant Colonel John Garland took charge in the place of the indisposed general. Twiggs's division consisted of Garland's own 1st Brigade with four companies of the 2nd US Dragoons under May (detached to aid Worth), Capt. Braxton Bragg's and Lt. Randolph Ridgely's batteries, the 3rd US Infantry under Maj. William W. Lear, and the 4th US Infantry under Capt. George W. Allen. Captain William R. Shivors' Independent Company of Mississippians and Texans was also attached to Garland's brigade. Twiggs' 2nd Brigade was composed of Capt. John J. Abercrombe and the 1st US Infantry along with Lt. Col. William H. Watson's battalion of volunteers from Baltimore and the District of Columbia. Lieutenant Colonel Henry Wilson commanded the 2nd Brigade. Two engineering officers, Maj. Joseph K. F. Mansfield and Capt. William G. Williams led the way for Garland's assault as they scouted ahead to find the best way for the troops to enter the city.[6] Unlike in the western suburbs, here the Americans met serious resistance, and Taylor's feint soon turned into a bloody affair that forced Taylor to commit more men to the battle in order to help extract Garland's battered column from Monterrey's streets.

Advancing under fire from the guns of the Black Fort and other smaller enemy redoubts located about Monterrey, Garland's troops had entered the city's narrow streets at the place indicated by Mansfield. Mexican soldiers firing from rooftops and from behind barricades took deadly aim at the Americans clustered in the narrow streets below. A hidden battery roared into action, and the US casualties quickly began to mount. Although wounded, Major Mansfield continued to guide Garland's column. Taylor sent Bragg's battery into the city to add its weight to the American assault. The general ordered its recall because the narrow streets limited the artillery's effectiveness and only endangered the gunners and horses. Garland decided to retreat, but, fortunately for the Americans, Capt. Electus Backus of the 1st US Infantry did not receive word that his brigade had been ordered to leave the city. Backus positioned his men on the roof of a building overlooking a strongly fortified building known as La Tenería (the Tannery). This important Mexican position was one of the primary forts that guarded the eastern approach to Monterrey. From their elevated position, Backus's men could fire directly through the gorge or opening to the fort. The action of Backus and his men proved to be instrumental in the capture of the Tannery.[7]

Upon learning that Garland's assault had stalled, Taylor ordered Butler's field division to advance into Monterrey. At this point the American commander had determined to carry the city by storm. Held in reserve by Taylor, Butler's division was situated behind Ramsey's 10-inch mortar near the Marin junction. The division's normal order in the line of battle for the regiments from right to left was the following: the 1st Kentucky and 1st Ohio (Gen. Thomas L. Hamer's 1st Brigade) next to the 1st Tennessee and 1st Mississippi (Gen. John A. Quitman's brigade). Positioned directly behind Ramsey's mortar, the Mississippians were in a dangerous spot. Ramsey commented in an off-hand manner, "Col. Davis, move your men from that position, or they will all be killed: they are firing at my mortar and have already wounded one of my men, and knocked down some of my boxes." Quitman ordered the regiment to leave its customary position in the line of battle and repositioned it in a more sheltered location to the left of Ramsey's mortar. Davis ordered his men to lie down, a move that was "executed with promptness." The artillery piece split the regiments of the brigade with Davis's regiment to the left and the division's other three regiments to the right of the gun. This small gap separating Butler's division resulted in much confusion and controversy in the fighting that was to come.[8]

The sudden crash of musketry and cannonading coming from the town's eastern environs indicated that Ampudia's troops were putting up a fight. Taylor ordered Butler's division to support and relieve the bloodied troops under Garland's command. The division marched by the left flank following a path that would carry it first south and then east from where it could enter the city by its eastern approaches. The gap that separated the 1st Mississippi from the rest of the division prevented Colonel Davis from hearing the command to march. Davis's only clue that the order had been given was his view of the 1st Tennessee and 1st Ohio advancing toward Monterrey, leaving his regiment behind. (The 1st Kentucky did not go with these two regiments as it had been ordered to stay and protect the mortar.) After allowing the 1st Tennessee to pass along the front of his regiment, Davis ordered the 1st Mississippi Rifles to rise up and follow the Tennessee regiment, filing into column ahead of the Ohioans. A member of the regiment recalled Davis's words that sent them to battle: "Riflemen, to your feet! FORWARD! in double quick time—march!"[9] This command placed Davis's men between the Tennessee and the Ohio regiments. The movement kept the two regiments of Quitman's brigade together but reversed the order of the regiments by placing the 1st Mississippi on the right flank of the Tennesseans instead of its normal position on the left flank. This arrangement apparently disoriented many officers and men of both regiments, most of whom had never been in battle before. Colonel William B. Campbell, commander of the Tennesseans, later wrote that the small arms and cannon fire they received added to the confusion in his regiment.[10]

The 1st Tennessee Infantry and the 1st Mississippi Rifles branched off from the Ohio regiment and formed a line of battle about 300 yards in front of the Tannery. Quitman ordered his brigade to lie down to keep his troops from being easy targets of the Mexican guns in the city. A single cannon ball had killed four Tennesseans and wounded three others. According to Capt. Douglas H. Cooper (Company B, Wilkinson Volunteers), the Mississippians were marching by the left flank when Davis gave the order "Companies into Line." This would have caused the regiment to form a column of companies, left in front. Davis then ordered his regiment to form a line of battle to the front, which would have been accomplished by the second company in the column forming on the right of the first company, the third company in the column forming on the right of the second, and so on until all companies were deployed onto the line. Due to the confusion inherent on the battlefield, several companies of the Mississippi regiment had advanced further than others. To correct the irregularity in his line, Davis requested permission from Quitman to advance the rest of his companies on line with his furthest forward Mississippians. With Quitman's approval, Davis began to move his Mississippians forward and to the left by an oblique movement that placed Davis's regiment between the 1st Tennessee on its left and Garland's retiring command on its right. Their objective, the Tannery, was now approximately 180 yards away. Davis instructed his captains to commence firing as soon as they placed their companies on the new line. Conducted by Adjutant Richard Griffith, the companies marched by the left flank and arrived on the new line of battle in the following order, left to right: G, E, C, K, I, D, H, and B. At this stage in the battle, Davis commanded the left wing of the regiment (Marshall Guards, Carroll County Volunteers, Vicksburg Volunteers, and Wilkinson Volunteers) while McClung commanded the right wing (Raymond Fencibles, State Fencibles, Vicksburg Southrons, and Tombigbee Volunteers).[11]

Davis ordered the regiment to continue firing, and the Mississippians needed no other urging. The fire began as soon as the left-most company was on the new line of battle. Each succeeding company joined the fray once it arrived in the line of battle. The colonel commanded "fire advancing," which would have caused the line to move steadily forward. It appears that this order was carried out by individual companies instead of on a solid battalion front. The mode of firing required a company to advance, fire, load, advance, fire, load, and so on. While effective, it certainly would have been more difficult for Davis, McClung, and Bradford to oversee than a standard battalion front. This ragged advance helps explain why the participants' perspectives differed.[12]

The battle seemed to progress slowly for the Mississippians. Lieutenant Daniel R. Russell, commanding Company D (Carroll County Volunteers) in place of the ailing Capt. Bainbridge D. Howard, recalled seeing Colonel Davis sitting coolly astride his horse. Davis called out in frustration, "Damn it, why don't the men get nearer the fort? Why waste ammunition at such a distance?" John L. McManus, captain of Company E (State Fensibles), later claimed that he heard Davis loudly lament, "Now is the time, Great God, if I had 30 men with knives I could take that fort!" Davis cautioned his men to fire only at distinct targets, but the excited riflemen loaded and fired as quickly as they could, advancing all the while. Noted Lieutenant Russell,

"The attempt was made to make the firing regular, but it was futile for every man loaded & fired with the utmost rapidity." He and the other officers tried without results to maintain an orderly advance, but the men were eager to drive the Mexicans from the Tannery, and they steadily pushed ahead. Their accounts differ significantly from one Mississippian who recalled steadiness of his comrades, writing, "They fired steady and slowly, each man taking good aim . . . ere he pulled the fatal trigger." Recounted Joseph Davis Howell, Davis's brother-in-law, of this stage of the fight, "we were deployed and our firing commenced, every mexican who showed his head above fort was immediately cut off by our rifles."[13]

The time was about noon. The next event proved to be a point of controversy for years to come. The Tennesseans and the Mississippians charged and carried the Tannery. The controversy was over who actually ordered the charge, as General Quitman, Colonel Campbell of the 1st Tennessee, Colonel Davis, and Lieutenant McClung all later claimed credit for the deed. According to the accounts of all the Mississippians, the last movement of the regiment had placed Company K (Tombigbee Volunteers) directly opposite the sally porte that led into the fort. Those close to McClung heard him call out to the men of his old company, "Charge! Charge! Tombigbee Volunteers follow me!" Howell recalled the moment, writing home that "suddenly the order to charge was given by Col Davis and away we went like so many devils hooting and yelling, with nothing but our naked rifles no bayonets even." No matter who gave the initial order, the race was on. There was no doubt in the minds of the Mississippians who first reached and entered the fort: this honor went to Lieutenant Colonel McClung. Close behind McClung were Lts. William Purnell Townsend and William H. H. Patterson and Pvt. Edward Gregory, all members of the Tombigbee Volunteers. With the Tannery now in the hands of the Americans, Davis instructed Lieutenant Townsend to take charge of the prisoners.[14]

The rapid advance had broken the ranks of the Mississippi regiment. Officers became separated from their companies as the men swarmed over, through, and around the works. The rush continued on to a fortified stone building in the rear of the Tannery. Again, Alexander K. McClung led the charge. This time, though, the lieutenant colonel was shot down as he was receiving the sword from a surrendering Mexican officer. McClung's wound was serious enough to end his career with the 1st Mississippi Rifles. The regiment's officers gathered around the fallen man as Captain McManus (Company E, State Fencibles) offered his coat as a makeshift stretcher on which to carry the gravely wounded man from the battlefield.[15]

But these "Rifle Charging Mississippians" were not finished. A witness recalled that an officer he thought to be Twiggs's appeared about this time, "mounted, shouting, go on! go on, secure your victory &c." The officers and the men of the Mississippi regiment, however, required no additional encouragement as they pressed on into the city. The charge had broken the regiment into small groups of men—some under the control of officers, others acting on their own. Recounted Joseph Davis Howell, "Brother Jeff however still cheered us to the charge, and called upon us to follow him, myself Bob Davis, and about forty others rushed after him." Davis crossed a waist-deep stream that ran behind the fortified building just captured and advanced nearly 150 yards into the city. There he tried to rally his men for an attack on the next enemy fort in line, Ricon del Diablo. Lieutenant Russell (Company D, Carroll County Volunteers) and twenty to twenty-five other Mississippians had taken cover behind a small hillock. Another twenty or so ducked behind a chaparral fence to the rear of the first group. Captain Rogers (Company K, Tombigbee Volunteers) had also crossed the stream with about twenty members of his company. The rest of the regiment, in pursuit of the retreating Mexicans, had scattered in different directions. Davis prepared to charge Ricon del Diablo with the sixty-odd men still under his immediate command. This assault did not take place, however. Quitman's aide-de-camp, Lt. William Augustus Nichols, arrived and ordered Davis and his Mississippians to fall back across the stream, leaving Ricon del Diablo still in the hands of the Mexicans. Davis thought the withdrawal was a mistake. The colonel angrily swore to Russell that if given another five minutes they would have taken the works. Nevertheless, Davis obeyed Quitman's order and crossed back over the stream with his men.[16]

Once on the north bank of the stream, Davis tried to locate other Mississippians belonging to his regiment. He could find only Capt. Douglas Hancock Cooper (Company B, Wilkinson Volunteers), who had about thirty men with him. Captain George P. Field, 3rd US Infantry, led Davis and his men to a spot where the Mississippians were directed to fire on a tete-du-pointe guarding La Purisma bridge. Davis was concerned at the amount of firing the Mississippians had already done, so he asked the men how their ammunition was holding out. Even in the midst of battle, men still kept their sense of humor. One private held his hat in the air and cheerfully answered Davis, "Send us powder colonel; we can catch plenty of balls in our caps."[17] Major Mansfield was still in town, and he and Davis planned to assault the tete-de-pointe as soon as more Mississippians rejoined the colonel. But this attack, too, was called off. General Hamer arrived with his brigade and informed Davis that the Americans were withdrawing from the city. Hamer had assumed command of the field division in place of Butler, who had been wounded in the fighting.[18] Davis reluctantly ordered the Mississippians with him to follow Hamer's column. The general and his troops were about a half mile in advance of the Mississippians. Many of Davis's men, fatigued from the exertions and excitement of the day, began to straggle. Men from other commands also lagged behind. Outside the city, Mexican lancers suddenly appeared and threatened to run down the stragglers. Davis commanded his Mississippians to face about and marched them back to save the hapless Americans. A spirited fire from the Mississippians drove off the lancers. Soon afterward, Major Bradford rejoined Davis, bringing with him a portion of the regiment that had fallen under his command after the attack on the Tannery and stone building. General Quitman informed Davis where another group of Mississippians could be found and instructed the colonel to consolidate his regiment.[19]

Many Mississippians were upset at having been ordered out of the city and forced to relinquish the gains they had made. Some agreed with Davis that, had they been left alone, they would have captured several more enemy works before nightfall. General Hamer's conduct outside the city drew even more criticism. Lieutenant Russell complained that the general needlessly marched the brigade back and forth in front of the city's guns as many as five times, all while exposed to enemy fire. General Taylor cancelled his plans to send the men back into the city that evening, explaining that they were exhausted and low on ammunition. Instead, the Mississippians and other volunteers of Butler's field division returned to Walnut Springs to spend the night there.[20] Taylor attached the 1st Kentucky, which had been kept out of the fighting so far, to the 1st Division and posted this force at the Tannery in order to prevent the Mexicans from reoccupying the fort under the cover of darkness. Back at Walnut Springs, Joseph Davis Howell summed up his pride in his regiment's performance, stating, "[we] were marched back to camp for the night, after having performed an action hitherto unheard of in the annuals of war, viz moving, attacked, charged, and then taken in less than ten minutes with our rifles two strongly fortified forts, charging too as Gen. Taylor said, under the most galling fire he had ever seen or had any idea of."[21]

The gains made by the Mississippians during the day had not been without frightful losses for the regiment. That evening, Colonel Davis asked for volunteers to return to the city to help retrieve the regiment's wounded who had been left behind. It came to light that, in the confusion of the battle, McClung had not been carried from town as believed but still lay wounded near the stone building where he had been shot down. At dusk, Lt. William H. H. Patterson and Pvts. Edward Gregory, Argyle Kerr, Jack King, and Thomas Broom—all members of the Company K, Tombigbee Volunteers—went into the city, found the wounded officer, and carried him back to camp. The task, performed under fire from the enemy, was made even more difficult by a heavy rain that had begun to fall. Seven members of the regiment lay dead on the battlefield. Another forty-seven had been wounded, two of whose wounds proved to be mortal.[22]

The fight for Monterrey recommenced before sunrise on Tuesday, September 22. General Worth's division again started the action. At 3 AM, an assault force commanded by Lieutenant Colonel Childs—composed of three companies of the 8th US Infantry, three companies of the 3rd and 4th US Artillery, and 200 Texans—climbed the steep, rain-slickened slopes leading to the hilltop fortresses of Independence Hill and the Obispada (Bishop's Palace). Charging out of the darkness, the Americans quickly drove the Mexican defenders from both forts.[23]

Little movement took place on the eastern side of the city during the second day of the battle. Taylor planned no diversion to support Worth, as he had on the previous day. According to Joseph Davis Howell, "the Mississippi Regiment remained in camp the men being too much fatigued by their unusual exertions, to be able to march to the attack again, in fact many of them were so stiff and sore as to not be capable of working at all." That evening, however, Taylor ordered Quitman's brigade into Monterrey to relieve the troops who had spent the previous night at the Tannery. The Americans merely exchanged shots with the enemy without trying to advance their position. Because of the light fighting, the Mississippians suffered fewer casualties than the day before. That night Quitman's brigade slept in the works surrounding the Tannery.[24]

The action resumed early on the morning of September 23, the third and final day of the battle. One half hour before sunrise, Quitman instructed Davis to take two companies of Mississippians, G (Raymond Fencibles) and H (Vicksburg Volunteers), and two companies of the 1st Tennessee on a reconnaissance to see what lay before the Tannery. Davis quickly reported back to Quitman that the Mexicans had quietly abandoned El Diablo during the night and the entrance to the city was now open. Company G along with one of the Tennessee companies returned to the Tannery while Companies B (Wilkinson Volunteers) and D (Carroll County Volunteers) of the 1st Mississippi Rifles moved forward to join Davis. Many of the regiment's junior officers had assumed positions of command as wounds and illness were taking their toll on the 1st Mississippi Rifles. The regiment's adjutant, Lt. Richard Griffith, had been forced to remain in camp to nurse his injured shoulder, and Lt. Henry Felix Cook (Company C, Vicksburg Southron) volunteered to take his duty. Captain Rogers (Company K, Tombigbee Volunteers) had to remain in camp because he had lost his shoes and had marched "through the chapparel barefoot," lamenting that his "feet are literally torn to pieces." His place was taken by Lt. William H. H. Patterson, his second in command.[25]

Although Mexican soldiers still occupied many of Monterrey's buildings, the main body of Ampudia's army was thought to be dug in around the city's main plaza. The plaza was located near a bend of the Santa Catarina River. The capture of this plaza now became General Taylor's objective. Davis, under orders from Quitman, continued to advance. Prisoners taken by Lt. William Henry Hampton's men (Company G, Raymond Fencibles) confirmed that the Mexicans were gathering at the plaza for the final defense of the city. Davis moved forward, accompanied by an officer of engineers who was supposed to help him determine the best approach to the plaza. The Americans faced a hail of fire from windows, rooftops, and barricades as they advanced up the narrow streets toward their goal.[26]

Preparations were made for the final assault. Major Bradford joined Davis with companies C (Vicksburg Southrons), E (State Fencibles), G (Raymond Fencibles), and K (Tombigbee Volunteers). He had left Company I at the Tannery to cover their rear, just in case the Americans were forced to retreat. The Mississippians were also joined by Col. George T. Wood and the 2nd Mounted Texas Volunteers and Gov. J. Pinckney Henderson. The Texans showed the Mississippians a way to advance toward the plaza without facing the enemy's fire. They entered the buildings along the streets and began burrowing through the adobe walls of the Mexican houses. Although it took about 20 minutes to break through the two-foot-thick walls, the Americans steadily advanced toward the plaza. This method of fighting was one with which the Texans were very familiar: they had employed the same procedure in the 1835 battle for San Antonio against Gen. Martín Perfecto de Cos during the Texas Revolution. Davis later wrote, "I derived great support from [the Texans] as well from their gallantry as their better knowledge of the construction of Mexican houses." One Texas volunteer in Wood's regiment, James K. Holland, wrote, "Miss and Texas fought together and bravely too." He declared, "Bradford and [former President Mirabeau B.] Lamar were our heroes." General Worth's troops, following the example of Hays's Texans in their ranks, advanced building by building toward the plaza from the west in the same manner. Taylor ordered Bragg's battery, supported by the 3rd US Infantry, into the city from the east, but the light field pieces were no more effective in town than they had been on the first day of the battle.[27]

Davis's brother-in-law provided a firsthand account of this portion of the battle. Wrote Joseph Davis Howell:

> having forced our way by dint of hard knocks and sharp shooting, about half a mile, the weather became a *leetle* too warm for us, Gen Quitman was with us and ordered us all to take cover of which invitation I for one was not slow to avail myself—a call was then made for Captain Brags artillery which advanced gallantly in the face of a murderous fire, wheeled his artillery, opened his fire upon and immediately cleared the street of the mexicans who were

> annoying us, as soon as he had fired, on *we* rushed shooting and shouting, to the best of our ability advancing nearly to the Plaza, where suddenly the sound of bells and bugles from the mexican forces was heard, leading us to expect a charge from the mexican lancers or Rancheros as they are called, we were however mistaken it being instead of a charge a retreat, for they began running to the Plaza with all their might and main the worst scared looking fellows you ever saw in your life.[28]

Not all the Americans' time in the city that day was spent in fighting. Captain William S. Henry and his men of the 3rd US Infantry found time to partake of ripe limes and cool water offered to them by the owner of an apothecary shop located in one of the buildings they entered. Some of the men combined the two ingredients to make a "first rate" drink.[29] A group of Mississippians under the command of Major Bradford took refuge for a time in a hotel near the plaza. Once there, the landlady prepared beef and tortillas for the hungry men. Bradford, though, made sure that the Mississippians paid the woman for their meal.[30]

Similar incidents occurred in other parts of the city. At one spot near the Plaza, Davis ordered some of the Mississippians to break into a warehouse to obtain pack saddles and other items stored there in order to build a barricade across the street. In one part of the building were bundles of Mexican blankets, highly valued by the Americans in Mexico, but, under the watchful eye of their colonel, none were taken by the Mississippians. Davis allowed at least one of his men to replace his worn-out shoes from a pile found in the warehouse. By their own accounts, the Mississippians respected all private property they encountered in Monterrey. This was not the case with the Texans. One Texan explained to Sergeant William Estes (Company E, State Fencibles) that he had taken a purse belonging to a Mexican woman as payment for ponies the "greasers" had once stolen from him.[31] The Texas Revolution had taken place only 10 short years before and was still very fresh in the minds of many Americans—especially Texas veterans of that war and battles that continued during the life of the Republic of Texas.

According to Mexican sources, General Ampudia had concentrated 4,000 Mexican soldiers around the plaza. On the afternoon of September 23, General Taylor once more instructed his troops to leave Monterrey. His men were shocked by the order—many had worked their way to within one block of the plaza. The volunteers, reluctant to abandon the gains they had made during the day, were ordered to leave first. Noted a disappointed Joseph Davis Howell, "I really believe if the combined forces of Gen. Worth and Gen. Quitman had then attacked the Plaza that every rascal of them would have left the town or surrendered." Many shared his view. They were followed by the regulars who had remained behind to cover the withdrawal and make sure the volunteers obeyed Taylor's instructions.[32]

The American commander's new plan called for the plaza to be bombarded with shells from Ramey's 10-inch mortar. Taylor sent the mortar to General Worth, who had it placed in the city's cemetery from where its fire would be the most effective. The mortar began hurling shells into the plaza just before nightfall. Earlier that afternoon, the Mexicans had sent a flag of truce to Taylor's headquarters asking to be allowed to evacuate the women and children from the city. Taylor refused their request—he and his officers took it as a sign that the enemy was weakening and the battle was drawing to a close. Indeed, the end was near. On the morning of September 24, 1846, General Ampudia sent a message to the American commander asking Taylor his terms for the surrender of Monterrey.[33]

5
Life under the Armistice

We do not wish to lead the dull inactive life we are leading now.
—Capt. William P. Rogers

REPRESENTATIVES FROM THE ARMIES of the United States and Mexico met on the morning of September 24, 1846, to discuss terms for the surrender of Monterrey. General Taylor appointed General Worth (US Army), General Henderson (Texas Volunteers), and Colonel Davis (1st Mississippi Rifles) to the American delegation. Generals Tomas Requena and José María Ortega of the Mexican Army and Señor Manuel M. Llano, the governor of Nuevo León, represented General Ampudia.[1] Two separate issues faced the delegation: the surrender of the city of Monterrey and the surrender of the Mexican Army. The threat of renewed fighting hung over the heads of the representatives of both nations should they fail to agree on a solution acceptable to both sides.

The Mexican representatives were firm. Although willing to give up the city to the Americans, they refused to surrender their military forces in and around Monterrey. The Mexican delegation argued that the Mexican Army had not been defeated and was still capable of fighting. Taylor had sent his representatives to the conference hoping to achieve both goals. Eager to end the hostilities, though, the American commander advised his delegation to accept the Mexican offer to surrender the city without the surrender of the army. The following day, September 25, the Mexican and American representatives signed an armistice agreement that ended the battle.

But the document signed by both sides did more than end the fighting at Monterrey—for a time it halted the war in northern Mexico. Under the agreement, the Mexican government turned over all public property in Monterrey to the American Army. However, the Mexican Army retained its small arms and one six-gun battery of field artillery. The Mexican Army was required to evacuate the city and retire to a position south of a line passing through Rinconada Pass, Linares, and San Fernado de Pusos. No American troops were to advance beyond that line for the next eight weeks. One clause of the armistice allowed either side to revoke the truce at any time by notifying the other government of its intentions.[2]

Taylor agreed to the terms of the armistice for several reasons. He believed that he did not have enough troops at Monterrey to force the unconditional surrender of the Mexican Army. The Americans, running low on supplies and ammunition, had to be provisioned over lines stretching back to the Rio Grande and beyond. The Mexican Army still occupied the Black Fort, the city's most formidable fortification. This fort commanded Monterrey from its vantage point on the city's north side and could rake the attackers with its guns almost at all points. Taylor had no siege artillery with which to batter down the impregnable Mexican fortress, and his only chance to take it would have been by means of a costly frontal attack or a siege for which he lacked the resources. Inside Monterrey, a cathedral on the main plaza used as a powder magazine by the Mexican Army alarmed the American commander. If the fighting continued, a direct hit on the munitions store there would result in the death and maiming of many civilians as well as Americans. Finally, Taylor and Ampudia had recently learned of changes at the Mexican capital that had supposedly placed a government in power that wanted a negotiated end to the war. Convinced that the deal was the best that could be achieved under the circumstances, Taylor felt satisfied that the terms of the armistice met his primary objective—the capture of Monterrey.[3]

Ampudia surrendered Monterrey on September 26, 1846. Members of General Worth's division escorted General Taylor into the city to claim the prize his army had won. The Mexican Army began evacuating Monterrey on September 27. The retreating army rendered an eight-gun salute when the Mexican flag came down, and an American band played "Yankee Doodle" as the Stars and Stripes rose in its place. A twenty-one gun salute fired by the US batteries drowned out the cheering Americans. The Mexican withdrawal continued throughout September 28. Except for the US regulars who occupied the city and necessary medical personnel to care for the many wounded, no Americans were supposed to enter Monterrey until the last of the Mexican Army had departed. A number of volunteers from the field division, including members of the 1st Mississippi Rifles, ignored the stipulation in the treaty and went into the city to watch the exodus. Perhaps knowing he could do little to keep the volunteers out of town, Taylor ordered them to leave their weapons in camp to prevent any breach in the armistice on their part. According to Sgt. William Estes (Company E, State Fencibles), many of the Mississippians noted the dark complexions of Ampudia's officers and soldiers. He and others harangued the departing soldiers, insinuating that they were little more than slaves. They thought it a great joke to ask the dark-skinned soldiers who their owners were. One of the Mexican officers seen exiting the city was the notorious deserter John Riley of the San Patricio Battalion, a Mexican artillery unit containing deserters from the US Army. Taylor asked for the return of the Irishman, but Mexican officials refused to give him up, and he was allowed to accompany his artillery battery out of town. Unable to seize him, the Americans had to be satisfied with shouting curses at Riley as he rode past.[4] Despite this type of verbal harassment engaged in by the Americans, no serious violations of the armistice took place during the evacuation of the city.

Care of the many wounded proved to be the first task that faced the Americans after the battle. Taylor's official losses totaled 488 to 492 killed, wounded, and missing. However, many who witnessed or participated in the battle believed the actual number was much higher. The army's medical department established several general hospitals around Monterrey to care for the wounded of each division. Solid shot and grape from the Mexican artillery inflicted many severe wounds on the first day of the battle. Escopette and musket balls also produced their share of wounds. Flying stones, knocked loose by Mexican cannon fire, injured several Americans. Although lancers had killed a number of Americans outside the city, surgeons noted they treated few lance or bayonet wounds, an indication that an encounter with such weapons was usually fatal for the victim. Some of the unfortunate wounded lay on the ground on blankets in their blood-soaked clothing for several days before being moved to a hospital. Many of those with only slight wounds did not even seek the care of a surgeon. One unnamed Mississippian expressed the lack of confidence many soldiers had in army doctors to heal the sick and wounded when he wrote to the *Woodville Republican* that a sick man "may as well bid farewell to this world of ours, and look to the God of all good for protection."[5]

Monterrey had given the 1st Mississippi Rifles its first taste of battle. Davis wrote his brother, "The town is ours after a severe conflict."[6] The regiment saw fourteen killed and forty-seven wounded during the three days of fighting. One Mississippian wrote home to say that the regiment had been "cut to pieces." Capt. William P. Rogers (Company K, Tombigbee Volunteers) concurred, writing, "It was indeed dreadful—We lost a great many men and our chief officers are much to blame."[7] Mississippians took advantage of the armistice to write home to inform their friends and families that they had survived the battle and boast of the role that their regiment had played in the victory. In Mississippi, the news of the battle was received with both pride and fear: pride in the achievements of their warriors but fear of learning of the death or maiming of a loved one. Throughout the state, anxious citizens read accounts of the battles in local newspapers and letters from the front. Joseph Davis, typical of those who waited for news of the battle, informed his brother Jefferson that "Yesterday we read accounts of the Battle of Monterrey. You may easily imagine the feeling intense anxiety with which the news was read and listened to by all parties. I came to the list of killed and wounded, here my eyes failed me, my voice grew tremulous. But Heaven be praised you were not on the list."[8]

The Mississippi Democrat published a letter from Maj. Alexander B.

Bradford in which he announced to friends and family that "The Great City of Monterey is taken." He also sent word of acquaintances who had either been killed or survived. The same edition published a full list of the regiment's casualties broken down by company. Despite loss of personal friends, some "with their entrails torn out heads arms and legs shot off," Joseph Davis Howell wrote home, pleased that the Mississippians' loss had not been for naught. He noted "our Regiment wear the palm of honor for enough courage and hard fighting by universal acclamation. Brother Jeffs influence in the army here, and Gen Taylor is equaled by no other officers, the old Gen, calls us his striped tigers, from our uniform being all striped, and says damn the boys, they make their little brass mounted rifles do more execution in an hour than my regulars can do with musket and bayonet in a day." When news of the battle reached the troops stationed at Mier, James C. Browning noted with pride, "the Volunteers all fought Bravely Especially the 1st Tenn. and the Miss. Regiments."[9]

With the fighting over, the Americans at Monterrey had time to reflect on the events of the past few days. Many of the Mississippians, including Gen. John A. Quitman, disapproved of the armistice and voiced their opposition to the terms of surrender. Captain Rogers went so far as to label the armistice a folly. Many of the volunteers lacked confidence in Taylor, whom the captain thought did not have "the appearance of a great man." Most believed that they would have to face Ampudia's men in battle again. If that happened "Gen. Taylor and all his referees deserve the execretation of the whole American people." In his view, the enemy could have been captured. Others agreed with Rogers, including the nation's leaders in Washington, DC. Even Joseph Davis asked his brother, "why after forcing them into the narrow streets under circumstances that compelled a surrender unconditionally, were such terms accepted?"[10] Davis's answer was: "They were whipped, and we could afford to be generous."[11] Taylor and Davis, both with political futures ahead of them, would often find themselves fending off the charge of allowing the Mexicans at Monterrey to escape only to fight another day.

In addition to having to defend the armistice, Davis also became embroiled in a dispute involving the honor of his regiment. A disagreement developed over which unit should receive the credit for capturing the Tannery, an honor claimed by the 1st Mississippi Rifles, the 1st Tennessee Infantry, and the 3rd US Infantry. Captain Backus insisted, with some truth to his claim, that the fire delivered by his regulars from the roof of the building overlooking the Tannery had driven the enemy from their post. But both volunteer regiments emphatically stated that they alone had been responsible for the fort's capture.[12] The Tennessee volunteers argued that the Mississippians had played only a supporting role in the attack. Wrote

Col. William B. Campbell, "The Mississippi Regt. was on my right and gallantly came up to the charge and rushed forward with my men, but my Regt. being more directly in front of the fort and nearer to it than the Miss. Regt. reached it sooner and were the command that stormed the fort." Moreover, claimed some Tennesseans, a comparison of the weapons of the two regiments would convince most parties interested in the truth of the matter. The Tennesseans were armed with the standard flintlock musket, fitted with an eighteen-inch bayonet. The Mississippians, on the other hand, carried rifles without bayonets. They reasoned, a regiment equipped with bayonets would be the logical choice to charge a fortification while a regiment with only rifles would stay behind to provide covering fire. One Tennessean offered proof that his regiment had led the charge that drove the Mexicans from the fort. He claimed that, after the battle, doctors from his regiment removed rifle balls from the backs of several Tennesseans—balls that he insisted were fired by the Mississippians who were to the rear of his regiment.[13]

The Mississippians did not take this accusation from the Tennessee regiment without offering their own side of the story. Davis's sense of honor compelled him to defend his regiment's claim to the fort's capture. He sent the commander of the Tennessee regiment a letter asserting Mississippi's right to claim the disputed honor. When Colonel Campbell failed to give a satisfactory reply to the letter, Davis sought the help of his brigade commander and fellow Mississippian General Quitman. The general, not wanting to exhibit favoritism among the units in his brigade, tried to remain neutral in the dispute. Quitman's failure to vigorously support the Mississippians' initiated a rift in the once strong friendship between the general and Davis.[14] Letters from Tennesseans and Mississippians appeared throughout the United States for several months after the battle, all offering evidence to prove their respective claims.[15]

Discord between the two regiments grew worse as bickering broke out over who deserved the credit for ordering the charge on the Tannery. Quitman, Davis, and Campbell all voiced the opinion that they had been the first to order their men forward. Davis asked each of his company commanders to submit a report to help him secure his and the regiment's laurels. Several diplomatically wrote that they heard no command and only moved when they saw the line advancing. McClung, recognized by the Mississippians to be the first American to enter the Tannery, strongly asserted that the order to charge had originated with him. Officers near McClung during the battle supported the wounded man's claim. McClung even challenged Davis over statements his commander had made that cast doubt on his assertions. The scramble for credit disgusted some officers of the Mississippi regiment. Captain Rogers wrote his wife, "I understand that Colonel Davis has just finished his report of the battle and if it is as I have it, it is both partial and false." The concern over one's own reputation, though, also extended to Rogers, who contended "If he has done me injustice he must give me satisfaction."[16] These squabbles soiled the true accomplishments of the Mississippi volunteers in Monterrey.

Life in Monterrey after the battle proved to be monotonous for the Mississippians. Rogers lamented the lack of refined entertainment available to the men and blasted his fellow volunteers for their disregard of the Sabbath. Only a person who had commanded a group of idle volunteer soldiers, Rogers complained to his wife, could know of the difficulty facing volunteer officers such as him. Hardly a day passed without the murder of a Mexican or a volunteer. He reported that "Every day or two a straggling soldier from our camp is killed and then the Texians kill two of three Mexicans to pay for it." Then another killing could be expected in retaliation for the previous one, and so the deadly cycle continued. Lamented Rogers, "We do not wish to lead the dull inactive life we are leading now."[17]

Seeking diversion from their boredom of camp life, the volunteers went into the city as often as they could. One of the regiment's members, Pvt. George H. Hise (Company H, Vicksburg Volunteers), paid a high price for his visit to Monterrey—a dishonorable discharge from the service. Assigned guard duty one night, Hise paid another man to take his place so he could go on a spree. An infraction such as this was usually handled by a regimental court martial, but because the volunteers were deep in enemy territory, General Quitman recommended that Hise receive a general court martial instead. Confessing his guilt at his trial, Hise claimed that hiring a substitute was a common practice in his company. The remorseful volunteer pleaded for mercy from the court, saying that he could never return home with such a cloud of disgrace over his head. Found guilty, Hise was dishonorably discharged from the service, cut off from his family and friends, and set adrift to fend for himself in a hostile country.[18]

During the same time, Joseph Davis Howell recounted an unexpected reunion during one of his visits to town. "I was walking about seeing sights one day when suddenly an old woman ran out of a house near me caught my arm and insisted with many vehement exclamations in my coming into her house, understanding what she wanted having learned to speak a little and understand a good deal of their language I went in." He found inside a Mexican soldier whose life he had saved in the attack on the Tannery who was about to be bayonetted by a Tennessee volunteer. "[He] shook me by the hand, while she kissed and cried over him and me until she made me ashamed of myself for having done nothing more than my duty in protecting a poor wounded prisoner." The elated mother "offered me every thing to eat she had in the house, and tried to make me take a costly blanket which the poor fellow had on when he was shot, I was sorely tempted, for it was the most beautiful thing I ever saw, and I wanted it for father, but it looked too much like being paid for doing my duty and I could not take it." Nevertheless, she did not intend for her son's savior to go away empty-handed. "[She] loaded my pockets however with all kinds of fruits and filled a hankerchief with their delicate tortillas which are very acceptable, particularly as provisions were rather scarce in our camp." Howell exclaimed that his and others' "humanity and gentlemanly conduct during and after the conflict" prompted the grateful residents to call them "los buenos Americanos."[19] Howell's story serves as a counterpoint to the many tales of abusive behavior by volunteers toward the Mexican populace.

The odds of another battle seemed remote. Joseph Davis Howell predicted to his mother that he would be home in a "month or six weeks."[20] The volunteers had come to Mexico to fight, and many of them, with their curiosity satisfied by the recent combat, longed to return home. The Mississippians in Capt. William Shivors's Independent Company, disbanded by Taylor in his release of the Texas volunteers, hurriedly made their way home. Invalids from the Mississippi regiment streamed northward during the lull in fighting resulting from the armistice.[21] Colonel Davis, granted a sixty-day furlough by Taylor, traveled to his Mississippi home in mid-October, leaving Major Bradford in command of the regiment at Monterrey.[22] The *News Orleans Picayune* noted his return to the United States, saying "We notice that a collation was to have been given on Tuesday evening last at Vicksburg, including compliments to Colonel Jefferson Davis, Capt. George P. Crump, of the [Vicksburg] volunteers; Capt. John Willis, of the Southrons, and *all* the volunteers of said companies." The writer praised "all of those brave Mississippi regiment who have returned from Mexico, on furlough and on account of ill health. . . . We say 'Honor to the Brave.'"[23]

In a letter to his mother written shortly after the battle, Howell wrote that men of the regiment were pleased with Davis, indicating that they had come to see the reason for his insistence on discipline. "If . . . our Colonel, Jeff Davis, even thinks we could be useful, there is not a man in his regiment who would not sacrifice his life to obey him, so much has his gallant conduct raised him in their estimation." He contended that Davis's reputation with the army for "coolness, courage, and discretion" would not be believed at home. "I verily believe that if he should tell his men to jump into a cannon's mouth they would think it alright, and would say, 'Colonel Jeff,' as they call him, 'knows best, so hurrah, boys, let's go ahead.'" Davis could always be found in front of his regiment, leading the way. He ended the letter by saying "I never wish to be commanded by a truer soldier than Colonel Davis."[24]

Papers throughout the state praised Davis and his regiment. *The Mississippi Democrat* carried a short laudatory piece that extolled the virtue of its fellow Mississippians. "The Mississippi Regiment, Commanded by Davis, was as we learn from various quarters, the bravest of the brave at the dreadful siege of Monterrey. They have shown themselves to be among the best soldiers in the world. The bravery of the American Volunteer troops hitherto has been exhibited in the *defence* of their own homes, but here is the same kind of troops in a war of *assault*. The Mississippians were the leaders in those terrific storms of death. We feel proud of that troop." The soldiers' actions showed that they not only excelled in civil life but on the battlefield as well: "Hurrah! for 'the young planters and professional gentlemen constituting the Mississippi regiment.'" A few days later, the paper announced that there would be a public meeting at the courthouse to "pay a tribute of respect to the memory of our fellow-citizens who have died in the service of their common country."[25]

Davis, by his absence, missed one of the army's saddest occurrences of the war—the tragic accidental death of Bvt. Capt. Randolph Ridgley. This popular officer from the 3rd US Artillery had served with distinction in the battles along the Rio Grande and had assumed command of Capt. Samuel Ringgold's light battery after Ringgold's death at Palo Alto. During the Battle of Monterrey, soldiers from both sides tore loose sharp volcanic stones from the city's streets to obtain material to build barricades. Many of the streets remained unrepaired in the weeks following the fighting. On the evening of October 25, Ridgley's horse stumbled on some of the loose paving stones and threw its rider head first to the ground. The talented artilleryman died shortly after the accident, an ironic end for an officer reputed to be one of the best horsemen in the army. Taylor and his regular and volunteer officers attended Ridgley's elaborate funeral.[26] Money was raised by subscription to return some of the officers who had died at Monterrey to their home states. The bodies of these officers, including Ridgley's, were disinterred, and they were then placed in storage until they could be transported to the United States.[27]

In December, quartermaster Capt. Franklin Smith received permission from Gen. Robert Patterson to leave his post at Camargo and visit Monterrey. The Mississippian had been plagued by illness and had asked the general to be allowed to go to the city to recuperate. While in Monterrey, Smith had the opportunity to see his friends in the Mississippi regiment. After meeting Major Bradford and Captain Rogers, Smith called on Lieutenant Colonel McClung. McClung, recovering from his wounds, greeted his visitor by calling out, "Why Smith is that you, when the Hell did you get here? Tie your horse and come in!" Everyone Smith met, including McClung himself, told him that the lieutenant colonel had been the first man to enter the Tannery. He also likely described the wound he had received on that day that ended his career with the regiment. A musket ball had struck his left hand in which McClung was holding his sword scabbard. The projectile drove five finger bones and pieces of the scabbard deep into his hip, requiring surgeons to remove these objects later when his wound would not heal. During the few days Smith spent in the city, several officers from the regiment acted as guides and escorted him to the places where the Mississippians had fought. Before returning to Camargo, Smith visited the warehouse that held the remains of Ridgely and the other deceased officers awaiting the journey home. Stacked up in plain boxes that resembled musket crates that he was so used to seeing at Camargo, Smith thought the resting place did not sufficiently honor these American heroes. With his furlough about to expire, Captain Smith returned to Camargo to resume his quartermaster duties.[28]

The eight weeks of peace promised by the armistice ended early. President Polk and his administration in Washington, DC, unlike Taylor on the scene in Mexico, did not think the truce was in the nation's best interest. Upset at the general for allowing the Mexican Army to leave the city as well as granting Mexico time to rebuild its forces for the next battle, Polk told Secretary of War Marcy to instruct Taylor to suspend the armistice. On October 13, Marcy sent Taylor a letter containing this new order. Taylor, in turn, notified the Mexican government that hostilities would recommence on November 15, 1846.[29]

Monterrey began to stir as Taylor prepared his army for a new campaign. Taylor planned to penetrate deeper into Mexico and occupy more territory. Accordingly, on November 12, Taylor left Monterrey and accompanied General Worth's division southwest through Rinconada Pass to take possession of the city of Saltillo, the capital of Coahuila.[30] Taylor thought it necessary to control the road through Saltillo and its nearby mountain passes in order to secure all the gains his army had made so far. Taylor wanted to explore the feasibility of using the road from Saltillo to San Luis Potosi as the invasion route to Mexico's heartland. Leaving Worth to tend to these tasks, Taylor returned to Monterrey.[31] Soon the general would be on the road again—this time in the company of the restless men of the 1st Mississippi Rifles.

Depicted in this drawing at Buena Vista, General Zachary Taylor later praised the men of the 1st Mississippi Rifles and their colonel for their role in the American success at the battle. Drawing by Gary Zaboly.

"The Battle of Buena Vista." Painting by Samuel Chamberlain, courtesy West Point Museum Collection, United States Military Academy.

Samuel Chamberlain's postwar drawings depict the volunteers of both Mississippi regiments wearing red overshirts similar to the one shown here. While it and the accouterments are period-correct reproductions, the M1841 Rifle is original and bears the date 1847. Photo by Ernesto Rodriguez III.

6
The Victoria Expedition

The war has not been prosecuted in such a manner to bring the enemy to peace.
—Capt. William P. Rogers

MEXICO'S REFUSAL TO ADMIT DEFEAT after a series of military reverses was unexpected. Back in the United States, the public and the politicians were beginning to express dismay that no end was in sight. Captain Rogers (Company K, Tombigbee Volunteers) shared his opinion of the situation: "Either more active operations or an entire cessation of hostilities—But [of] the latter there is little prospect—The war has not been prosecuted in such a manner to bring the enemy to peace."[1]

Since the army's early days at Corpus Christi, President James K. Polk and Secretary of War William L. Marcy had allowed Zachary Taylor freedom to interpret and execute his instructions. The army's victories at Palo Alto, Resaca de la Palma, and Monterrey had increased Taylor's popularity with both his troops and the American public. Now that the armistice had been terminated, the general had every intention of continuing his string of successes by vigorously pushing on to the very gates of the enemy nation's capital at Mexico City. Unknown to Taylor, control of the war would soon slip from his hands into those of another general.

President Polk received advice early in the war from three informed men: Bvt. Maj. Gen. Zachary Taylor, Maj. Gen. Winfield Scott, and Missouri Senator Thomas Hart Benton. All three urged the capture of Mexico City, and each offered the president a plan to accomplish the feat.[2] These men reasoned that the occupation of Mexican territory alone would not be enough to force Mexico to surrender, and with much of northern Mexico, including New Mexico, and California under American control, peace seemed to be no closer. Only the capture of the capital, they warned, would break the enemy's will to fight and bring an end to hostilities. Polk agreed and began to formulate a plan. But certain problems had to be solved before Polk could put the plan into action.

The most serious—and politically thorny—was the selection of a leader for the proposed campaign. Applicants for the position abounded. Compounding the problem for Polk, the plan's originators all laid claim to the post. Taylor, proud of his victories in the war, expected the administration to allow him to continue in his role as the commander of American forces in Mexico. Scott, the highest ranking officer in the US Army and its commanding general, thought his position entitled him to lead the expedition. Benton's claim to the post, although weaker than either Taylor's or Scott's, greatly appealed to Polk. Both Taylor and Scott were Whigs, and the examples of George Washington, Andrew Jackson, and William Henry Harrison reminded Polk that victorious generals often captured the votes of the American public and, the greatest prize of all, the White House. Polk hoped to use Senator Benton, whose military experience consisted of his position as a lieutenant colonel in the War of 1812, to prevent the Whigs from gaining any more political advantages by placing this leading Democrat in control of the war's prosecution. Ultimately, Polk's maneuverings failed, and he reluctantly gave the command of the expedition to Winfield Scott.[3]

Yet another problem existed though. Scott needed troops. The volunteers already in the field had only agreed to a one-year term of service, and that time already was half up. As a matter of expediency, Scott would have to assume command of the bulk of Taylor's army if his campaign was to begin on schedule. Even then, replacement troops would be needed to garrison the towns Taylor had seized as well as replenish Scott's column once the one-year volunteers headed home. To solve this problem, the War Department issued a call in November 1846 for a second wave of volunteers for Mexico. This time, however, the term of enlistment was "for the war." The administration did not want to end up in the situation of a mass exodus from the seat of war, which was what was expected to happen the following June. For Mississippi and other states, this new call offered men who were shut out of the first call a second chance to soldier in Mexico.[4]

In Mexico, Taylor forged ahead with his own plans, unaware that Scott had superseded him and was on his way to take command of the American Army in Mexico. With Worth holding Saltillo, Taylor proposed to occupy another key city; thus he gathered a force for the purpose of capturing Victoria, the capital of Tamaulipas. The route to Mexico City via the road from Saltillo had proven to be impractical as the army's supply line would have to stretch back over 800 miles of dry, mountainous roads to the vital depots on the Rio Grande.[5] The occupation of Victoria would secure the state of Tamaulipas, preventing the Mexican Army from accessing the rear as well as open an overland path to the port at Tampico. A base at one of Mexico's ports would greatly shorten the supply line for an American advance on Mexico City from the coast.

In December 1846 Taylor reorganized his troops to meet the requirements of his new objectives. Twiggs now commanded Col. William S. Harney's brigade of regulars, composed of Bragg's battery, four companies of the 2nd US Dragoons, five companies of the 2nd US Infantry, and the 3rd US Infantry, and Col. Persifor F. Smith's brigade, composed of Sherman's battery, two companies of the US Mounted Rifles, the 1st US Infantry, and the 7th US Infantry. Taylor reincorporated the Baltimore Battalion and the 1st Georgia back into Quitman's volunteer brigade. On December 13, Harney's brigade left Monterrey for Victoria. Quitman's brigade, which still included the 1st Mississippi and the 1st Tennessee, followed the next day. According to John S. Holt, a Mississippian detailed to serve as the general's secretary, "The men were in fine spirits. Those who, when they had marched before, were lean and sickly, let out their belts a notch or two, and, slinging their rifles and muskets over their shoulders, took the route-step with a springiness which, however, was changed before night."[6]

The 200-mile journey took the column two weeks to complete. Marches along dry, dusty roads produced familiar complaints from Taylor's soldiers. The further south the men progressed toward Victoria, the more tropical the landscape and climate became. The men marveled at the many new varieties of plants and animals they encountered, feasting on such delicacies as bananas, pineapples, oranges, lemons, limes, sugar cane, guava, parrots, and armadillos.[7] In Captain Rogers' opinion, the Mexican people of this region possessed a better character than those living in and around Monterrey. Here he found them to be gentle in disposition and fair in complexion. John S. Holt, however, warned that not all inhabitants they encountered were to be trusted, writing, "To-day one of our Mississippians, foot-weary and straggling in the rear of the column, got up behind a ranchero for a ride, giving him his rifle to carry. The Mexican soon dexterously twitched him off the horse and rode away with the weapon!"[8]

Rumored resistance to Taylor's advance by the Mexicans failed to materialize. Unfortunately for Mexico, the governor of Tamaulipas did not receive the support from his government for which he had pleaded. The inhabitants of the towns and villages through which the Americans passed warned that there would soon be a big "fandango," but Rogers and others doubted a battle would take place.[9] The Mississippi captain boasted that, if such a fight did occur, he would distinguish himself or die in the attempt.

Hoping to make the march easier, some volunteers purchased horses with their own money. Without dragoons in his brigade, Quitman relied on these self-mounted volunteers to scout the way. Mississippi Lt. William H. H. Paterson, a member of Company K, was selected to command the ad hoc unit.[10] On December 29, 1846, one year to the day that Polk signed Texas annexation into law, the Americans entered Victoria. Noted Rogers of their arrival, "We marched into Victoria with great pomp and show—raised the flag of our country and saluted it in good style."[11]

A serious threat appeared that demanded Taylor's attention elsewhere during his march to Victoria—the return of Antonio López de Santa Anna to Mexico. The former president had been living in exile in Cuba when the war broke out. He sent a representative to convince Polk and his advisers that he would work for peace between the two countries if allowed to return home. Gambling that Santa Anna would do what he said, Polk agreed. With the knowledge and approval of the United States, the charismatic leader was allowed to slip through the US Navy's blockade. Welcomed home, Santa Anna accepted the Mexican presidency once more and abandoned his promise of peace. The "Napoleon of the West" took to the field and, at San Lois Potosi, began rebuilding the Mexican Army after its defeat at Monterrey. He eyed Worth's small, isolated force at Saltillo, hoping he could deal the Americans a smashing blow while their army was divided. Luckily for Worth, help was nearby. Upon learning of the impending attack, Gen. John E. Wool quickly marched to Saltillo with his command to reinforce Worth. Having lost the advantage he sought, Santa Anna decided to build a larger force before advancing northward.[12]

General Wool had recently arrived in Mexico. Following his orders from the War Department, the general had assembled a force of regulars and volunteers throughout the summer and fall. Troops from the Mississippi River Valley received word to rendezvous at San Antonio, Texas. Part of the administration's early war strategy had called for Wool to lead a column from Texas across the Rio Grande and into Chihuahua. He and his troops were to take possession of the Mexican state for the United States. Wool's force consisted of the 1st and 2nd Illinois Infantry, the 1st Kentucky Cavalry, the 1st Arkansas Cavalry, Capt. John Macrae Washington's Battery of the 4th US Artillery, a battalion of the 6th US Infantry, and Colonel Harney with four companies of the 2nd US Dragoons.[13] Events in northern Mexico and New Mexico had rendered the advance on Chihuahua unnecessary, and Wool received word from Taylor to join him instead in order to support the general's new campaign. Harney and his dragoons joined Twiggs's division, but Wool retained the rest of his troops at the town of Parras. A rapid march from Parras enabled Wool to come to Worth's rescue.[14]

On December 16, while at Montemorelos, Taylor received Worth's frantic message informing the general of Santa Anna's expected advance on Saltillo. The Mexicans had learned of Scott's plans when they intercepted and killed an officer carrying dispatches to Taylor that told of the new developments, including the reduction in the number of troops in northern Mexico. Instructing Quitman's volunteer brigade to proceed to Victoria as planned, Taylor took Twiggs's division and returned to Monterrey to ward off the threatened attack. News of Wool's timely arrival on the scene reached Taylor as he traveled the road between Monterrey and Saltillo. With the situation again under control, Taylor retraced his route to Victoria and entered that city on January 4, 1847.[15]

Captain Franklin Smith, still on duty at Camargo with the Quartermaster Department, took the news of Santa Anna's threat to northern Mexico to mean that he might finally have a chance to rejoin his friends in the 1st Mississippi Rifles. A letter from home had convinced him that continued service at Camargo was not worth being away from home with his "wife's health . . . delicate one of [his] children sick the negroes disobedient [and his] business neglected and ruinous." He hoped to be reassigned to the regiment, shouldering a rifle if that was the only position open for him. Explained Smith, "I would not wish to open new accounts or be compelled to assume the quarter master's duties there for the present, that would defeat my object but to have a chance to mingle in the fight and that if I escaped unhurt to get a leave of absence immediately." When his request was denied, the disappointed Mississippian wrote, "I will now resign I have seen no fight it is true but I have done all I can to get into one. . . . I resign solely on account of my wife." His last diary entry related that he was waiting for his superior, Captain Crossman, to return to Carmargo so he could submit his resignation and start his homeward journey.[16]

Events in Washington, DC finally caught up with General Taylor. On December 20, 1846, while in route to Victoria, Taylor received a letter from his commanding general. Scott informed Taylor that he was coming to Mexico to take personal command of a new front that would soon be opened. He asked Taylor to join him on the Rio Grande to discuss the new campaign, but unfortunately for both Scott and Taylor his letter arrived too late for the meeting to take place. The letter instructed Taylor to hold a defensive line and not advance beyond Monterrey. This change in strategy was necessary because Scott wanted to capture Vera Cruz and march inland before the onset of the yellow fever season. To do this, however, he would have to take most of Taylor's troops from northern Mexico so the new offensive in central Mexico could begin as soon as possible.[17] Taylor's disbelief turned to outrage when he learned that Scott had already put this new plan in motion. Not being able to communicate directly with Taylor, Scott issued orders to William O. Butler to start 9,000 of Taylor's troops on their way to Brazos Island and Tampico from where they would embark for the upcoming campaign. Scott promised Taylor that he could resume his operations once new regiments arrived in Mexico—the volunteers who were just now being raised in the United States. This did little to soothe the general's injured pride or make up for the loss of so many of his veteran troops.[18]

The men in Taylor's command felt that Polk and his administration had betrayed General Taylor. Their hostility toward the president spilled over to Scott as well. At Camargo, Franklin Smith noted Scott's unsuccessful attempt to meet with Taylor with the irreverent entry, "The great mogul of the army Maj. Gen. W. Scott commander in chief . . . arrived this morning." Colonel Davis claimed that Scott wanted to be the next president and had seized command of the army in Mexico as a way to eliminate Taylor as a rival for the office. Despite his earlier misgivings about the general, Rogers contended that he had great confidence in Taylor and saw him as the victim of political intrigue between the president and the commanding general.[19]

With Taylor gone to attend to Santa Anna's threatened attack, the Mississippians and other volunteers of their brigade settled into their camps at Victoria. Quitman, the highest-ranking American officer in the area upon the departure of Taylor and Twiggs, commanded the troops at Victoria. He appointed Maj. Charles J. Williams of the 1st Georgia to command the town's garrison. Each of the brigade's regiments, including the 1st Mississippi, provided two companies for the garrison.[20] Rogers recorded that the wife of one of the 1st Georgia's lieutenants had accompanied her husband to Victoria. Modest and lady-like in person, she presented an amusing sight to the men as she rode by on her mustang, armed with pistols tucked into her belt and sash.[21] With McClung in Monterrey recovering from his wound and Davis still on furlough in Mississippi, the task of leading the regiment fell to Major Bradford. Serving as acting major, Capt. John McNutt Sharp (Company A, Yazoo Volunteers) assisted Bradford in his duties. While not questioning the personal character of Bradford and Sharp, one Mississippian gave both men low marks for their performance, saying that "they do not excel as tacticians."[22]

The 1st Mississippi Rifles underwent minor reorganization while at Victoria. The men elected six new company officers during January to fill vacancies caused by illness and battle. Horace H. Miller (Company H, Vicksburg Volunteers) received the important appointment to sergeant major. Though the health of the Mississippians was generally good, the hardships of service had shrunk the size of the regiment. Seventy-one Mississippians had died. An even greater number had returned home. Some still occupied hospital beds at Monterrey, Camargo, and Matamoros. Company A had only thirty-six of its original ninety-three members.[23] Many changes had taken place since the regiment left Mississippi only seven months earlier.

On January 4, 1847, Davis rejoined his regiment at Victoria just in time to witness the redistribution of forces.[24] General Patterson's division, following Scott's instructions, had recently arrived at Victoria. In mid-January, Taylor sent both Quitman's and Patterson's divisions southward to Tampico where they joined the forces being assembled for Scott's campaign.[25] In a speech reminiscent of Washington's farewell address to his officers, Taylor thanked the departing troops for their loyalty and commended them on the service they had performed for their country.[26] With the great demand for troops placed on Taylor by Scott, none could be spared to garrison Victoria. Taylor selected a small detail to accompany him on his return to Monterrey. The general honored the Mississippians by choosing their regiment to be a part of his personal bodyguard. The light artillery batteries of Bragg and Sherman as well as several companies of May's 2nd US Dragoons completed the escort.[27] Although disappointed to miss the opportunity to march on Mexico City, Davis felt he could not desert Taylor during this difficult period in his former father-in-law's career. For Taylor, detaching Davis from Quitman and the 1st Tennessee Infantry could have had the added benefit of separating the two quarreling regiments as well as quashing the growing rivalry between the colonel and his brigade commander.[28]

The escort encountered no Mexican soldiers—regular or guerrillas—on the four-day journey, and Taylor arrived safely at Monterrey on January 25, 1847. One incident marred the trip for Captain Rogers. The captain, who had often complained of the rowdy behavior that went on in the volunteer camp, had become concerned about the excess drinking by the Mississippians. One night, Lt. William H. H. Patterson (Company K, Tombigbee Volunteers) became drunk and, in a fit of anger, struck Rogers. The captain knocked Patterson to the ground and proceeded to choke him. Rogers released the man only after realizing he was too intoxicated to know the offense he had committed. Rogers' anger was intensified by the fact that the brawl took place only a few feet away from the body of a fellow officer, Josephus J. Tatum (Company F, Lafayette Volunteer) who had died only a short time before. Patterson, claimed the captain, later tried desperately to atone for his indiscretion, but Rogers never forgave his first lieutenant for the incident.[29]

Taylor spent only four days in Monterrey before starting for Saltillo. He and his escort left Monterrey on January 31 and entered Saltillo two days later. The journey had taken the Mississippians over the mountainous Rinconada Pass on to the high plateau on which Saltillo rested. Hemmed in on the east and west by mountains, the city impressed many of the volunteers. Not as large as Monterrey, Saltillo appeared clean and industrious. A fountain in the main plaza shot water 10 feet into the air. Saltillo's church, the third largest in Mexico, became a major point of attraction for Americans visiting the city. Rogers noted that the priest had removed some of the most valuable art work from the church to prevent its theft by the Americans.[30] Taylor did not quarter his troops in Saltillo but instead marched 5 miles south of the town to a small hacienda. There he established his camp on the plains of Buena Vista.

In just a few short months, the course of the war had significantly changed. Interest in the United States now focused on the proposed capture of Vera Cruz, and northern Mexico no longer seemed important. Taylor's victories had made him a popular figure and a potential candidate for president. Relegated to a small defensive command, his chances to add to his successes seemed remote. Taylor's troops felt dejected and excluded from the action. With more than half of their term of service completed, the volunteers prepared to settle down to the dull routine of army life. Unknown to Taylor and his small army at Saltillo, the general would soon fight the greatest battle of his career at a narrow pass called Angostura near the hacienda of Buena Vista. The deeds of Colonel Davis and the 1st Mississippi Rifles under Taylor at Buena Vista would forever secure for them a prominent place in the history of the war.

7
Glory Bound

Excited by the sound [of artillery], the regiment pressed rapidly forward, manifesting upon this, as on other occasions, their more than willingness to meet the enemy.
—Col. Jefferson Davis

General Taylor disregarded his instructions from the War Department to halt his advance, choosing instead to remain in the vicinity of Saltillo. Scott and Marcy had wanted Taylor to fall back to Monterrey until he could be reinforced by a second wave of volunteers who were on their way to Mexico. Taylor, partly out of stubbornness and partly out of real concern, reasoned that Monterrey could not safely be protected without first securing the mountain passes that led to the city.[1] The general established the main base for the troops still under his command at the hacienda of Agua Nueva, 12 miles south of Saltillo. His actions helped set the stage for the upcoming Battle of Buena Vista.

Rumors of another advance by Santa Anna reached the Americans at their camp at Agua Nueva. Taylor, who had returned to Monterrey with the 1st Mississippi Rifles as his escort, left General Wool in command at Saltillo. Needing to find out if the reports were true, Wool sent out mounted patrols to investigate. Proof of a hostile force in the area soon came when one patrol failed to return to camp. The scouting party, consisting of about seventy members of the Arkansas and Kentucky cavalry, went to bed on the night of January 22 without taking the simple precaution of posting pickets. They awoke the next morning to find themselves surrounded by a party of several thousand Mexican lancers and surrendered. Daniel Drake Henrie, a Texan who had been guiding the volunteers, escaped to carry word of the incident back to Wool. Five days later, the Mexicans captured another small detachment of Kentucky cavalry.[2] Despite these encounters with the enemy, security by the volunteers in the area remained extremely lax. Lieutenant Robert L. Moore (Company H, Vicksburg Volunteers) and Lt. Samuel French of Bragg's battery even ventured off alone on a hunting trip together only a few days before the Battle of Buena Vista. Most Americans thought the main body of the Mexican Army had gone east to meet Scott's attack on Vera Cruz and discounted the possibility of a large enemy force in the area as another "stampede" like the one in December.[3]

Taylor and his escort returned to Saltillo around the middle of February. On the 20th, the general sent Captain May with 300 dragoons, Captain Ben McCulloch's (Texas) Spy Company, and one section of Washington's battery south on the road to San Luis Potosi to survey the situation and locate the Mexicans. The patrol returned to Agua Nueva that night with the news that Santa Anna's army had indeed arrived. Taylor and Wool decided to abandon Agua Nueva in the morning in favor of a stronger position closer to the hacienda at Buena Vista.[4] Taylor ordered all supplies that could not be removed from his forward base destroyed in order to prevent them from falling into the hands of the Mexican Army. He assigned the Arkansas and Kentucky cavalry the task of loading the supplies into the waiting quartermaster wagons, but the dragoons had to finish the job because the volunteers proved unwilling to perform manual labor. The Mexican Army's approach interrupted the work of the Americans, causing panic in the ranks of the untried volunteers. Taylor's rear guard set torches to the hacienda and burned the supplies they could not carry away before hurriedly abandoning Agua Nueva.[5]

Santa Anna's advance elements had left San Luis Potosi on January 27, 1847, after listening to a speech in which he announced, "Let our motto be conquer or die." Units continued to depart over the next three days. His artillery train consisted of three 24-pounders, three 16-pounders, five 12-pounders, eight 8-pounders, and one howitzer with the appropriate ammunition. The shells, canister, and grape, as well as 500 boxes of musket cartridges, were transported in twenty-one wagons the army had contracted to carry the ammunition. What would not fit in the wagon was carried by 450 mules. "The sick, the weak, and unarmed" were to be left behind at San Luis Potosi. A minimal medical staff remained to care for the sick, as did a small number of officers to train recruits. Santa Anna placed Gen. Juan Amador in charge of the city.[6]

The Mexican Army under Santa Anna had made a rapid and grueling march from San Luis Potosi over inhospitable terrain. Not often given credit for his military ability, Santa Anna's career was marked by several incidents in which he had quickly appeared before his enemy expected him. He had reminded his men what was expected of them before they left San Luis Potosi: "The Mexican solider is well known for the frugality and his capability of sufferance." He intended to hold them to that standard. Santa Anna set out with an army that numbered over 20,000 men. Several thousand women and children, the families of Mexican soldiers, accompanied the army. Shortages of food and water caused great suffering on the march. Santa Anna drove the army northward toward Taylor. Many of his soldiers died from exposure—many more deserted the column.[7]

Santa Anna's army had shrunk to 15,142 as it neared Taylor's forces on February 19, but the Mexican leader still had good reason to expect success. Stragglers caught up with the main body, and his force soon numbered 21,000. Moreover, Taylor had only 4,759 effectives in the immediate area.[8] Thus Santa Anna outnumbered Taylor four to one. The American general, deprived of most of his veteran regulars by Scott, now faced the Mexicans with a generally inexperienced army of volunteers. If Santa Anna could position part of his larger army in the Americans' rear at Saltillo, he could both block the retreat of his enemy and prevent reinforcements from reaching Taylor. If Santa Anna could defeat Taylor's small army, the Americans would then be trapped in the mountain valley and be forced to surrender. Such a victory for the Mexicans would reverse the American gains and drastically affect the outcome of the war. Writing as Santa Anna's troops neared Agua Nueva, Lt. Carnot Posey (Company B, Wilkinson Volunteers) expressed the thoughts of most of Taylor's troops when he said "Every man feels that the honor of his country is now placed in his hands."[9]

The few remaining veteran troops still with Taylor played a crucial role in the approaching battle. The general's veteran regulars included Capts. Braxton Bragg's and Thomas W. Sherman's batteries of the 3rd US Artillery; Capt. John M. Washington's battery of the 4th US Artillery; Capt. Charles May's company of 2nd US Dragoons; and Capt. Enoch Steen's squadron (two companies) of the 1st US Dragoons. The veteran volunteers of Taylor's command included Capt. Ben McCulloch's Texas Spy Company, Capt. Patrick Edward Connor's Company of Texas Rifles, and Col. Jefferson Davis's 1st Mississippi Rifles. Of these veteran troops, the artillery and the Mississippians would be instrumental in winning the day for the Americans. The untested 1st Illinois Infantry, 2nd Illinois Infantry, 2nd Indiana Infantry, 3rd Indiana Infantry, 2nd Kentucky Infantry, 1st Arkansas Cavalry, and 1st Kentucky Cavalry completed Taylor's scant force at Buena Vista.[10]

According to James C. Browning, the opening rounds of the Battle of Buena Vista were fired by a Mexican battery on February 22, 1847.[11] The day happened to be the 115th anniversary of George Washington's birthday, a fact that bolstered the Americans' morale as Taylor's troops celebrated the life of the nation's first president. Taylor had left the battlefield placement of the troops to General Wool while he made arrangements for the defense of the hacienda and the town of Saltillo. The American line of battle stretched across the mouth of the valley that led to Saltillo and the mountain pass to Monterrey. Wool placed Washington's battery facing south on the road from San Luis Potosi to block the important route. Ravines cut deeply into the plateau, limiting access to the plains of Buena Vista. The valley was constricted here, giving it the local name of La Angostura (the Narrows), a name by which the battle is known in Mexico. A mass of impassable ravines protected the American line on the right. From west to east, starting behind Washington's battery, the Americans' main line of battle consisted of the 1st Illinois Infantry (aided by Connor's Texas Rifles), the 2nd Illinois Infantry, the 2nd Kentucky Infantry, the 1st Arkansas Cavalry, and the 1st Kentucky Cavalry. To the rear of those troops sat the reserves, again from west to east, consisting of the 2nd and 3rd Indiana Infantry, the 1st Mississippi Rifles, the 1st and 2nd US Dragoons, and the batteries of Bragg and Sherman.[12] As they waited for the Mexican attack, the American bands played the patriotic tune "Hail Columbia."[13]

At about 11 a.m. on February 22, a Mexican officer approached the American line carrying a message from Santa Anna for General Taylor. The Mexican general informed his opponent that his small, outnumbered force was surrounded and asked the American commander to surrender in order to prevent unnecessary bloodshed on both sides. Taylor sent the officer back to his own lines carrying the courteous but firm reply, "I beg to say that I decline acceding to your request." Soon afterward, as already noted by Browning, Mexican artillery boomed and announced the battle had commenced.[14]

Only a few units from the two armies engaged in the fighting on February 22. The majority of both sides sat as spectators to the events that unfolded in the foothills to the east. In an attempt to gain access to the plateau behind Taylor's small army, Santa Anna sent a body of light infantry into the hills that overlooked the American left (east) flank. (Critics of the questionable armistice could point to the fact that these troops were commanded by none other than Gen. Pedro Ampudia.) Taylor ordered the Kentucky cavalry to dismount and ascend the heights to counter the threat. Eventually, the general sent Maj. Willis A. Gorman and four rifle companies from the Indiana regiments to assist the Kentuckians. Muzzle flashes marked the progress of the combatants as they climbed high and higher. Taylor broke off the engagement at dusk and recalled the volunteers from the mountainside. Both sides laid down on their arms to pass a cold and rainy fireless night as darkness cloaked the battlefield.[15]

When it appeared that Santa Anna would wait until morning to launch his major attack, Taylor took May's dragoons and the Mississippi Regiment with him to check on the situation around Saltillo. Major William B. Warren had been left to guard Saltillo with four companies of the 1st Illinois Infantry. Captain Lucien B. Webster's two 24-pound howitzers commanded the southern approach to the town from his position in an earthen redoubt on the edge of Saltillo. First Lieutenant William Shover, supported by Companies B (Wilkinson Volunteers) and E (State Fencibles) of the 1st Mississippi Rifles, had been detailed to guard Taylor's headquarters at the hacienda of Buena Vista and the Americans' supply train that had been parked there. Although large bodies of Mexican cavalry had been seen off in the mountains earlier in the day, all seemed quiet for the night.[16]

A dispute had arisen earlier in the day over which companies of Mississippians would have to remain at the hacienda and thereby miss any action on the front line. Colonel Davis had requested Captain Rogers to stay there with his and one other company to guard the rear. Rogers flatly refused. The colonel allowed him to take his place on the field that day, assigning two other companies the duty instead. That night Davis again went to Rogers and explained that all the other companies in the regiment, with the exception of his (Company K, Tombigbee Volunteers), had been on detached duty at some time. Besides it being Rogers' turn to accept the duty, Davis explained that he wished to offer him the honor of leading an independent command in battle. Under these circumstances, Rogers could not refuse again, and he reluctantly agreed to remain behind at Taylor's headquarters. In addition to Rogers' Company K, Davis also assigned Lt. Daniel R. Russell and Company D (Carroll County Volunteers) to the post as well. This left Colonel Davis eight companies, an aggregate of 341, to lead into battle the next day.[17]

Fighting resumed early on the morning of February 23, 1846, and the Mexicans quickly gained the upper hand. Santa Anna's light troops used the night to reach the heights above the American left flank. Wool had reinforced the Americans already fighting in the mountains with several Illinois rifle companies under the command of Maj. Xerxes Trail. However, the Mexicans could not be dislodged and even progressed toward the American rear.[18] Mexican troops relentlessly pressed the left flank of the American line, anchored at the base of the mountains by 1st Lt. John Paul O'Brian's three guns from the 4th US Artillery and the 2nd Illinois and 2nd Indiana regiments of volunteer infantry. Indiana Brig. Gen. Joseph Lane, in immediate command of that section of the battlefield, issued the order to advance to meet the oncoming Mexicans. Disaster for the Americans followed Lane's fateful order. The colonel of the 2nd Indiana, William A. Bowles, instead of giving the order to advance commanded the 2nd Indiana to retire from the field. As the other American units watched in disbelief, his action created a wide gap in the American line. Both the 3rd Indiana and O'Brian fell back to a new defensive line but not before the artilleryman was forced to abandon one of his pieces to the enemy after all their horses were killed or disabled. The Mexicans quickly took advantage of the confusion in the Americans' ranks and poured through the open hole that now led to Taylor's rear. This was the situation as Jefferson Davis and the 1st Mississippi Rifles advanced onto the battlefield. Noted the colonel of the moment, "We had approached to within about two miles of that position, when the report of artillery-firing, which reached us, gave assurance that a battle had commenced. Excited by the sound [of artillery], the regiment pressed rapidly forward, manifesting upon this, as on other occasions, their more than willingness to meet the enemy."[19] And meet the enemy they would.

8
The 1st Mississippi Rifles at Buena Vista

At this critical juncture, the Mississippi regiment, commanded by Colonel Davis, arrived on the field.
—Gen. Joseph Lane

TAYLOR HAD SPENT A TENSE but quiet night on February 22, 1847, at Saltillo. After attending to last-minute details for the defense of the town on the morning of the 23rd, the general and his escort—including the 1st Mississippi Rifles—made their way to the battlefield. Around 9 a.m., Davis halted his regiment for a brief rest at the springs near the hacienda of Buena Vista before proceeding to the lower end of the valley. After quickly filling their canteens, the Mississippians left the hacienda and headed for the front line. Although the regiment was still several miles away from the fighting, they clearly heard the sounds of battle. Davis and his men soon encountered a mass of Arkansas, Kentucky, and Indiana volunteers streaming to the rear. Many cried out that the day was lost and warned the Mississippians to turn back. The Mississippians, instead of being shaken by the rout, called to frantic men who were running away and offered them a refreshing drink of water if they would only come back and join their ranks. Colonel Davis, Major Bradford, and Adjutant Griffith passed through the crowd, attempting to calm the distraught volunteers and pleading for them to stand and do their duty. Colonel Bowles and a number of the 2nd Indiana attached themselves to the right flank of the Mississippians and served with the regiment the rest of the day. A private from the 2nd Illinois, Augustus Ehinger, captured the confusion of the moment. Separated from his regiment and unable to rejoin it, Ehinger wrote, "I could make myself useful where I was; and if I had lost my life while I was fighting with the Mississippians, none of my comrades would have known what had become of me."[1]

Davis approached General Wool, who was also trying to rally the unnerved volunteers, and asked him to send help. As Wool rushed off in search of another unit to put into the fray, the 1st Mississippi Rifles hurried to the faltering American left flank, leaving the frantic crowd behind them.[2] Noted General Joseph Lane, "At this critical juncture, the Mississippi regiment, commanded by Colonel Davis, arrived on the field." Davis rode ahead of his regiment to survey the terrain and assess the situation. Several Mexican infantry and cavalry regiments had already made their way on to the plateau, with others moving up the ravines that debauched

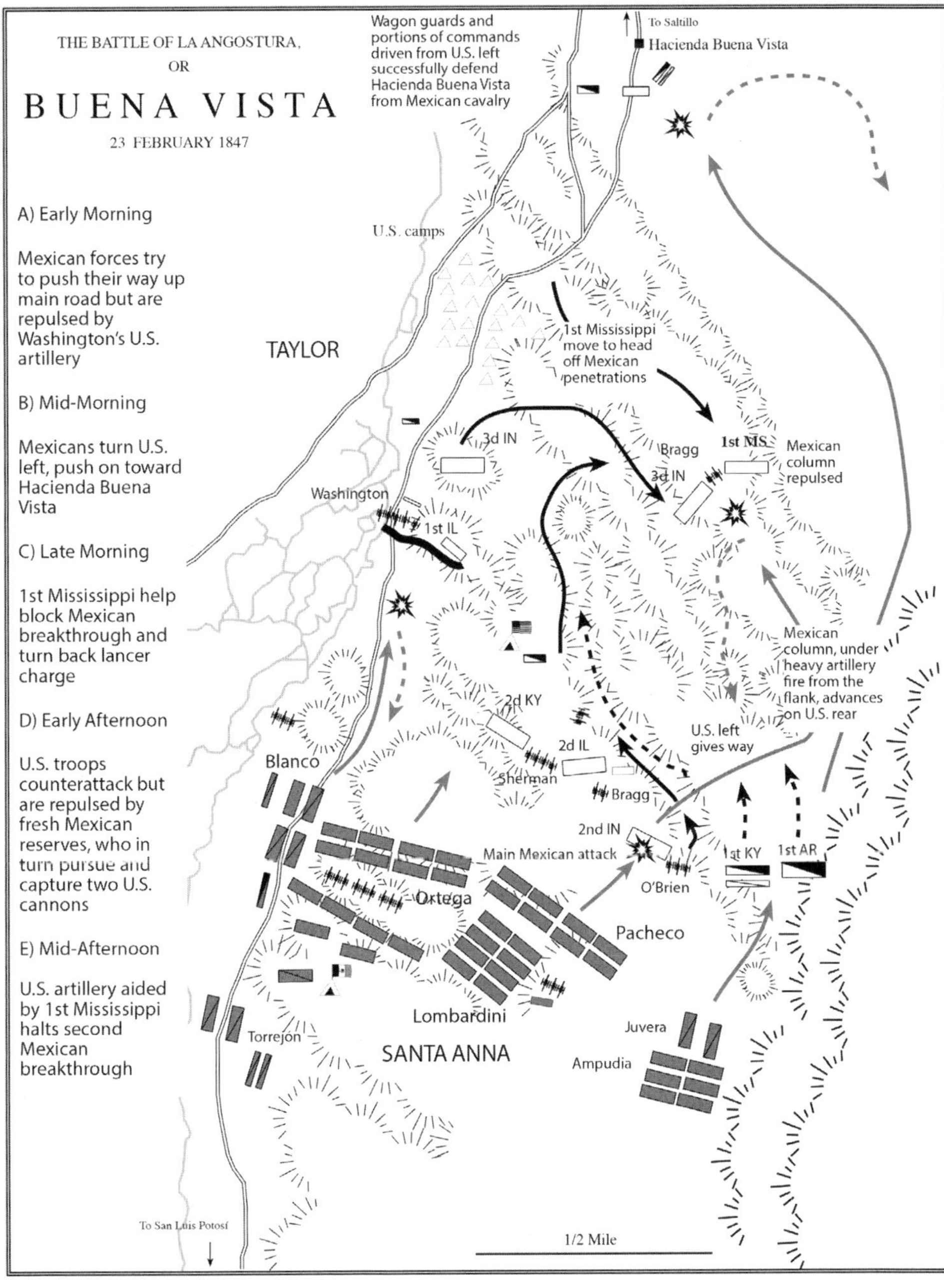
THE BATTLE OF LA ANGOSTURA,
OR
BUENA VISTA
23 FEBRUARY 1847
A) Early Morning
Mexican forces try to push their way up main road but are repulsed by Washington's U.S. artillery
B) Mid-Morning
Mexicans turn U.S. left, push on toward Hacienda Buena Vista
C) Late Morning
1st Mississippi help block Mexican breakthrough and turn back lancer charge
D) Early Afternoon
U.S. troops counterattack but are repulsed by fresh Mexican reserves, who in turn pursue and capture two U.S. cannons
E) Mid-Afternoon
U.S. artillery aided by 1st Mississippi halts second Mexican breakthrough
Wagon guards and portions of commands driven from U.S. left successfully defend Hacienda Buena Vista from Mexican cavalry
To Saltillo
Hacienda Buena Vista
U.S. camps
TAYLOR
1st Mississippi move to head off Mexican penetrations
3d IN
Bragg
1st MS
Mexican column repulsed
3d IN
Washington
1st IL
Mexican column, under heavy artillery fire from the flank, advances on U.S. rear
2d KY
2d IL
U.S. left gives way
Blanco
Sherman
Bragg
2nd IN
Main Mexican attack
1st KY
1st AR
Ortega
O'Brien
Pacheco
Lombardini
Juvera
Torrejón
SANTA ANNA
Ampudia
To San Luis Potosí
1/2 Mile

onto the plain. Colonel Davis formed his regiment into a line of battle at the edge of a ravine that cut deeply across the plain. Ordering his men to "fire advancing," the Mississippians climbed down, and then up, the steep sides of the ravine. Once on the opposite side, they delivered a withering fire that brought the Mexican advance to a halt. The outnumbered Mississippians continued to move forward, even pushing the enemy back. At this point, a body of lancers was seen moving around the regiment's right flank in an attempt to reach the ravine the Mississippians had crossed minutes earlier. If the lancers were successful in gaining the ravine, the Mississippians would be surrounded with no avenue of escape. Captain Rueben N. Downing (Company G, Raymond Fencibles), wounded at Monterrey and only reunited with his company the day before, acted quickly and called on the men around him to recross the ravine in order to head off the advancing lancers. The fire from these few Mississippians slowed the attackers and gave Davis and the rest of the regiment time to rejoin Downing on the other side of the ravine. One witness reported that Major Bradford, failing to hear Davis's order to retire, saw the Mississippians falling back and cried out, "Shoot me! The Mississippi regt. has run and I don't want to live another minute!" Fortunately, the help promised by Wool arrived on the scene. Hard-pressed but resolute, the Mississippians had been fighting almost single-handedly to save the American left flank from collapsing. Second Lieutenant Charles L. Kilburn quickly unlimbered the one gun he had brought from Bragg's battery and set up near the Mississippians. At about the same time, the 3rd Indiana Infantry rushed up and hurriedly formed on the left flank of Davis's regiment. The combined fire from these American units put an end to the Mexican advance.[3]

The effort of the 1st Mississippi Rifles had been costly to the regiment. The Mississippi volunteers had over thirty killed and another forty wounded in their brief, lone stand against the Mexicans. Davis had been shot in the foot as he sat astride his horse. Several of the wounded, including the injured colonel, refused to go to the rear for medical attention.[4] Captain John M. Sharp (Company A, Yazoo Volunteers), painfully wounded in both thighs, turned command of his company over to Lt. Amos B. Corwine. The captain followed his company on horseback the remainder of the day, repeatedly encouraging his men to "stand to their arms."[5]

In their haste to recross the ravine in order to keep from being cut off from the rest of the Americans, the Mississippians left their dead and seriously wounded behind. After he broke the Mexican assault, Davis sent a small party back across the ravine to aid the wounded Mississippians. The detail returned with word that the lancers had killed some of the wounded Mississippians as they lay helplessly on the ground.[6] The 1st Mississippi Rifles soon had the opportunity to avenge their dead in what would be one of the most famous episodes of the war. The action would also propelled Davis and his regiment into the national spotlight.

Another large body of lancers appeared on the left of Davis's regiment. The colonel changed his front to meet the new threat. He dispatched Sgt. Maj. Horace H. Miller to Captain Sherman's battery to ask for more artillery support to replace the piece that Kilburn had withdrawn. The 3rd Indiana Infantry, commanded by Col. James H. Lane, had moved from the left to the right flank of the Mississippi regiment in order to take shelter in a nearby depression from the fire of a Mexican battery. By design or chance, the Mississippians (with the remnants of the 2nd Indiana on its right flank) and the 3rd Indiana now formed almost a right angle (Davis and others would later describe the formation as a "V"). The lancers, almost perfectly aligned, charged down upon Davis's thin line. The colonel cautioned his men to hold their fire until he gave the order. The Mexican horsemen thundered on toward Davis and his men and then, amazingly, when only 80 to 100 yards away, reigned in to almost a complete halt. A few Mississippians, no longer able to restrain themselves, fired without waiting for Davis's command. Shots immediately erupted from the rest of the Mississippians, as well as the 3rd Indiana. Scores of Mexican saddles emptied of their riders. An artillery piece from Sherman's battery arrived and helped to make the rout of the lancers complete.[7] These few short moments captured the imaginations of Americans at home and made heroes of the Mississippians.[8]

Fighting had been raging on other parts of the battlefield other than the ground occupied by Davis's regiment. The gap created by the withdrawal of the 2nd Indiana Infantry earlier in the day had caused the 2nd Illinois Infantry to be outflanked. As the regiment fell back, a section of Sherman's battery came forward to support the hard-pressed Illinoisans. Taylor, just arrived on the field from Saltillo, rushed the 2nd Kentucky Infantry and a section from Bragg's battery to their aid. Joined by a portion of the 1st Illinois Infantry, this concentration of American forces halted the Mexican advance and even recaptured a portion of the field that had been lost earlier.[9]

With the American front line stable, Taylor turned his attention to a new Mexican threat to his rear. A large body of Mexican cavalry and infantry had successfully made its way unnoticed through the deep ravines at the base of the mountains on the east and advanced unchecked toward Buena Vista and Saltillo. Taylor ordered Captain Charles May to take all the US Dragoons, along with several companies of Arkansas cavalry under Capt. Albert Pike, to intercept this force before it reached the American rear. The 1st Arkansas Cavalry and the 1st Kentucky Cavalry, driven from the mountainsides and onto the plain below by the Mexican light infantry, blocked the path of the advancing Mexicans. The clash that followed resulted in heavy losses of the volunteer cavalry, including Archibald Yell, the former governor of Arkansas and the colonel of the 1st Arkansas Cavalry. With the timely arrival of several guns from Bragg's and Sherman's batteries, the assault was broken up, leaving the Mexican soldiers milling about in confusion. The Mississippians, having just defeated the Mexican lancers, received orders from Taylor to proceed to the scene to lend their support. But the outcome had already been decided by the time they arrived on that part of the field.[10]

A Mexican officer appeared from Santa Anna's lines bearing a white flag and a note from the Mexican leader for General Taylor. In the message, Santa Anna asked the American commander what he wanted. Not understanding the meaning of the inquiry, Taylor sent General Wool forward to the enemy lines to arrange a conference with Santa Anna. Wool was unable to cause the Mexicans to cease fire. Failing in his mission to affect a truce, Wool returned to his own lines. It was commonly believed by the Americans that Santa Anna had used the break in fighting to extract his troops who were being pounded behind the American lines. Some Mexican soldiers did escape during the short lull, but the firing from either side never entirely stopped.[11]

A threat appeared to the Americans at Saltillo from another direction. Several days earlier, Gen. José Vincente Miñon and a force of 1,800 cavalry had been sent by Santa Anna on a mission to seize the pass above Saltillo and thereby cut off the American retreat. This thrust behind his enemy's lines was what Santa Anna had referred to the previous day when he told Taylor that the US Army was surrounded. Traveling a different route from Santa Anna, Miñon successfully completed his task and, early on the morning of February 23, led his cavalry in an attack on Saltillo. As he neared the town, Webster's entrenched guns opened up and caused Miñon's troopers to take up a position on the road south of town out of range of American artillery. Although Miñon failed to capture the town, his action cut off communication between Taylor and his troops in Saltillo. Additionally, his lancers captured a number of hapless American volunteers who had fled to Saltillo and the safety they thought the town offered.[12]

At the hacienda of Buena Vista, the units placed there to protect the headquarters and supply train could clearly see Miñon's cavalry on the road. Around noon, roughly 600 fleeing volunteers reached the hacienda with the same tale told to Davis and his men earlier in the morning: the day was lost. Captain Rogers (Company K, Tombigbee Volunteers), assisted by Capt. John L. McManus (too ill to accompany his own Company E onto the field), 1st Lt. Daniel R. Russell (Company D, Carroll County Volunteers), 2nd Lt. Thomas P. Slade (Company A, Wilkinson Volunteers but acting quartermaster in charge of the Mississippians' wagons), and his own company officers, tried to stem the tide of routed men. Rogers succeeded in rallying over 200 of the fleeing volunteers. He added these men to his own detail, placing those who were mounted under the command of Lieutenant Slade. The Americans at the headquarters had no difficulty fending off a detachment of Mexican cavalry that eluded Captain May's force and made a half-hearted dash against the hacienda.[13]

First Lieutenant William H. Shover, commanding the artillery piece left at the hacienda by Captain Bragg, climbed to a high point from which he could observe through his spyglass the events then unfolding on the battlefield. From his elevated post he saw that a portion of the American line held firm. Shover also could see that Miñon's cavalry were forming up for an attack on Taylor's headquarters and supply train. Seizing the initiative, Shover limbered his gun and rode out from the hacienda onto the open plain to meet the enemy. Accompanying him was Mississippi Lieutenant Slade with his motley collection of 100 mounted teamsters and rallied volunteers. This bold move on the part of Shover and Slade prevented the attack on the hacienda from materializing. The small, outnumbered command chased the enemy for 3 miles before halting. Captain Webster sent one of his howitzers, supported by one company of Illinois Infantry, to assist Shover in driving the Mexicans from the plains around Saltillo. Their bold action ended the threat to the American rearguard at Saltillo.[14]

Trouble arose again for Taylor back at the Narrows. After several close calls for the Americans throughout the day, all was at the point of truly being lost. Three volunteer regiments, the 1st Illinois Infantry, the 2nd Illinois Infantry, and the 1st Kentucky Infantry, had advanced down the valley ahead of the American front line. It is unclear what prompted their action. Both Taylor and Wool later denied ordering the ill-fated charge. As these regiments marched forward, they approached a large ravine that had been hidden from their former position. From this deep depression rose up a large force of fresh Mexican lancers and infantrymen, estimated by witnesses to number between 6,000 to 7,000. Horror filled the Americans as they realized that they had marched into a trap; the volunteers fired only a few shots before fleeing back up the valley. Pursued by Santa Anna's soldiers, many of the Illinoisans and Kentuckians fell victim to Mexican bayonets and lances. The American dead included both the colonel of the 2nd Kentucky Infantry as well as the colonel of the 2nd Illinois Infantry, William R. McKee and John J. Hardin. Of particular note here was the death of the 2nd Kentucky regiment's lieutenant colonel, Henry Clay Jr., the son of the famous statesman.[15]

Only a few pieces of American artillery stood between the Mexican onslaught and American defeat. Lieutenant John Paul O'Brian, who had helped plug the gap left by the sudden departure of Bowles's 2nd Indiana earlier in the day, found himself once again forced to buy precious time for Taylor's small army. Knowing that holding his ground could might mean the difference between victory or defeat, O'Brian chose to stay put and deliver as much damage as he could before the enemy overran his position. Firing until the charging Mexicans were almost at the muzzles of his guns, O'Brian finally was forced to abandon his pieces to the enemy.[16]

Fortunately for Taylor, another American artilleryman, Capt. Braxton Bragg, arrived on the scene to help blunt the Mexican advance. With the Mexicans rapidly approaching, the captain asked Taylor if he should unlimber and fight or take his battery to the rear in order to save it from certain capture. The general instructed Bragg to double-shot his guns with canister and give them "hell"—an incident that has been handed down to us by the period press as "A little more grape, Captain Bragg!" The officer obeyed and poured shot after shot into the oncoming Mexicans.[17]

The Mexican advance had reached its high-water mark. Taylor had sent word calling for the 1st Mississippi Rifles, 3rd Indiana Infantry, and Sherman's battery to come as rapidly as possible. The men of the Mississippi and Indiana regiments marched at the double quick, running when the ground permitted, over the rocky plain and through ravines to reach the scene in the nick of time. Bragg and his guns were on the verge of falling into the hands of the Mexicans. Sherman's Battery galloped up and quickly unlimbered, adding its firepower to Bragg's. Davis and his regiment again sprang into action. Deploying on the right flank of the advancing Mexicans, the Mississippians and the 3rd Indiana delivered hot fire into the enemy's exposed ranks. Santa Anna's troops now found themselves in a situation similar to the Illinois and Kentucky regiments they had just demolished. Breaking at last, the Mexicans withdrew down the valley, leaving Taylor's troops bloodied and breathless. According to James C. Browning, the action had lasted 6½ hours.[18]

The Americans prepared for another assault they thought most certainly would come the next day. Taylor sent seven fresh companies of infantry, including Rogers' and Russell's Mississippians (Company K, Tombigbee Volunteers and Company D, Carroll County Volunteers), to man the front lines during the night. Help arrived unexpectedly when reinforcements commanded by Brig. Gen. Thomas Marshall reached Saltillo after pushing their way through Rinconada Pass. Notified of the battle while it was in progress, Marshall rushed forward elements of the Kentucky cavalry as well as Capt. James H. Prentiss and four guns of the 1st US Artillery. Unknown to the Americans near Buena Vista, Santa Anna had taken O'Brian's three guns and several flags captured during the day as proof of his victory and ordered his army to retrace its steps back to San Luis Potosi. The battle of Buena Vista was over.[19]

In his after-action report, Taylor summed up the immediate result of the battle. He wrote, "The enemy had fully reckoned upon our total rout, and had made arrangements to intercept our retreat and cut off the army, [and] stationed for that purpose corps of cavalry not only immediately in our rear, but even below Monterey." He had "no doubt that the defeat of the [enemy's] main army at Buena Vista will secure our line of communication from further interruption." Taylor must have taken satisfaction in announcing "The dispositions made to harass our rear vindicate the policy and necessity of defending a position in front of Saltillo, where a defeat has thrown the enemy far back into the interior. No result so decisive could have been obtained by holding Monterrey, and our communications would have been constantly in jeopardy." This last remark was clearly a jab at Polk's intention of preventing him from advancing deeper into Mexico while Scott prepared to invade Vera Cruz.[20]

In most wars, one campaign or battle can be pointed to as a critical turning point. Buena Vista was the turning point of the Mexican War. A victory by Santa Anna would have thrown the Americans back to Monterrey, perhaps even farther. General Scott's invasion of Vera Cruz would have been postponed, or even canceled, in order to rush troops back to northern Mexico to counter the new Mexican offensive. The war's length would have been extended, possibly ending in a stalemate or even a negotiated settlement more favorable to Mexico. Although several opportunities still existed for Santa Anna to halt Scott's advance to Mexico City, after Buena Vista northern Mexico was firmly in the hands of the Americans. Taylor's victory insured that Scott would be free to begin his campaign in central Mexico that ultimately ended with the capture of Mexico City and the Treaty of Guadalupe Hidalgo.

9
Homeward Bound

Our regiment is cut to pieces and we all begin to want to go home.
—Anonymous Mississippi Volunteer

Taylor's army collected its wounded, buried its dead, and counted its losses. Total American casualties—killed, wounded, and missing—numbered 673. The general reported the astonishing fact that between 1,500 and 1,800 of his soldiers had quit the field while the outcome of the battle was still undecided. He estimated that Santa Anna had lost between 1,500 and 2,000 in wounded and killed with another 2,000 to 3,000 deserting the Mexican cause. Buena Vista had been a costly battle for both sides, and both generals eagerly claimed it as a victory. But four days after the fight, elements of Gen. Zachary Taylor's force were back at Agua Nueva and Santa Anna's troops were still retreating to San Luis Potosi.[1]

The Mississippians gathered and cared for their wounded. Jefferson Davis, who spent most the battle astride his horse because he could not stand or walk on his wounded foot, turned the regiment over to Maj. Alexander B. Bradford. He and the other wounded men traveled to Saltillo for medical attention in common quartermaster wagons pressed into service as ambulances. (The wounded Davis returned to the battlefield in a wagon when it was believed that the fighting would resume on the morning of February 24.) In Saltillo, Taylor's medical staff set up impromptu hospitals in the church and other buildings—both public and private. The Mississippians had lost forty-one killed and fifty-two wounded. Ambulance details returning from the battlefield reported that the Mexicans had murdered and stripped many of the American wounded, including some men of the 1st Mississippi Rifles. This practice did not extend to all Americans, as one wounded Mississippian, Corp. James E. Stewart (Company H, Vicksburg Volunteers) returned to his regiment after spending a week as prisoner of the Mexicans. Two other Mississippians also rejoined their comrades unharmed. The pair had reportedly been taken prisoner after running away from the battle during the regiment's first engagement on the 23rd. One letter writer summed up the feeling of the Mississippians in the battle's aftermath when he wrote, "Our regiment is cut to pieces and we all begin to want to go home."[2]

The American surgeons had more to contend with than their own wounded. The Mexican medical department had been unable to care for the great number of Mexican casualties that Santa Anna abandoned in order to speed his retreat. Captain Rogers (Company K, Tombigbee Volunteers) walked over the battlefield the morning following the fighting and observed Mexican dead and wounded lying together in heaps. Some of the unfortunate wounded begged for "Agua and Pan" while a few pleaded for the Americans to kill them and end their suffering. The captain did not record if the latter request was granted. Mexican wounded lined the road from the battlefield southward to Agua Nueva and beyond. Many Mexican soldiers received aid from the very men Santa Anna had hoped to conquer.[3]

In a battle largely characterized by shirking and running, the outstanding performance of the 1st Mississippi Rifles received great acclaim. Davis praised the regiment in his official report saying, "my regiment equalled . . . my expectations." Captain Braxton Bragg lauded both the Mississippians and their colonel. He wrote that at one point in the battle, "I saw the Mississippi regiment gallantly led against a force immensely superior." From Capt. Thomas Sherman, an officer who had worked closely with the Mississippi regiment during the battle, came the words "The unwavering firmness and deadly fire of the Mississippi regiment on this occasion showed them equal to the most veteran troops." Taylor's report commended the Mississippians for their "conspicuous gallantry" and credited the regiment with saving the American left flank from being turned by the enemy. As for Davis himself, noted Taylor, "though severely wounded, he remained in the saddle until the close of the action." General John E. Wool praised Davis and his regiment for "their conspicuous gallantry, which caused them to be a rallying point." General Joseph Lane, who was in position to observe the colonel, wrote "justice compels me to mention Colonel Davis and his regiment of Mississippians, who so nobly and so bravely came to the rescue at the proper time to save the fortunes of the day." Newspapers across the United States carried words praising these gallant heroes from Mississippi.[4]

As at Monterrey, however, controversy arose over the competing claims of glory. Taylor had awarded Davis and the 1st Mississippi Rifles the lion's share of battlefield laurels. The Indiana regiments not only felt slighted; they believed they had been maligned. It is true that the 2nd Indiana Volunteers had moved to the rear under questionable circumstances, but many had rallied and stayed on the battlefield. Its individual members apparently served in the ranks of both the 1st Mississippi Rifles and the 3rd Indiana Volunteers. One group even held together as the 2nd Indiana Volunteers under the command of their own officers, taking up a position on the right flank of Davis's regiment. As for the 3rd Indiana Volunteers, the regiment had made up the left flank of Davis' heralded "V" and had rushed to the scene of O'Brien and Bragg's desperate stand against Santa Anna's last charge of the day. The rancor caused by the uneven distribution of praise would dog both Taylor and Davis for years to come.[5]

The belief that the fighting in northern Mexico was over settled on the American troops at Saltillo. The Mississippians anxiously passed the time at Buena Vista, waiting for the orders that would send them home. Spring was near, but the nights were still bitterly cold at this high altitude. Captain Rogers had the luxury of sleeping on a bed composed of three wool blankets placed on a church pew that some of his men had brought to him as a favor. (The priest had been correct in his fears that Americans would remove items from his church.) Camp life was dull, and the men were restless—a combination that almost always spelled trouble for volunteers. In the camp of another regiment of volunteers, one soldier murdered one of his comrades, prompting the moody captain to muse that even in the midst of war such sad acts were committed against one another.

Additionally, the men now suffered from the want of clothing because theirs had either worn out or had been discarded to lighten their loads on the many long marches across northern Mexico. The shortage apparently existed even though Taylor had sent Joseph D. Howell, a member of the regiment and Jefferson Davis's brother-in-law, to Camargo to ask the Quartermaster Department to forward clothing for his command. The volunteers paid exorbitant prices to replace lost items. At Saltillo, pants that cost $2 at home were as high as $7, with a simple ticking shirt going for $3 and shoes for $3.50 a pair—all this out of a soldier's pay that was set as low as $8 per month for a private. These shortages were made more acute by the fact that the government had not paid the regiment's enlisted men since the past October. Happily, Rogers reported that the regiment would soon leave for Monterrey.[6]

On March 9, 1847, the 1st Mississippi Rifles bid farewell to the plains of Buena Vista and headed for Monterrey and home. Augmented by several companies of Kentucky cavalry, the Mississippians once again served as Taylor's personal escort. Although the road was hot, dusty, and dry, for once the men did not have to march. Riding in empty quartermaster wagons on the return leg of a supply train, the Mississippians arrived in Monterrey three days later to a warm welcome from the Americans there who had heard of their deeds. Rogers noted the reception they received, writing, "We are all Lions here." The regiment returned to its old camp near Walnut Springs and settled into a familiar routine: reveille at daybreak, surgeon's call at 7 AM, peas on a trencher at 8 AM, guard mounting at 9 AM, roast beef at 1 PM, retreat at sundown, and tattoo at 10 PM.[7]

Opportunities for action still existed for the war-weary Mississippians. Mexican cavalry constantly harassed supply trains on the way to and from Camargo. The trains had to be escorted to prevent them from falling into the hands of the enemy. Large escorts, though, were no guarantee against attack by brazen bands of irregulars. Shortly after arriving at Monterrey, word reached the Americans there that one such band had attacked an army supply train outside the town of Marin. Taylor called on 150 Mississippians to go to the train's relief. The men marched at the double quick for 12 miles, reaching Agua Frio, where they spent the night. Arising early the next morning, they hurriedly resumed their rescue mission. Arriving at Marin shortly before noon, the Mississippians learned that the report that had caused them to undertake the grueling forced march was false. They then returned to Monterrey, angry and worn out.[8]

The Mississippians looked for ways to pass the time in Monterrey. Rogers again complained of the rude nature of his companions who treated the Sabbath as just another day in the week. Befriended by the alcalde of San Nicholas, Rogers spent much of his spare time visiting the mayor and his family. Americans lucky enough to have access to horses rode about the city. Fraternization with the Mexicans provided the Americans with the opportunity to brush up on their Spanish and learn the local customs. According to Rogers, many local citizens held American officers in awe, and the town's residents willingly received them as guests in their homes. Still, lone "Yankees" had to be wary as they were easy prey for the many guerrillas and bandits in the area. In an effort to make their stay more bearable, the Mississippians moved their camp about 1½ miles to a new location that provided more shade and shelter from the Mexican sun and wind.[9]

The opportunity to escort supply trains offered a welcome change from the inactivity of camp life. In April, Captain Rogers took three companies of the 1st Mississippi Rifles on such a trip to Camargo. His account of the journey contrasts greatly with his regiment's impressive record and showed volunteers at their worst. The weather was hot and dry, and tempers were on edge. One drunken Mississippian fell beneath a wagon and was run over. "So it is with drunkenness," noted the captain. One of Rogers' lieutenants, William Purnell Townsend, received a beating from one of his own men. It appears the lieutenant angered the man with his abrupt manner in giving orders. Rogers had little sympathy for his junior officer and thought that Townsend was a "dog" who got what he deserved. At Camargo, Rogers took part in a fight himself when he pounded a "Dutchman" who dared to insult him. The Mississippians still had enough energy left to deal with Mexicans who got in their way. One man lagged behind and failed to show up at camp when the train stopped for the evening. Searchers located the man's body and his two supposed killers. Dispensing justice, volunteer-style, the officers of the command held a brief conference to study the evidence and then, upon deliberation, ordered the two Mexicans shot. Rogers felt sorry for the two men, but he was convinced of their guilt. Writing of the two men who were shot, the captain said, "One of them was game to the last, the other begged like a dog." After spending three weeks on escort duty, Rogers' detachment finally returned to Monterrey on April 17, 1847.[10]

Rogers noted that a new regiment had reached Monterrey during his absence: the 2nd Mississippi Rifles. He had encountered Reuben Davis, whom he had known before the war near Cerralvo. The colonel of the 2nd Mississippi Rifles, who was on his way back to Mississippi, told Rogers a tale of woe. Rogers soon found out for himself how bad things were for the new regiment when he visited their camp outside Monterey: "The Regt. is suffering under small pox. They are discontented poor fellows."[11]

The 1st Mississippi prepared to leave Monterrey and Mexico as they neared the end of their term of service. At the time of enlistment, few thought that the war would last more than a year. Most men of the 1st Mississippi Rifles felt they had done enough for their state and the nation and wanted to go home. Celebrating the approaching departure, one band of Mississippians held a drunken spree on the night of April 20 that left one young Mississippian maimed for life. Led by William H. H. Patterson, the first lieutenant of Rogers' Company K (Tombigbee Volunteers), the Mississippians became involved in a dispute with Capt. Charles May's orderly and another soldier from the Quartermaster Department. The provost guard arrived and took the two men with whom the volunteers had been fighting into custody, placing the pair in jail partly for their own protection. Soon to be independent citizens again, the Mississippians chafed under military discipline and refused to disband and return to their camp. A scuffle ensued outside the jail in which Patterson attempted to wrestle away a musket from one of the guards. The Mississippians brandished their bowie knives, and the officer of the guard, believing his men were in danger, gave the command to fire. Patterson fell wounded, struck in the leg. The injured limb required amputation. Rogers, in an unconcerned tone, recorded that the Ohio officer who had ordered his men to fire on the Mississippians had turned down a request from a friend of the wounded man to fight a duel over the affair.[12]

As the regiment passed its time away at Monterrey, a court of inquiry held at Buena Vista reviewed Colonel Bowles' battlefield performance. Witnesses swore that Bowles was more at home exploring the countryside for plants and lacked the knowledge and ability to command his regiment. Ultimately, the court determined Bowles, while not lacking in personal courage, guilty of incompetently handling his regiment on the battlefield. Additionally, the finding absolved the men of the 2nd Indiana from the charge of cowardice, many of whom had rallied and fought alongside the Mississippians. With Davis still recovering from his painful wound, Major Bradford carried the colonel's deposition to the court of inquiry meeting at Buena Vista. In his letter to the court, Davis stated that he had no knowledge of Bowles before he and his men joined the Mississippians. He affirmed, though, that the Indiana colonel had exhibited genuine courage while serving with the 1st Mississippi Rifles. In fact, the men of the 1st Mississippi Rifles held Bowles in high esteem. According to a report in *The Mississippi Democrat*, "the morning after the battle, as Bowles was passing over the field, the Mississippi regiment rose voluntarily and presented arms, in a token of their sense of compliment he had paid them in seeking their ranks when deserted by the mass of his own regiment." Nevertheless, the verdict of the court failed to settle the question in the public's mind of the conduct of the 2nd Indiana and its colonel. The controversy, especially resented by Indianans, raged for years after the war's end and even played a role in the 1848 presidential election.[13]

Davis held an interesting and solemn ceremony for his regiment before its departure from Monterrey. The colonel marched his men to the spot the 1st Mississippi Rifles had occupied on the eve of the regiment's first battle. He instructed the Mississippians, as near as they could remember, to stand where they had on that day in the not-too-distant past. Large gaps separated the regiment's few survivors. More than half of the men who had originally joined the 1st Mississippi Rifles were no longer in its ranks, the victims of disease and battle.[14]

On April 27, 1847, with only two months remaining in their term of service, the 1st Mississippi Rifles left Monterrey on their return journey to the United States. On the road to Cerralvo, the regiment saw its final action when a small party of Mexicans attacked Maurice K. Simons, the regimental butcher who had ridden ahead of the column. Although severely wounded in the leg, Simons killed one of his assailants and drove the rest away before assistance arrived. A doctor, using the butcher's own tools, amputated Simons' leg near the hip, and he was left with a Mexican family. His friends did not believe he would survive, but he eventually recovered. The regiment spent four hot, dusty weeks at Cerralvo before moving on. Rogers, depressed by the extended stay at the small town, passed the long hours by drinking hot chocolate and shooting targets with his pistol. Regrettably, this officer who had chronicled the exploits of his regiment gave up writing in his diary at this time. His last entry reveals the despair that he and other men of the regiment likely felt as they waited for their enlistment to expire: "The day I will record as one of the blackest days of my life when gloom and melancholy have claimed me for their own."[15]

By May 22, the Mississippians had passed Camargo, headed for the mouth of the Rio Grande. They were not alone. The Kentucky regiments had reached the expiration of their terms of service and were as eager as the Mississippians to go home. Davis tried to arrange for the steamer

Rough and Ready to carry the 1st Mississippi Regiment to New Orleans, but the Quartermaster Department was swamped by the multitudes of anxiously waiting volunteers. After waiting their turn for transportation, the regiment made its way down the Rio Grande. After spending several days at the river's mouth, Davis finally secured transportation for his regiment. On May 29, Davis embarked on the brig *Forest* with Companies A (Yazoo Volunteers), B (Wilkinson Volunteers), C Vicksburg Southrons), E (State Fencibles), and H (Vicksburg Volunteers). The schooner *P.B. Savoy* left Brazos Santiago the next day with Companies F (Lafayette Volunteers), K (Tombigbee Volunteers), and I (Marshall Guards). The remaining two companies, D (Carrol County Volunteers) and G (Raymond Fencibles), followed several days later. After a few short days at sea, the first elements of the 1st Mississippi Rifles arrived in the Crescent City.[16]

The citizens of New Orleans had prepared an elaborate homecoming for the heroes of Buena Vista. In a city constantly filled with volunteers on their way to and from the front, members of 1st Mississippi Rifles stood out as special. On June 5, 1847, the *New Orleans Picayune* reported that a committee had been formed to make plans to receive the regiment. In the reporter's judgments, there was "no doubt the 'star regiment' will receive the welcome at New Orleans which their deeds at Monterey and Buena Vista merit."[17] The welcoming committee explained that it considered it a privilege to be the first city to greet the regiment on its return home: "It is the purpose of our citizens to evidence the admiration of all. To each and every man a sincere greeting is offered. They all have done nobly; they have all won the gratitude and reward of their fellow-countrymen." The article lamented that "Many a bright face and flashing eye will be missed from the ranks. They who saw these troops on their way to the wars will ask in vain for many of the sturdy spirits whose high and soldier-like bearing was prophetic of victory. . . . They are gone, they are dead; but their deeds live on after them, rejoicing over the achievements of valor they will not be forgotten."[18]

The grand reception of the 1st Mississippi Rifles took place on June 10, 1847. Gone now were the red shirts and ragged duck cloth pants as the men once more donned civilian garb. Escorted by detachments from local militia regiments, 250 Mississippians—one-fourth of their original number—paraded down Canal Street. The procession made its way to Lafayette Square where a huge crowd had gathered to glimpse Davis and his famous regiment. The cheering spectators were drowned out at times by the fifty-gun salute rendered by local artillery companies. Dignitaries on the platform included Mississippi Governor Albert G. Brown, Brig. Gen. George M. Brooke, Col. Jefferson Davis, and Lt. Col. Alexander K. McClung. Also on the platform were Col. Robert M. Echols (13th US Infantry,) Colonel

James P. Drake (1st Indiana Infantry), the mayor of New Orleans, and the city's aldermen. After listening to a speech given by ex-Mississippi Congressman Sgt. S. Prentiss that heaped praise upon the Mississippi regiment, Colonel Davis, who had been sitting with his wounded foot propped on a chair, was helped to his feet so he could deliver his reply. He remarks began with a work of thanks to his hosts: "Citizens of New Orleans—no language can express the emotions of the returned volunteers under the reception you give them. But the heart feels, and it spontaneously thanks you. We are unconscious of having done any thing which merits a reception like this. When our country called us, we went, as dutiful children, to her defence; and if you think we have been fortunate in the discharge of our duty we thank you. Next to the approval of his own conscience, the soldier values the approbation of his country."

Davis then reviewed the actions of the 1st Mississippi Rifles at the battles of Monterrey and Buena Vista for the gathered crowd. He praised his men and the role of volunteers in general, claiming for these citizen-soldiers a share in winning the war. At the conclusion of Davis's speech, Lieutenant Colonel McClung, still on crutches from his grievous wound, gave a few words of thanks for the help and support he had received during his slow recovery.[19]

Some of Davis's remarks could have been meant for the volunteers' sister regiment, the 2nd Mississippi Rifles, which he and Bradford encountered at Monterrey. The colonel admitted that not all war was glory. He cautioned his listeners that "To die is sometimes a privilege. For many of the returned volunteers there was a harder task than to die—to thirst for glory and not be able to realize it—to burn with desire to mingle in the strife, and not to be able—to know that friends search their names in vain upon the public records. This is the volunteer's hardest fate—unknown heroes. The courage to submit in silence, and in the discharge of duty to be inactive, where action is glory."[20] While meant for his own men, Davis's words would be even more meaningful to other Mississippian still in the field.

The next day the *New Orleans Picayune* carried a short piece describing the event. "Yesterday was a day devoted by our citizens to the reward of patriotism and historic deeds. . . . From Lafayette Square the procession moved to the *Place d' Armes*, where it was received with a salute from the artillery, and partook of an excellent collation prepared by Mr. Victor. For several hours the company remained there, and with the stirring airs of the bands of music the festivity was continued up to a late hour in the evening." A separate section informed readers that other heroes were in town as the "The bodies of MCKEE and CLAY and VAUGHN lay in the public arsenal." This was a reminder that other heroes of Buena Vista had returned home.[21]

On June 12, 1847, Col. Sylvester Churchill mustered the 1st Mississippi Rifles out of service, officially disbanding the regiment.[22] Davis received back pay in the amount of $1,685 for himself and his two servants.[23] Soon after mustering out, the members of the regiment began the journey to their homes, families, and friends. Rogers' company separated from the regiment and traveled to Mobile, Alabama. From there they proceeded up the Tombigbee River to their homes. The company was unaware that the citizens of Lowndes County had sent ten to twelve carriages to Bayou Sara to greet and carry the Tombigbee Volunteers home. The townspeople learned that the volunteers were already on their way home via Mobile, having traveled some 150 miles on their journey. Although most of the party turned back, two wagons were sent ahead for the use of Lt. Col. Alexander K. McClung and Lt. William H. H. Patterson. The rest of the regiment boarded the steamers *Saint Mary* and *Belle Creole* for the trip up the Mississippi River, feted along the way by the citizens of their states. The Wilkinson County Volunteers bade farewell to Davis and their comrades near the Louisiana–Mississippi border at Bayou Sara. The remainder of the Mississippians disembarked at Natchez to attend a celebration given in their honor. At the courthouse, one speaker praised the men of the 1st Mississippi Rifles using a play on words, saying, "The work was 'Rough' but you were 'Ready.'" Davis answered, comparing Taylor's victory at Buena Vista to that of Jackson at New Orleans. He also spoke about the regiment's return to civilian life as its veterans once again became "the mechanic, the professional man, the husbandman, and the peaceful citizen."[24] Proceeding on to Vicksburg, the members of the 1st Mississippi Rifles dispersed even further. Most volunteers used that city as the beginning point for the last leg of the trip home. The companies from Marshall and Lafayette counties again boarded a steamer in order to reach their homes further up the river.[25]

For the next several weeks, the men of the 1st Mississippi Rifles continued to be the center of attention. Barbecues were held for them at Amite, Woodville, and other towns around the state. The largest of the celebrations took place in Clinton on Saturday, July 3, 1847. Clinton was selected as the site because of its central location midway on the rail line between Vicksburg and Jackson. Special trains were scheduled to carry people to and from the two cities to attend the festivities. A crowd of nearly 3,000 of the regiment's many admirers gathered for the barbecue.[26] The citizens had hoped that Jefferson Davis would attend, but the colonel sent word that duties at home prevented his participation in the festive event.

Gradually, the men of the 1st Mississippi Rifles returned to civilian life. Some used their fame to help campaign for political office.[27] These candidates included Capt. John L. McManus, Clerk of the Circuit Court of Hinds

County; Maj. Alexander B. Bradford, US House of Representatives; Pvt. Samuel C. Hubbs, Ranger of Hinds County; and Lt. Richard Griffith, Mississippi State Treasurer. Davis returned to Congress, appointed by Governor Brown to fill the empty seat left by the death of Mississippi Senator Jesse Speight. Others wished for another look at the "elephant" and sought ways to continue their military careers, both in the present and future conflicts that loomed on the horizon.[28]

Colonel Davis turned down two offers to return to Mexico. The first came from James K. Polk in the form of a commission as brigadier general of volunteers. Davis thanked the president but said his interpretation of the US Constitution would not allow him to accept the position. He explained that, in his opinion, volunteers were a form of militia and the national government had no authority to make appointments on the state level. Thus his conviction forced him to decline the honor of the appointment. The *New Orleans Picayune* was already discussing a second offer for Davis to return to the field as the city planned to receive the colonel and his regiment home from Mexico, reporting, "There is a rumor, the *Vicksburg Sentinel* say of some circumstances which may induce Col. Davis to decline the appointment of brigadier general tendered him by the President, and take command of the 2nd Mississippi Regiment in case of Col. Rueben Davis's resignation." Davis had indeed received an invitation from the men of the 2nd Mississippi Rifles, which read, in part, "Knowing and appreciating the high reputation you have acquired as commander of the 1st Mississippi Regiment, there was on the part of the meeting a unanimous expression of opinion in your favor." Although honored, he informed them that he has already accepted Brown's appointment to the US Senate and therefore could not join them in the field. He told them, "To you now is Mississippi's standard confided. Rent and blood-stained it may be; but in your hands, can never be dishonored. It may droop with the cypress, but will be crowned with the laurel." Davis had left his days in Mexico behind, but one can only think that the 2nd Mississippi Rifles would have benefited with him as it commander.[29]

Colonel Davis and the men of his regiment carried the glow of their fame for the rest of their lives. Indeed, as one Mississippi newspaper noted, "The 1st Mississippi, under the command of Colonel Jefferson Davis, coated itself over with immortal glory." In the future, it would be "sufficient to mark a man for distinction and honor for him to say, 'I was one of the 1st Mississippi Regiment.'"[30]

10
The 2nd Mississippi Rifles Go To Mexico

The First Mississippi won honors at Monterey; the Second will emulate the glorious example, if opportunity is given.
—*The Mississippi Democrat*

President James K. Polk and his advisors had received word of Gen. Zachary Taylor's victory at Monterrey with mixed emotions. Pleased for the American public to learn of another important triumph, the president expressed disappointment in Old Rough and Ready at the slow progress of the war. In retrospect, the administration's and public's expectations had proven unrealistic. After six months of fighting had passed and Mexico showed no signs of giving up the struggle, the administration determined that a second call for volunteers must be issued.

With the terms of the volunteers already in service, including the 1st Mississippi Rifles, soon to expire, replacements had to be found. Mississippi's Governor Albert G. Brown received notification of the second call for volunteers and in November 1846 announced the formation of the 2nd Mississippi Rifles.[1] Governor Brown had been authorized to accept ten more companies to form another regiment of riflemen. State militia officials once again named Vicksburg as the rendezvous site and instructed captains to have their companies there by the first of the new year.[2]

Interest in the war was still high as this second call up came closely on the heels of the Battle of Monterrey. Still, some pundits doubted that the state's quota could be met. "It would indeed be discreditable if the regiment could not be raised. Let our friends remember that we have given those who were disappointed in the Spring [another] chance to service their country."[3] The thought that Mississippians would choose to remain at home while their service was still needed drew a sharp rebuke from the editors of *The Mississippi Democrat*, who posed the question to their readers: "Does anyone seriously apprehend that all the chivalry and patriotism of Mississippi has been sent off in one regiment? Is it not provokingly illiberal towards the volunteers who were so eager to go last summer, to be saying that they are not as patriotic now as they were then?" They then chided, "It is an insult to these gallant spirits to say that they will not buckle on their armor with the same earnest zeal, for this second term, that characterized their conduct in the first instance."[4]

Indeed, rumors that the new regiment would rendezvous at Tampico with other troops intended for Gen. Winfield Scott's new invasion of Mexico had Mississippians rushing to organize their companies. Local editors boosted martial spirit with the same promises of fame and glory as already won by the members of the 1st Mississippi Rifles, then boasting one victory under Taylor to their credit. In Jackson, the state's capital, *The Southron* extolled, "Let the recollection of the renown won by the First Regiment, stimulate the young men of Mississippi to rally to our country's call" and reminded potential volunteers that "Laurels are yet to be won." Another local paper urged the citizens of Carrollton to battle by saying, "the First Mississippi won honors at Monterrey; the Second will emulate the glorious example, if opportunity is given." *The Mississippi Democrat* stated that, once formed, the new regiment would be taken to Tampico by steamer.[5]

Glad to be granted this second chance to serve their state, volunteers quickly enrolled in the various companies being raised throughout Mississippi. The organization of companies and the election of officers did not all proceed smoothly, however. One group of thirty volunteers became angry when their candidate failed to win. Disgusted with the process of forming the regiment, they bolted and went to Mexico on their own to offer their services to Scott as an independent company. But on January 1, 1847, *The Southron* declared the regiment filled and printed the names of the ten companies accepted for the 2nd Mississippi Rifles. The ten companies chosen by the governor converged on Vicksburg. They included

Company A	Lowndes Guards	Capt. Andrew K. Blythe
Company B	Marshall Relief Guards	Capt. Joseph H. Kilpatrick
Company C	Choctaw Volunteers	Capt. Enos Elder
Company D	Monroe Volunteers	Capt. Joel M. Acker
Company E	Tippah Guards	Capt. Alexander M. Jackson
Company F	Lauderdale Volunteers	Capt. William J. Daniels
Company G	Thomas Hinds Guards	Capt. Charles Clark
Company H	Union Greys	Capt. Adam McWillie
Company I	Panola Boys	Capt. Alfred A. Overton
Company K	Union Company	Capt. Benjamin C. Buckley

Noted *The Southron* with pride, "They have done it too, with the earnestness and rapidity which must afford every citizen of the State the most honorable pride."[6]

A volunteer with the Lowndes Guards left a detailed record of his company's journey from home to Vicksburg. Dr. Thomas Neely Love joined, hoping to be named to the post of regimental surgeon for the 2nd Mississippi Rifles. His description of the parting of the volunteers from their families and friends mirrored similar scenes in other towns around the state. The company was presented with a flag on which were inscribed the words

"The Lowndes Guards—Victory or Death." The townspeople sent the men off with a grand feast held in Mrs. Musgrove's dining room. Love noted the company's impending departure, saying, "Our friends came around us with hearts and countenance of deep emotion, with their lips trembling with the farewell words of 'God bless you. Farewell.'" He believed that the memory of this event would "nerve our arms and give our hearts courage to know that our friends love us." As a physician and possible future regimental surgeon, Love received numerous heartfelt requests from parents: "You must take care of my son . . . when he gets sick—if he dies have him buryed decently." All seemed to recognize that "Many a beloved boy has gone forth from under the roof of an indulging parent to return no more." Making the parting even more poignant was the fact that they left home on Christmas Day.[7]

The march to Vicksburg started off like a pleasure excursion, with few indications of the hardships to come. The company was feted in each town they passed, and patriotic citizens made sure they did not run short of food and liquor. Unseasonably spring-like weather graced most of their march across the state. Discipline was lax, leading to at least one incident in which some members of the company raided a woman's chicken yard. Outraged at their conduct, she demanded that the men return a bag of flour she had given them. This rebuke ended the chicken-stealing.

After several days of marching, the volunteers began to get just a small taste of what lay ahead for them. Wrote Love, "the boys moved out this morning like stiff plough horses—great complaints about sore feet, blistered toes and heels." In one town Love had to treat a volunteer who was wounded by a pistol ball fired by another man in a drunken brawl. The wound proved superficial, and the injured volunteer was able to march the next morning, but the incident caused Love to reflect on such rowdy behavior. Wondered Love, "[is] this to serve as a prelude to some of our battles in Mexico—They will be more credible I hope."[8] Had he only known what was ahead, he might have turned around and gone back home then.

The company passed through Jackson on its march to Vicksburg. Love met with Governor Brown, who informed him that he was not alone in the hope of obtaining the post of surgeon for the new regiment. The governor told Love that he had already been approached by "15 to 20" men about the position. He recommended that Love write to President Polk immediately as well as secure as many written recommendations from the regimental officers as soon as possible. The young doctor thanked Brown and followed the governor's advice. Before leaving Jackson, the Lowndes Guards, the Union Grays, and the Lauderdale Volunteers paraded before Brown, who spoke briefly to the volunteers on their way to the rendezvous. Love's company had evidently been noticed attending church services the previous day. According to Love, "Governor Brown thought us the finest looking volunteers he had ever seen."[9]

Officials in Vicksburg had prepared for the second onslaught of arriving volunteers. On January 5, the Lowndes Guards disembarked from the train that carried them from Jackson and found five companies already at the depot. Noted Love of the gathered volunteers, "as we passed the long line of these companies I began to feel the magnitude of an army." The volunteers marched to a vacant warehouse the state had rented for use as a barracks. Most men stayed there, eating the provisions provided and making fires near the entrances. Others, like Love, found more comfortable quarters in town and proceeded to gather support for their ambitions. With the regimental elections on the horizon, coalitions were built and patronage promised. On January 5, each company present at the rendezvous officially elected its company officers and noncommissioned officers, clearing the way for the volunteers to be sworn into service. Love quipped, "This thing of being 'mustered into service' is a little like getting married—easy to get into, but devilish to get out of." He noted his change in his life, recording that "I am now a soldier in the service of the US at seven dollars a month and fed on lean beef and crackers."[10] By January 11, Capt. Charles S. Lovell, US Army, had mustered the last company of the 2nd Mississippi Rifles into service.

The following day, the newly sworn in regiment left the warehouse and marched to a campground located 2½ miles north of Vicksburg. The site, called Camp McClung in honor of the 1st Mississippi Rifles' wounded lieutenant colonel, sat at the foot of the city's bluffs near the river's edge.[11] Here the regiment erected its tents and waited for the formalities associated with becoming soldiers to be completed. Love felt uneasy about the campground, noting that "It is exposed to an open bank of the river—very low and damp. . . . I begin to notice and count up the cost of whipping these Mexicans and really feel that we will pay dearly for the whistle." As an omen of things to come, rain began to fall while the men were still erecting their tents. Over the next few days, the camp of the 2nd Mississippi Rifles became a sea of mud and standing water. Their pleasure excursion came to a soggy, cold end as the spring-like weather was replaced with near-freezing temperatures and sleet.[12]

Regardless of the change in the weather, one important task yet remained before the 2nd Mississippi Rifles: the election of field officers. *The Mississippi Democrat* warned, "It is of the utmost importance to the honor, efficiency, [and] health of the New Regiment, that a gentleman of military abilities and experience . . . should be selected for their Commander." *The Southron* had its own favorite for "the office of *Colonel Commandant of the Mississippi Regiment* now being raised for the Mexican service," telling its readers that "Gen. Brandon is an old soldier and has seen much service, and thoroughly understands the spirit and genius of our Mississippi boys."[13] He would have his chance, but only if he could secure enough support.

Adhering to the custom in volunteer regiments, companies nominated their local favorites for these important positions. The usual rounds of campaigning had already begun. Charles Clark of the Thomas Hind Guards was the favorite of many of the men for the office of colonel, including most of the Lowndes Guards. Love and his friends thought that they had arranged for his election, but their plans were thwarted by another faction that was conspiring on the behalf of their own candidate. Clark had promised to accept the post only if he received a clear majority of the men's votes. Although he garnered more votes combined than the other candidates, he called for a second ballot. Many of his supporters deserted him, opening the door for others to seek the office. The candidate who benefited from Clark's refusal to accept the results of the first vote was Rueben Davis. Love and his friends had not been the only ones busy trying to influence the vote. Davis claimed that he had the support of three companies prior to the first ballot. He credited his friend, John A. Wilcox of the Monroe Volunteers, for moving the election in his favor. The election for colonel occurred on January 8, and the election for lieutenant colonel and major followed on January 13. As in the race for colonel, these two contests were also determined by political machinations.[14]

The local papers carried the election returns. The men of the regiment selected Col. Reuben Davis (no relation to Jefferson Davis), Lt. Col. Joseph H. Kilpatrick, and Maj. Ezra R. Price to lead them to Mexico.[15] Only Price, the man who had walked from Camargo to fight at Monterrey, retained his position throughout the regiment's service.[16] The elections pitted volunteers from different parts of the state against one another. Hard feelings over the results lingered for months. According to Davis, the man who was most affected by the results was Capt. Benjamin C. Buckley, whom he had defeated for colonel. "He had been warmly supported by Governor Albert G. Brown, who, some days before the election, presented him with a handsome sword." The loss remained a lifelong disappointment for Buckley.[17]

A few officers stood out for either their abilities or their deficiencies. According to Rueben Davis, the man selected to lead the regiment, Lieutenant Colonel Kilpatrick, was "prompt and efficient" when active service required it but had "an insuperable aversion to the routine duties of his office." This did not bode well for the men who had placed their trust in him. Major Price, on the other hand, "was devoted to the least detail of his department, and performed every duty with punctual observance." Davis had appointed Lt. Beverly Matthews to the important post of regimental adjutant, even though he believed he was not up to the task. Matthews received the position as a conciliatory gesture to the Lowndes Guards. Davis contended that Matthews must realize that he was not qualified and would resign before the regiment reached Mexico. When Matthews refused to give up the position, Davis replaced him with a more able officer, his friend John A. Wilcox. Of the company commanders, Capt. Charles Clark was the most talented. Noted Davis, Clark "had from early life displayed a passion for anything like military affairs, and always had command of a company in whatever town be happened to remain long enough."[18] Subsequent events would eventually place Clark and Wilcox at the head of the regiment.

Reuben Davis, a Democratic candidate in the upcoming gubernatorial campaign, reluctantly accepted command of the 2nd Mississippi Rifles. Just that fall *The Southron* reported that "Gen. Rueben Davis, of Aberdeen, is mentioned by the Southron Tribune as a very suitable person to be run by the Democratic party for next Governor. The General has the popularity with his party in the North, is a skillful and active tactician."[19] Caught up in the same war fever that infected his friends, he had originally enlisted in the regiment as a private in Capt. Joel M. Acker's Monroe Guards. Writing later in life, Davis discussed the position he had accepted. His own words lead us to conclude that the regiment had made a mistake in selecting him as its commander: "I had always considered the position of colonel peculiarly trying, as it places a man in such an attitude both to his superior officers and to the men under his command, as to make him a target for complaint on both sides. It was not long before I was more than ever impressed with this, and my want of military training made matters much less easy for me." He added, "How I got through the first day without resigning my command has always been a mystery to me."[20] A review of the regiment's history makes it clear that it would have been better for all if he had.

Davis quickly regretted his decision, stating, "My affairs [in life] were progressing in accordance with long-settled plans, and to jump from law into the army and from the army into politics must inevitably change the current of my life to my own ultimate disaster." Called to service by his fellow Mississippians, Davis could not refuse their offer of leadership and still retain their respect and friendship. Yet he feared that a poor showing on the battlefield by the new regiment would result in less support for him at the polls. His premonition about a life-changing experience proved to be accurate: Reuben Davis would be blamed by his opponents for the regiment's hardships, and he never became governor of his state. After resigning from his post in the summer of 1847, Reuben Davis answered his detractors by claiming he had always discharged his duties faithfully if not efficiently.

One well-fought battle, he thought, would have gone far in building a memorable reputation for both him and his regiment.[21]

There was much for which to answer. The problems that plagued the 2nd Mississippi Rifles began in Vicksburg during the regiment's formation. The bitter cold front left the men as defeated as any opponent they could have met on the battlefield. The volunteers, expecting to be quickly sent on their way to the warm climate of Mexico, did not bring winter clothing with them and sat shivering at Camp McClung. Love described the pitiful volunteers camped down by the river: "They were a lean, gaunt, smokey looking set of fellows—muddy up to their knees. They wrapped up in their blankets like Indians. . . . O how cold—the whole camp was about six inches deep in mud and water. The boys were trying to keep warm, some in their tents, & some by their little fires." Love moved a step closer to his goal of being named the regiment's surgeon when the US medical officer in charge at Vicksburg allowed him access to medicines to treat the men in any company who were reported sick. With patients in camp and spread out through the town, Love soon had his hands full. Sick himself, he struggled to relieve the suffering volunteers.[22]

The drastic change in weather ravaged the regiment. The weakened men of the 2nd Mississippi Rifles quickly succumbed to influenza, rheumatism, pneumonia, and a disease known only as the "cold plague." Captain Charles Clark, the candidate Love had supported for colonel, somehow provided extra blankets for his company because he was concerned for their welfare. However, Capt. Alfred A. Overton did not let the inclement weather prevent him from marching and drilling his Panola Boys in the streets of Vicksburg, an act that increased the number of sick recruits in his ranks. Love claimed the individual actions of the company officers helped determine the level of sickness in their respective commands. Men from rural areas of Mississippi suffered more cases of disease, resulting in more deaths among that group, than did the recruits from towns and cities.[23]

After spending two dreadful weeks at Vicksburg, the regiment received instructions to proceed to New Orleans. The trip, though, did little to improve conditions for the Mississippians. On January 14, the steamer *Sam Dale* picked up Colonel Davis and the first three companies and headed down the Mississippi River. Arriving at the Crescent City, Davis and his regiment disembarked outside the city where they pitched their tents at Chalmette, the site of Jackson's famous 1815 victory over the British. The *Sam Dale* then returned to Vicksburg to retrieve companies that had been left behind. On January 20, they rejoined the regiment on the old battleground. The 1st Mississippi Rifles had occupied the same site only six months earlier.[24]

Dr. Love was one of the volunteers who was left behind at Vicksburg. The health of many volunteers continued to decline. Love described one case of the disease called the "cold plague." The patient showed no perceptible pulse and had purple and pale lips and large black spots over his legs and feet. Love and others were at a loss as to what to do, as he exclaimed, "Mustard and stimulants have no effect." He continued ministering to the sick once he boarded the *Sam Dale* for the trip to New Orleans. He reported that of 160 men on board, only 10 were not suffering some degree of respiratory distress, writing that "the cabin [is] full of men constantly coughing."[25] The *New Orleans Picayune* noted that "two members of the Panola Boys died on the passage down—John Hall who was buried at Franklin's plantation, near the mouth of the Red River, and a man named [James H.] Templeton, who was taken down to the Battle-Ground . . . for internment."[26]

The Mississippians had not escaped the winter weather by traveling south. They shared their miserable camp with several other volunteer regiments who were also on their way to Mexico. One member of the 1st Pennsylvania Volunteers witnessed the arrival of several companies of the 2nd Mississippi Rifles and wrote they "encamped about five hundred yards above us, nearer the river." He further added, "I am sorry to say that they are the hardest and most delicate looking set of men, for new arrivals, that I ever saw."[27] Two weeks of exposure to nature's elements had begun to break down the regiment even before it left the shores of the United States.

The Mississippians later looked back in horror on the days they spent at New Orleans. Noted Colonel Davis, "New Orleans is a place to dream about when the sun shines and soft breezes blow, but in cold and rainy weather the fair city turns shrewish. . . . I think I never saw her so deadly chill[y] and bitter as she was that winter."[28] Water covered the low ground where soldiers had pitched their tents. Equipment became lost in the mud, as did men's lives. Dampness and cold worked together to produce an epidemic that the regiment's officers worked desperately to check. Unfortunately, many officers became ill themselves and could offer little assistance to their men. The *New Orleans Picayune* reported on the mounting death toll, blaming the situation on the "neglect of proper precaution on the part of the Government." One article erroneously reported that the overzealous Captain Overton had died from "fatigue and exposure."[29] The regiment lost as many as seven men a day while camped on the battleground. Love summed up the regiment's plight: "I saw more suffering . . . than I ever saw before." As for the sick stranded at the old battlefield, the doctor wrote, "Here the sick lay upon the cold wet ground, the tents above them wet—their blankets wet—nothing to eat—no one to nurse them—to make warm tea, or even to give them a cup of water in kindness and affection." Lamented Love, "Our brave boys are dying day and night."[30] The *New Orleans Picayune* reported that the stricken volunteers "suffered with the heroism of soldiers" even though they continue to "suffer for the want of comfortable quarters."[31] Tired of being blamed for the problems that the regiment faced, army officials in New Orleans published a report absolving the government of any culpability. Comparing the health of the Pennsylvania and Mississippi volunteers, both camped on the old battleground, they concluded that the Mississippians were not used to cold weather like the Pennsylvanians who came from and higher latitude and therefore were not affected by the harsh weather.[32]

The citizens of New Orleans soon became aware of the dire situation facing the volunteers and offered aid. Some of the sick were taken to medical facilities in the city for treatment. At one time, Dr. Charles A. Luzenberg's Franklin Infirmary at the intersection of Port and Moreau alone housed more than fifty of the regiment's sick—one half of the two-story brick hospital's 100-bed capacity. When these sources were taxed, military authorities finally opened the hospital at Jackson Barracks to the Mississippians. More volunteers needed treatment than there were beds, meaning that some of the sick had to be laid out on the cold brick floors. As Love recorded, no matter how sick, soldiers hated and feared military hospitals. He overheard one volunteer remark, "that it was only twenty five cents between that and going to Hell." Wrote Love, "Some refused to go—some remained in Camp—and others went to Dr. Luzenbergs' Hospital or to private houses." Once Jackson Barracks became available, though, military authorities announced that volunteers taken to private hospitals and homes would be responsible for the cost of their own medical care or lodging.[33] Love mused on the effect of the debacle: "We have all seen and felt ten times the misery of a hard fought battle. Indeed we have fought a battle—disease has been our invincible enemy. How hard it is that our brave men have left their homes, their friends and before the scene of fame & honor fall a victim to disease and misfortune?[34]

Families and friends of the stricken men searched for someone to blame for this catastrophe. Naturally, political opponents of Reuben Davis blamed him and claimed that he did little to ease the suffering of his men.[35] The federal government drew its share of criticism for neglecting the volunteers by leaving them on the soggy campground in bad weather while Jackson Barracks stood vacant only a few miles away.[36] Mississippians demanded that the US Congress investigate why eighty of their sons had died needlessly at New Orleans. The editor of *The Southron* proclaimed "when we reflect that the government was bound to see them cared for at least as a humane man cares for his beasts of burden . . . whatever department, or officer of the government has thus been criminal, deserves the execration of the nation as well as the severest punishments."[37]

The sympathy exhibited by the people of New Orleans toward the men camped on the battleground quickly vanished with increasing reports of crimes committed against the city's citizens by volunteers. On January 22, 1847, the *New Orleans* Picayune carried a story titled "Rowdy Volunteers." The reporter contented that "A large portion of the volunteers enlisted for the Mexican war, are doubtlessly well disposed and orderly men, anxious to do their duty and serve their country; but there are those among them who seem to delight in every specie of rowdyism and ruffinism, unfortunately bringing disgrace as well upon the company or regiment to which they belong as to themselves."[38] Identification of the guilty parties was almost impossible: the city was playing the unwilling host to several regiments who were passing through on the way to Mexico. Approximately 3,000 volunteers were in or about the city. The city's newspapers, therefore, usually laid the blame on unknown parties of "volunteers," lumping the innocent and guilty together. The Mississippians, languishing in sickbeds at camp and in the city, resented the accusations and protested to editors and city officials. The *New Orleans Picayune* reported on January 30, 1847, that several officers from the regiment had visited their offices to deny the allegations. "These gentlemen, each for his own command, declared to us that their men had not been guilty of the excesses committed; that they could not be guilty of such without receiving instant punishment from the hands of their comrades; and they claim to be exempted from the indiscriminate censure of a few is bringing upon a body of innocent men." *The Southron* announced with relief "We rejoice to learn by the *Picayune*, of the 31st, that the alleged outrage upon a girl of 14 by some members of the Mississippi Regiment has turned out holy false. . . . We were astonished and mortified at the report; for if the people of Mississippi are distinguished for one virtue more than another it is their horror and disgust for the brutalizing manners that the rumor attributed to them."[39]

It appears that the real culprits of many of the outrages were members of Company D, 1st Pennsylvania Infantry, who had appropriately named themselves "The Killers." The band had wreaked havoc with the inhabitants of the Ohio River towns they passed through, taking what they wanted from stores and threatening the lives of anyone who dared to stand in their way. Now in New Orleans, their depredations continued. In one episode, these men stole, killed, cooked, and ate the pet deer belonging to a Spaniard who lived near the battleground. In a more outlandish incident, roughly sixty members of this company took over a private party at the city's Globe Ball Room and "arrested" the policemen who came to ask them to leave. The volunteers kept the policemen in their "custody" and were marching their prisoner back to camp when the lieutenant colonel of their regiment rode up and ordered them to release their captives. At least one member of The Killers met with justice when a tavern owner caught him in the act of stealing and shot and killed him. In order to clear the name of their regiment, the officers of the 2nd Mississippi Rifles sent a letter to the *New Orleans Picayune* denying any such riotous acts on the part of their men.[40]

The men of the 2nd Mississippi Rifles finally embarked the transports they hoped would take them to Mexico and away from their troubles. Once aboard, the volunteers spent several agonizing days on the ships at the city's docks awaiting their departure. More men sickened and had to be carried into the city.[41] In New Orleans, rumors flew that the 2nd Mississippi Rifles had rebelled against the city's authorities and were on their way to sack several plantations. Lieutenant Colonel Kilpatrick and other officers were reported to have been shot down. The local militia and armed citizens turned out to combat the fictitious rioters. The article related that "By 9 o'clock it began to be evident that the whole affair was a false alarm, but how got up or started we could not learn. . . . the bloody doings below the city proved to be unfounded, the military ordered to dispense, and quiet once more reigned." The reporter explained how such a story could and did spread so quickly through the city: "high-handed outrages, helped to increase the alarm, until finally our citizens were ready to believe and receive any rumor that reached them." The people of New Orleans celebrated the departure of the volunteers, prompting one paper to express a feeling common among the locals: "The volunteers, or the larger part of them, have gone, and for ourselves we are heartily glad for it. That they had indifferent treatment while here is granted by all: that the elements have conspired to add to their discomforts is equally true: and furthermore a portion of them, few in number but reckless and abandoned men, have conspired to add the mortification of an ill name to the many misfortunes that beset them." The next word that the city had of these volunteers, hoped the writer, was that their valor on the battlefield had allowed them to restore their good reputations. The *Picayune* was not the only newspaper happy to see them go. The *Courier* proclaimed, "We are glad of it for their own sake and for the sake of the inhabitants of the vicinity of the ground on which they were camped."[42]

By February 3, the regiment had sailed for Mexico, a fact that brought relief to both the citizens of the town and the volunteers. Exclaimed Love, "I am glad to leave this place—the city has treated us badly—they have cheated us—they have slandered us—they have rejoiced at our departure—they have refused to sympathize with us in all our misfortune." His final thought: "The God of Battles I hope will be with us, *while the Devil* will remain in N. Orleans, for if he has a habitation on this globe it is there."[43]

The voyage to Mexico proved to be another ordeal for the regiment. The remaining 800 Mississippians were crowded into the holds of three ships hired to transport them across the Gulf. Many of them, not yet recovered from their illness, found that conditions below the decks did little to promote their healing. The volunteers embarked wearing wet clothing and carrying soggy bedding. Rough seas and poor diet contributed to the declining health of many of the hapless men imprisoned on the ships. Love described the conditions endured by the volunteers while at sea; officers shared cramped cabins while the enlisted men were housed "between the decks." He wrote, "On each side of the ship there is three rows of shelves one above the other about two feet apart—four feet wide, each one to contain two men. Then in the middle of the ship from one end to the other, is a middle set of berths: they are about ten feet wide—one above the other making three shelves, as at the sides." The men and their clothing, bedding, and equipment never had a chance to dry. "The water, or dampness of the hold settles where the men had to sleep," where it formed drops and then rained on the men below. The moisture combined with the heat produced by the packed men to create "a perfect steam," observed Love. The space was "dark, damp, filthy & offensive." His fear that these conditions would led to more sickness proved true.[44]

Love worked endlessly to assist the stricken Mississippians aboard his ship. Many were still suffering from the effects of illnesses contracted at Vicksburg and New Orleans. The motion of the ship caused most of the Mississippians to be seasick at least part of the voyage. It also made it difficult for doctors such as Love to visit the men below decks and to dispense medicine. Love's words "The dead and dying were knocked about like hogs in a butcher's pen" certainly applied to the voyage. In addition to those already lost on land, the regiment lost twenty-eight more who died during the four-week journey. Love captured the heartbreaking scene of a burial at sea. The volunteer was sewn into his blanket with a weight placed at one end. The ship's captain read the "Episcopal form of burial" over the body stretched out on plank. Few heard the words over the howling wind though. The ceremony concluded, the plank was raised, and the poor man dropped into the sea. Love expressed the sadness he felt at witnessing the event: "The rugged sea—the rolling ship—the silent burial—the gloom of the volunteers, all tended to render this one of the most distressing scenes I ever beheld."[45]

Increasing the 2nd Mississippi Rifles' woes, the ships carrying them to Mexico encountered a fierce winter storm out in the gulf. Colonel Reuben Davis had received instructions at New Orleans to take his regiment to Lobos Island, the marshaling point for Scotts' proposed attack on Vera Cruz. The storm not only hampered the ships' progress but also caused the transports to become separated from one another. The two ships containing Colonel Davis and Lieutenant Colonel Kilpatrick's contingents landed at Lobos Island, but the ship carrying Major Price and his men never arrived, which caused much concern on the island. Davis was later relieved to learn that the ship's captain, who had lost his bearings due to stormy weather, had put in at Tampico instead of continuing on to Lobos Island.[46]

The regiment at last reached Lobos Island, the destination specified in the orders Colonel Davis had received before leaving New Orleans. The men of the 2nd Mississippi Rifles were glad to be among the troops gathering for Scott's attack on Vera Cruz. Davis reported the arrival of his regiment to General Scott. Scott had disappointing news for him. The regiment's orders had been changed before they left the United States, a fact the military authorities at New Orleans had failed relate to Davis or his ship's captain. The regiment would not be allowed to participate in the attack on Vera Cruz but would instead be sent to Taylor as part of the replacements promised to the general by Scott. In an effort to circumvent the new order, Reuben Davis sent Kilpatrick to see Scott with a request that his regiment be brigaded with the new South Carolina regiment already in Scott's command, but he received word from the general that the new orders would stand. The Mississippians, who had already disembarked and cleared a campground on the island, reluctantly returned to their cramped quarters aboard the transports. Most, like Love, felt betrayed by their own government and even talked of going home now that there was little chance of fighting. "We have been badly treated," exclaimed the doctor. "[Scott] is a mean contemptible man."[47]

The ships turned northward and sailed along the Mexican coast, taking the regiment to Brazos Santiago where the men again disembarked. Ironically, Davis and his men later learned that Jefferson Davis and the 1st Mississippi Rifles were busy winning more glory at Buena Vista while they were sailing to join General Taylor's army. *The Mississippian*, a Jackson newspaper, voiced the frustration felt by many of the regiment that the time lost due to mix-up in its orders kept the 2nd Mississippi Rifles from being at the side of her sister regiment at Buena Vista and thereby sharing in its glory. Although it would have been impossible to transport the regiment to Saltillo in time to take part in the battle, the men of the 2nd Mississippi Rifles would later feel that they had been cheated out of their chance at fame. If not subjected to the unnecessary trip to Lobos, surmised Love, "We might have been long ago at Monterey and our sick men recruited—now ready for action."[48] The travails of the regiment, however, were far from over.

11
Discontented Poor Fellows

We have had nearly as many plagues among us as was inflicted on the pharaoh.
—Lt. Andrew Jackson Trussell

THE 2ND MISSISSIPPI RIFLES' long shipboard ordeal was about to end. "Early this morning [March 1, 1847] the [ship's] Capt. and Col. Davis, went on land," noted Dr. Thomas Love. Many volunteers, including the doctor, took the opportunity to write home knowing that Brazos Santiago was a terminus in the army's line of communication back to the United States. The captain returned to Love's ship that evening with word that the colonel had stayed ashore arranging transportation inland. He uttered words that revived the men's sagging spirits: "Col. Davis says you will have your fill of fighting—Genl. Taylor is now fighting his way back to Monterey—He is attacked by 10,000 Mexicans."[1]

News that Taylor had been engaged in a desperate battle, the outcome of which was yet unknown, had arrived at Brazos Santiago at the same time as the regiment. Davis endeavored to have his men landed amidst the excitement. By March 3, word arrived that the Mexican force battling Taylor numbered 20,000. Two days later, a steam lighter took the volunteers to shore. Noted Love, "This place Brassos Santiago or Brazos St. Jago is a low flat sandy place—subject to overflow. I am surprised that Genl. Scott has left this place the mouth and Port Isabel so entirely unprotected." Accessing the current situation, Love contended, "If the Mexicans knew it they would avail themselves of it & they do know of it—for there is great communications between this [place] and the Mexican forces."[2]

Davis finally moved his regiment up river to Matamoros.[3] Given the uncertainty over Taylor's fate, the prospect of a battle seemed promising. On March 9, it appeared that the regiment's time for glory had arrived. Scouts reported a large cloud of dust approaching the town thought to be stirred up by advancing Mexican soldiers. "I took active steps for defence against the attack which seemed to threaten us," recalled Davis. Love noted that "Every arm was nerved and ready for the struggle. What a beautiful or rather grand spectacle to behold a long line of men drawn up with a view of meeting a foe that had conquered the invincible Taylor.—now was not the time for a craven heart to quail—not a quiver was seen on any lip." The source of the dust cloud was soon revealed to be a mule caravan bringing its load to town. The regiment was dismissed until brought back into line by the boom of cannon upstream. They wondered if it was another chance for battle. A steamboat came into view. Noted Love, "Lt. Col. Kilpatrick dashed off at full speed [on his charger] to meet the news at the river's edge. He returned, "crying at the top of his voice. 'Old Taylor gave them Hell at Saltillo—killed 4000 Mexicans!" "The men were fairly wild with pride and delight," said Davis. Cannons and muskets were fired off in salute to Old Rough and Ready.[4] The mystery of Taylor's fate had been solved, squashing the regiment's chance for battle.

Attention now shifted back to the fight with which the men were so familiar. The 2nd Mississippi Rifles had reached Mexico, but they had not escaped the sickness that had so plagued them. Major Price reported that a disease similar to smallpox had been observed in some of the men aboard his transport. Reuben Davis, who had practiced medicine before taking up the profession of law, did not think that the disease was smallpox, but Love believed that it was indeed the highly dangerous and contagious disease and recommended that a separate hospital be established for the stricken volunteers. Unfortunately, Love and Davis had developed a contentious relationship, and the colonel gave little weight to his surgeon's opinions. Others in the Mississippi regiment showed symptoms. According to Love, Davis once told him, "I can never be made to believe that we have small pox—it is nothing more than chicken pox." Eventually more than sixty of the Mississippians were afflicted by the epidemic with several deaths attributed to the new disease.[5] Amid this new crisis, Colonel Davis moved his regiment inland to Matamoros, leaving his sickest men behind as inmates of the army's smallpox hospital.[6]

The rift between Love and Davis, which was to add to the suffering of the ailing volunteers, began on the voyage to Lobos Island. Love took offense to Davis's suggestion that he had been drinking on duty. The proud young doctor admitted to the colonel that he had used wine and brandy but only for the medicinal value of warding off disease and reviving his constitution. After this incident, each man held the other in contempt. The colonel had little faith in the surgeon's ability, and Love laid the cause of his difficulties he faced in ministering to the regiment's sick squarely upon Davis's shoulders: "When the head officer is incompetent to the discharge of his duties no system prevails in the army." He was particularly annoyed that, contrary to regulations governing the army, the colonel would not allow nurses for the sick to be detailed from the ranks of the companies. Love had no support among the officers in his request, causing him to state, "They are not willing that their men shall be detailed to have anything to do with the hospitals as nurses or attendants, yet as soon as a man gets sick, they want to post him off to the hospital and expect me to feed, physic, & nurse him."[7]

In the meantime, the first official duty of the 2nd Mississippi Rifles was to relieve the 1st Indiana Infantry of its garrison duties so the Hoosiers could advance inland. The Indiana regiment had been left there by Taylor and had been guarding this important town on the south bank of the Rio Grande for several months. On observing the new arrivals, James P. Drake, the major of the 1st Indiana Infantry, remarked that the Mississippians "are fine looking and in a bowie knife fight they would have been some[thing?] but they are not drilled or disciplined for service."[8] An incident occurred in the Mississippian's camp during their second day at Matamoros that confirmed his observation. Company K's captain, Benjamin C. Buckley, had lost the election for colonel to his political rival, Davis. Still resenting his defeat, Buckley refused to form his company for dress parade. Only the threat of violence against the captain and his disobedient volunteers caused them to turn out. The climax came when Colonel Davis commanded two loyal companies to load their rifles and prepare to fire on their mutinous comrades. Buckley and his company then appeared on the parade ground, and bloodshed was avoided. Davis claimed that "After that one mutinous moment, I never had any trouble with the command." Others in the regiment thought otherwise.[9]

By the middle of March, the 2nd Mississippi Rifles turned the town over to three companies of the 1st North Carolina Infantry, the most recent arrivals to Matamoros, and started for Monterrey.[10] Marching along the river road in "shoe top high dust," Lt. Andrew Jackson Trussell of the Lauderdale Volunteers described the "Reo Grandy" as the "crookedest" river he had ever seen, comparing it in size to the Tombigbee River back home. Water from roadside ponds and the river did little to alleviate the men's thirst. Besides the amount of silt in the muddy water, the lieutenant noted a number of dead cows and horses in the river.[11] The unseasoned 2nd Mississippi Rifles reached Camargo after several days of exhausting marching that resulted in further hardship for the men.

At Camargo, Reuben Davis showed that he shared Captain Buckley's propensity for disobeying his instructions. The colonel of the 1st Ohio Infantry, Alexander M. Mitchell, instructed Davis and his regiment to remain behind to guard Camargo so the Ohio troops could take up the march for Monterrey. This additional delay was too much for Davis to bear. Eager to press on, he claimed that he had been given a letter at Matamoros by Taylor's brother, Lt. Col. Joseph P. Taylor, that instructed him to join the general without delay. Recalled Davis, "Now my men were wild to get on where there might be some chance of active service, and I was determined that it should not be my fault if they were not gratified." The Mississippian refused to halt his march, telling Mitchell that he was en route to join Taylor. The Buckeye colonel placed Davis under arrest and demanded his sword. The proud Mississippian told Mitchell that he was returning to his own camp and that he could come for his sword there, belligerently stating him to "send his whole regiment, as it may not be prudent for a small party to come on that errand." Fortunately, tempers cooled, and the next morning the Ohio regiment marched off to Monterrey while the Mississippians reluctantly stayed behind.[12]

The 2nd Mississippi Rifles' opportunity to move forward came when a supply train bound for Monterrey stopped at Camargo. The commander of the train's escort, Col. Humphrey Marshall of the 1st Kentucky Cavalry, invited Davis and his men to join his column. It seemed that a new route to Monterrey through the town of China had been proposed, and Marshall did not know what resistance the Mexicans might offer: thus he welcomed their added numbers. The Mississippians, on the other hand, welcomed the chance to move closer to the front.[13] The regiment's journey to Monterrey proved to be a repeat of its march to Camargo—dry and hot without an adequate water supply. At one point, the Mississippians had to march 20 miles before reaching a water hole. Adjutant John A. Wilcox sang songs to entertain and encourage his comrades and measured out water by the spoonful to those who lagged behind. The Kentucky cavalry guarded the head and rear of the column, with one company of Mississippians in the vanguard and the other nine companies posted one every fifteen wagons. An expected attack near Caidereta failed to materialize because the inhabitants feared the Americans would destroy the town in retaliation.[14] Recalled Davis of the rumored fight, "At very early dawn, every man was up and ready for action, but as had happened so often before, our hopes melted away with the dew before the morning son." The enemy did draw blood though, when a member of Company K fell behind on the march and had his throat cut, the fate of many stragglers in Mexico. The dead man's friends "arrested" the murderers and then shot them.[15] After a two-week march, the 2nd Mississippi Rifles reached Monterrey without having had any major encounters with the Mexicans.

The trip from Camargo to Monterrey was cause for more trouble between Davis and his surgeon. Love had determined that many of the sick were unfit to make the trip and should be discharged from the service. The morning reports listed 120 men sick, of which, upon examination, he determined 82 were actually ill. He received a visit from the colonel, who asked petulantly, "Dr. Love how many men have you discharged? . . . It must be stopped . . . You need not make out no more papers, for I shall not sign them." Angered at being chastised by Davis, Love invited the colonel to examine the men himself, a challenge Davis accepted. At the end of the inspection Davis remarked, "Well, indeed I did not know that so many men were sick here." A few days later Love asked Davis to visit his hospital again but was supposedly told "I have not time, your hospital is a matter I feel very little interest in."[16]

Davis's disinterest in the care of the sick caused unnecessary suffering on the march. Love, who wanted to leave the most serious cases behind, was ordered to send as many men forward as possible. The colonel still insisted that any cases of eruptive fever were only "chicken pox." Reported Love, "Instead of leaving *fifty one* as I recommended I found *only* 26 men in the hospital." Davis had said the sick men could ride, but there was little space for them on the heavily loaded wagons. When informed of the problem, Love said he told the captains "to get their [sick] men where ever they can." Love described the sorry condition of his patients: "It is heart sickening indeed to look at these poor fellows after hauling them 12 or 15 miles. Covered with dust—parched up by the sun, and famished for water. The small pox cases are horrid—Their faces are black with dust—they suffer greatly." The officers of the other units were dismayed that Davis would have brought smallpox along, which was beginning to make its appearance among Marshall's Kentuckians.[17]

Rumors reached the Mississippians as they approached Monterrey that Taylor planned to arrest Davis and send the 2nd Mississippi Rifles back to Camargo. Despite their colonel's assertion to the contrary, many of the Mississippians believed that Davis had marched the regiment to Monterrey without orders. Colonel Davis rode ahead to see the general and explain the tribulations he and his regiment had been through. To his relief, the rumors were untrue and Davis received a warm and friendly reception from "Old Zack." Taylor had two visitors in his tent at the time—Col. Jefferson Davis and Major Bradford of the 1st Mississippi Rifles. After spending a pleasant afternoon with these officers, Reuben Davis returned to his regiment amid their cheers. The next day, the jubilant 2nd Mississippi Rifles hailed General Taylor as they marched by his tent on their way to the army's camp at Walnut Springs. The Mississippians felt that they were at last a part of the American Army in Mexico. Even so, they could not escape the shadow of the 1st Mississippi Rifles. Noted Love about their sister regiment, "The first regt. is praised from the lips of every one—This will be an encouragement to us to fight with valor in order to support the reputation of the state."[18]

The regiment continued to be plagued by illness while at Camp Allen. One of the casualties was Rueben Davis. At Cerralvo, Capt. William P. Rogers, 1st Mississippi Rifles, chanced to meet Davis, who was then homeward bound. Davis, a prewar friend of Rogers,' told him that personal illness had forced him temporarily to give up the command of the 2nd Mississippi Rifles. The colonel said that he hoped to rejoin his regiment after a short period of recuperation in the United States.[19] Rogers, who had been escorting a supply train to Camargo, visited the camp of the 2nd Mississippi Rifles on his return to Monterrey. Rogers recorded in his diary that "The reg. [the 2nd Mississippi] is suffering under small pox. They are discontd [sic] poor fellows."[20] An officer of an Indiana regiment, Maj. Henry S. Lane, compared the sick list of his unit to the longer one of the 2nd Mississippi Rifles and found a four to one ratio. On April 30, 1847, Lane noted the health of his regiment to be good, but "The 2d Mississippi Regiment, however, are dreadfully scourged by sickness, having [lost] 11 persons in forty-eight hours past."[21]

Davis requested a furlough because his "business interests at home demanded that [he] should return immediately to Mississippi." Love noted Davis's departure and reflected on the effect it would have on the regiment. "Col. Davis has procured a furlough of 60 days and [has] gone home. He goes on private business." Davis's insistence on bringing the 2nd Mississippi Rifles to Monterrey had worked in his favor, prompting the doctor to write, "He has gained rapidly upon the affections of his regiment since we have been in camp. . . . But now, to leave us so suddenly," predicted Love, "will do him injury." Moreover, Davis's departure would discourage others and have "an injurious effect" on those who remained.[22] Although Davis may have gained favor with the men of his regiment, Love still thought little of the colonel, his ability, and his commitment to the men he led to a foreign land. "He has gone," exclaimed Love. "He has left us in a midst of trouble."[23] Nor did Love have faith in Lieutenant Colonel Kilpatrick, who Davis had left in charge. Wrote the doctor, "He is a good hearted man and a very clever fellow, as the saying is, but he is no military genius, and ought to resign his office."[24]

At Monterrey, however, Love finally found assistance for the regiment's numerous smallpox patients. He was approached by Taylor's medical director, who asked, "Well, well, have you, have you small pox in your regiment?" He replied that Assistant Surgeon David A. Kinchloe and he held the opinion that "we had small pox and had so considered it for sometimes." The officer then said in a "fatherly" tone, "The Drs. will go down with you, and see those cases, & try to figure out what they are." When Taylor's doctors examined the patients they "did not hesitate to pronounce them to be [afflicted with] small pox."[25]

After all he had been through with Davis, Love felt vindicated by Taylor's medical staff. Nevertheless, after a discussion with the medical director, Love decided that he needed to gather letters from officers in the regiment supporting his claim that he had warned Davis that the men had smallpox to help ward off any criticism that he was responsible for bring the disease to Monterrey. Although Taylor's quartermaster was unable to provide a hospital tent in which Love could house his smallpox patients, the department erected large tarpaulins supported by wooden frames for

Love's use: one for "fever and other diseases, and one for cases of smallpox." He then moved eighty-five patients under cover, more than sixty of them stricken men with smallpox. Wrote Love proudly, "It is also gratifying to my feelings to learn that the medical director who often visited my hospital, has expressed to Genl. Taylor a flattering account of my efforts to provide for the sick."[26]

Still, Love's task was daunting, as the number of smallpox patients continued to grow. On one day alone he received thirteen new cases. "The scene at the small Pox Hospital is yet heart rendering," wrote Love. A heavy rain one night caused him to lament, "Everything seems to be against us." Flies had laid eggs in many of the patients' sores, producing maggots in the men's "eyes, nose, and the flesh of the cheek." Noted the doctor, "[The maggots] are hard to [re]move from their dens which they have made deep in the skin." He also noted that "There is a peculiar smell about the small pox which has become so familiar to me, that I frequently pronounce a case to be small pox from this sign alone." He said of this ability, "I have not been deceived in a single case." He wondered that he had been so exposed but had so far escaped contracting the disease. Love contemplated his handling of the epidemic, musing, "I have now been exposed to this terrible disease for nearly two months, and I have not felt that danger which I thought I should have felt if this exposure had been presented to me before I engaged in the treatment of this formidable disease."[27]

Love laid the blame for part of his difficulty in tending to the sick on company officers. Coming from civilian life, they were ignorant of the procedures and routines associated with hospitals, especially those governed by military regulations. "Many of the Captains want to send their men to the hospital as soon as they get sick, without consulting me, or even knowing whether there is room for them in the Hospital or not," complained the doctor. He related one incident in which his control over the admission of a patient led to a fistfight with another officer. Captain Charles Clark and Lt. Chesley S. Coffey, both of Thomas Hinds Guards, came to his tent one evening to ask why Love had refused to accept one of the men who had been brought to him that afternoon. "I told him it was my privilege to say who should come into my hospital," replied Love. Clark told him that his lieutenant and orderly sergeant felt highly insulted by his rebuff. As a way of easing the situation, Love said he had not intended to insult anyone. Coffey then said, "I consider myself highly insulted." Knowing that a fight was in the making, Love told Coffey, who was "a large fleshy man about as heavy as a bale of cotton," to "help himself as quick as he pleased." The two men fought in the doctor's tent. Hearing the noise, Love's friends rushed in, separated the combatants, and ended the fight. Although Love did not want to fight, he believed it was inevitable since apology failed to satisfy Coffey.[28]

Love treated at least one Mississippian at Monterrey for gunshot wounds. William C. Faulkner—the grandfather of the famous Mississippi author by the same name—had gone riding outside the city limits when he was fired on from ambush. The first lieutenant of the Tippah Guards, Faulkner was struck twice by the shots with one ball entering his left foot and another carrying away the ends of three fingers from his left hand. Although not life-threatening, the painful wounds prevented Faulkner from effectively performing his duties, and the lieutenant asked for a medical discharge. Afterward, it was claimed by a fellow officer, 2nd Lt. Thomas C. Hindman, Faulkner had been shot while visiting Aguas Calientes, a popular village nearby that had been placed off limits by General Taylor. According to Hindman, the assailants were not guerrillas but instead Falkner's rival for the hand of a local señorita. The feud between the two officers continued after they both returned home, culminating when Faulkner killed Hindman's brother Robert with a bowie knife on the streets of Ripley, Mississippi. Like Faulkner and his brother, Thomas, Robert had been a member of the Tippah Guards although only a private.[29]

The 2nd Mississippi Rifles finally left Camp Allen at the end of May when it then moved on to Buena Vista. The march provided a welcome change from the inactivity of camp life. The Lauderdale Volunteers' Lieutenant Trussell wrote his brother that they had traveled through Rinconada Pass to reach Saltillo. Along the way he saw a mountain cove he judged "the bieutifulest [sic] Sight that I ever saw." The streams and wheat fields also impressed him. The regiment's new post, Camp Taylor, lay about seven miles south of Saltillo, near the site of the Americans' recent battle with Santa Anna. "We are now camped where the First Mississippi Regiment was camped at the time of the Battle of Buenavista," wrote Trussell. The locations encouraged sightseeing. Captain William Barksdale, the commissary officer for the 2nd Mississippi Rifles, walked the two miles to the battlefield soon after the regiment arrived at its new camp. He informed friends back home in Mississippi that hundreds of unburied Mexicans still covered the ground, a fact that Trussell confirmed. Barksdale wrote that the 1st Mississippi Rifles had disinterred some of its dead to take to Mississippi. He was correct. One of the dead men brought back to Mississippi was Lt. Robert L. Moore, a member of the Vicksburg Volunteers. Two members of the State Fencibles, Joseph C. Reville [Revell] and William Phillips, also were reinterred in Jackson on June 23, 1847, upon the first regiment's return. *The Mississippian* reported that flags in Jackson flew at half-mast as the Reserve State Fencibles escorted the bodies to the cemetery. The band form Mr. Stickney's New Orleans Circus provided the music for the funeral procession.[30]

Camp Taylor was situated on a treeless plain at the foot of the mountains. The men complained of the cold, but the higher altitude agreed with the Mississippians. Letters home proclaimed that the regiment's long, deadly bout with illness was finally at an end.[31] The 2nd Mississippi Rifles had suffered dearly, losing almost one-third of its members without once having participated in a single engagement against the enemy. Each company had lost an average of thirty-four men from its ranks, dead or discharged due to illness. One company, ninety strong at Vicksburg, could muster only forty-one by June.[32] Truly, these volunteers had experienced a long string of hard luck.

The stigma of the disease had been hard for the regiment to shake. Wrote Col. Samuel Ryan Curtis, who was also traveling to Saltillo, "I understand the 2nd Mississippi Volunteers start up country today. . . . The smallpox rages in the Mississippi regiment and I therefore determined to start very early so as to get the lead. We passed the regiment before day and traveled hard till we arrived at the watering place south of the pass [at] Los Muertos. We learned by one who had overtaken us, that the Mississippi Regiment did not march forward to day." At the camp near Buena Vista, Pvt. Augustus Ehinger of the 2nd Illinois Volunteers recorded the regiment's arrival on May 30, 1847: "Today at noon the remnant of the new Mississippi Regiment arrived. They had suffered terribly with the small pox." Ehinger had earlier recorded that the volunteers in northern Mexico, including at Saltillo, had been given vaccinations to present the spread of the disease.[33]

Finally, in July, Lieutenant Trussell was able to report good news from Saltillo. "The health of the regiment is now pretty good but I can assure you that if ever poor volunteers suffered under afflictions, it has been the 2nd Mississippians. We have had nearly as many plagues among us as was inflicted on the pharaoh. It has cost Mississippi the life of many a brave son and good citizen." As for the cases of smallpox, Trussell reported that "we have I believe got clear of the Desperate complainte Small Pox they was 22 of our company had the Small Pox at one time they was 84 of this Ridg- in Small Pox hospital but, fortunately, I did not have it marked Some of our boys very mutch."[34]

The transfer of the 2nd Mississippi Rifles to Saltillo had been part of the redistribution of the army in Mexico as a means to supply General Scott with the troops necessary for the capture of Mexico City. General Taylor remained at Camp Allen in Monterrey. General John E. Wool, instrumental in the American success at Buena Vista, was left in command of the regulars and volunteers at Saltillo. Wool's force included six companies of the 2nd US Dragoons and Company B of the 4th US Artillery—all seasoned regulars. Volunteers fresh from the United States, though, comprised the bulk of Wool's troops. He had one brigade of volunteer infantry made up of the 2nd Mississippi Rifles, the 1st Virginia Infantry, and the 1st North Carolina Infantry. None of these regiments had "seen the elephant," but all longed for the chance to prove themselves. Four companies of volunteer cavalry from the veteran 1st Arkansas and 3rd Texas rounded out Wool's command, bringing his total force to nearly 2,500 men.[35]

Frequent changes of commanders of the infantry brigade at Saltillo had an adverse effect on the discipline of the volunteers. Brigadier General Thomas Marshall, the brigade's first commander, soon left Saltillo to join Scott. A rumor passed through camp that Jefferson Davis had been promoted to brigadier general and would soon return to Mexico to lead the infantry at Saltillo. Although he had been offered such a position, he had declined it for several reasons.[36] With no brigadier general to command the infantry brigade at Camp Taylor, the duty passed to the colonels of the volunteer regiments in the brigade. On one occasion no field officers from the three volunteer regiments were present for duty for three days in a row.

The volunteers at Saltillo had not yet realized it, but the question of who was to be their commander no longer really mattered. The major fighting had shifted to the south, leaving them stranded in the backwaters of the war. Still, constant rumors of marches and countermarches kept their hopes of a fight alive for many months. General Wool developed a reputation as a "stampedest" among the Mississippians because of readiness to respond to any supposed threat. But it was dragoons and rangers who usually had the honor of chasing after the enemies, both real and imagined.[37]

The 2nd Mississippi Rifles settled into the routine of camp life at Camp Taylor. Lieutenant Coffey described the typical day: "we Get up at Revalle in the morning which is at the Brake of Day and form line. and have Rolls Cald. and then the Companeys ar properly policed and then we get our Breakfast then Regments police the waggans pass Round and take all the filth out from our Camps then offiscers Drill then Company Drill 2 hours. then nothing more until 2 Oclock. then Regmantal Drill 2 or hours and then at Sun Set we have Dress Parade at 9 Oclock we have another Roll Call half past nine taps on the Drum for all the mens lites out thus passes off one more Day and then we fall into our Little Cots and fall in a Dose."[38]

Other events marked camp life. The long period of illnesses had ravaged the regiment's officers, and most of the work now fell on the shoulders of the few junior officers fit for duty. A new ailment called the "black tongue" appeared in the camp of the North Carolina volunteers, but it mercifully missed the Mississippians. (The affliction was likely a bacterial infection brought on by poor oral hygiene and the lack of fresh fruits and vegetables.) The volunteers visited the local Mexican markets to augment their standard army fare of salt pork or beef with sweet bread, corn bread, wheat bread, sugar, milk, and, occasionally, fresh pork. Fatigue parties had to travel as far as 20 miles to gather wood for the cook fires because there were no trees left near the camp.[39]

Sunday, July 4, 1847, provided a welcome break in the regiment's dull routine. General Wool ordered his entire division to turn out for a dress parade, complete with a thirty-gun salute by the artillery. With an uncharacteristic show of goodwill that ran counter to his reputation as a strict disciplinarian, Wool told the men to enjoy themselves. Noted Trussell, "We had a glorious 4th [and] we enjoyed the day finely. Officers and privates, there being no distinction, the boys had full sway." Not all Americans in Saltillo were pleased with the general's actions. Susan S. Magoffin, the wife of a Santa Fe trader in Saltillo at the time, chastised Wool in her diary for allowing this public celebration to take place on a Sunday. In her opinion, the general should have set an example for the Mexicans on how to correctly observe the Sabbath. Back in Mississippi, the citizens had held their festivities at Clinton to welcome back the men of the 1st Mississippi Rifles on Saturday, July 3, in order to avoid the conflict between religious and patriotic duties.[40]

A party of the regiment's officers returned to Mississippi in June to sign up replacements to fill the gaps in the 2nd Mississippi's ranks. The recruiting party consisted of Capt. Charles Clark, Capt. Joel M. Acker, and Lt. Charles Gouveneaux. These officers had been authorized to receive 500 recruits, a number sufficient to fill their regiment to its limit of 1,000 volunteers. By July the officers had established recruiting offices at Natchez, Aberdeen, and Monticello. Notices placed in Mississippi newspapers alerted prospective volunteers of the opportunity that awaited them. Not all Mississippians, though, wished to have their friends and relatives join the hard-luck regiment. Chesley S. Coffey, the lieutenant with whom Love had fought in his tent, even went so far as to write his brothers in Mississippi to warn them not to enlist when the recruiters came around. His reason was "they [the volunteers] ar So much Exposed here that one man in 10 will not Stand it-."[41]

As so often in the career of the 2nd Mississippi Rifles, fate spoiled the regiment's plans. Shortly after these officers opened their recruiting stations to receive replacements for the 2nd Mississippi, Governor Brown announced the War Department's intention to accept yet another group of Mississippi volunteers. The government called for the formation of five companies of riflemen and promised that those who joined this new battalion would be sent to serve with General Scott. The battalion, commanded by James Patton Anderson, never reached Mexico, assigned instead to garrison Tampico. Recruitment for the 2nd Mississippi Rifles stalled in the face of this new competition for the limited number of men who still desired to serve their county in Mexico. Much of the enthusiasm for the war that the state had exhibited earlier in the conflict had cooled, and both units struggled to fill their quotas. Clark, Acker, and Gouveneaux achieved limited success in their efforts. Eventually, 158 recruits joined the 2nd Mississippi Rifles in Mexico. Thirteen more recruits had second thoughts and failed to show up at the rendezvous.[42] Mississippi's war fever had broken.

12
Life in the Backwaters of the War

If we could get in one hard battle and I could come out safe, we could then return home with some honor.
—Lt. Andrew Jackson Trussell

"WE MIGHT AS WELL BE AT HOME for all the good we are doing," exclaimed Lt. Everand Dowsing in a letter to a female friend back in Mississippi. "I sometimes think of resigning when I reflect upon the dull and cheerless prospect before us." He continued, "We fancy that we are as brave as the first Regt. and pant for an opportunity to show it."[1]

Dowsing may have had "a strong hankering to see a battle," but as the summer of 1847 came to an end he and the other Mississippi volunteers at Saltillo must have felt doubts about the prospects of any more fighting in northern Mexico.[2] The task of securing the gains that resulted from Taylor's victories had fallen to them: they were to be only the guardians instead of the conquering heroes. The American victories of August and September that ended in the capture of Mexico City would be won without their help.

Without the threat of a real enemy, the men considered the rigid discipline at Camp Taylor an unnecessary burden. The volunteers turned to the usual pastimes of idle soldiers. The long days of inactivity resulted in fights among the volunteers. The altercations were not confined to just the enlisted men. In the Virginia regiment, two lieutenants fought a duel that left both of the officers dead.[3] Major Montford Sidney Stokes, 1st North Carolina Infantry, received a bloody nose at a banquet when he was struck in the face with a champagne bottle swung by another officer who was trying to bash an uninvited guest.[4] Lieutenant Andrew Jackson Trussell informed his brother of an altercation he had with another volunteer: "I had a little difficulty the other day. I stabbed a man in the shoulder but did not hurt him very bad." He contended that his action was justified and that his captain supported him.[5]

With so much time on their hands, several members of the 2nd Mississippi Rifles formed their own Masonic Lodge at Saltillo. Those participating in this important fraternal order included the regiment's adjutant, John A. Wilcox, and two other officers, Capt. William J. Daniels (Lauderdale Volunteers), and Lt. Chesley S. Coffey (Thomas Hinds Guards). In the midst of the camp's daily routine, the members of the lodge went about the business of reviewing applications and inducting new members into their fraternity.

One volunteer whose application had been presented to the Thomas Hinds Lodge in Mississippi but was withdrawn for misconduct found redemption, earning his first degree at Saltillo.[6]

Samuel Chamberlain, an interesting if sometimes fanciful witness, left his impression of the volunteers who arrived to take the place of those who had served with Taylor at Buena Vista. He noted, "New regiments continued to arrive at Saltillo, composed of the roughs of the South, without drill or discipline." Chamberlain made an exception for the 1st Virginia Volunteers, saying their leadership was good and the "regiment bore a deserved character for efficiency." As for the other two units, however, the "men of the 2nd Mississippi Rifles, and the 1st North Carolina Volunteers under Colonel Payne, were especially unruly, committing many depredations and outrages on the inhabitants of the San Juan Valley." In true Chamberlain style, he recounts an episode in which he rushed in to save several women from a nearby ranch from the clutches of two red-shirted members of the 2nd Mississippi Rifles. Always the hero of his own stories—real or imagined—Chamberlain was in fact an astute observer. The term "unruly" could be accurately applied to the new replacement regiments.[7]

A serious affair occurred at Camp Taylor in August 1847 that involved the volunteer regiments at Saltillo, including the 2nd Mississippi Rifles. The trouble started in another regiment in the volunteer brigade, the 1st North Carolina. Dissatisfaction had existed in the North Carolina regiment since its formation. Colonel Robert T. Paine, an able but unpopular officer, had assumed command of the volunteer infantry brigade upon the departure of Col. Humphrey Marshall. Paine had three strikes against him when he took charge of the brigade at Buena Vista: he had been appointed by the governor of his state and not elected by his men; although a Whig, his men were predominantly Democrats; and he unrealistically expected all volunteers to behave like disciplined soldiers. He ordered a wooden punishment horse to be built and placed in back of his tent as a warning to those who might be tempted to misbehave. The device was well known to regulars. Soldiers guilty of minor infractions were ordered to straddle the tall sawhorse-like structure for hours while their feet dangled unsupported. Resenting what they considered to be Paine's attempt to impose cruel and unneeded punishment upon them, the volunteers made their plans. On the afternoon of August 14, 1847, men from the 1st Virginia entered the North Carolinians' camp, attacked the offending device, and destroyed it. Colonels Paine and John F. Hamtramck conferred over the incident but concluded that nothing could be done as no one had been apprehended in the act of committing the outrage. Paine had his company's carpenters repair the horse and placed it near his tent. The night passed without further incident, but the anger directed at the colonel and his horse had not been spent.[8]

Not yet satisfied, the mob returned the next night after tattoo, shouting and throwing rocks at Paine's tent. When the colonel's guard refused to come to his assistance, Paine fired his pistols into the crowd, causing it to disperse. The shots killed one volunteer and slightly wounded another. The next morning, Paine found a petition on his adjutant's desk signed by the officers of his regiment that called on him to resign. General Wool acted quickly and dismissed two North Carolina lieutenants, one North Carolina private, and one Virginia private for their involvement in mutiny and ordered the four to leave Saltillo immediately. In support of the beleaguered colonel, Wool wrote, "I have never known in the volunteer service an officer who possessed more zeal or efficiency. He is certainly one of the best officers I have known in any volunteer service, and because he was efficient, his officers, prompted no doubt by others, combined to drive him from the regiment." In the order dismissing the volunteers from the service, Wool stated, "Had the company officers of the North Carolina, *as a body*, uniformly and actively discharged their duties to their men and their government, the disgraceful and unfortunate affair of last night [would] had not happened." The event went down in the records as the Paine Mutiny.[9]

The matter was not ended though. The two disgraced lieutenants, Josiah S. Pender and George E. B. Singletery, took their case to President James K. Polk. Acting in his role as commander-in-chief, Polk ordered all four volunteers reinstated and returned to duty. He explained his action by saying that Wool had denied the men due process by dismissing them without giving them the opportunity of a defense. He did not absolve the volunteers but instead ordered authorities in Mexico to hold a court of inquiry to determine what had happened that August night.[10]

Pender and Singletery had gathered affidavits from officers and men at Saltillo before their departure. Some claimed that the two had not taken part in the riot that night and testified to the two volunteers' good character. They had the support of the officers of the 2nd Mississippi Rifles as well. On August 30, 1847, thirty officers of the regiment signed a written statement they sent to fellow Mississippian, Secretary of Treasury Robert Walker. The document expressed their belief that Wool's dismissal of the four volunteers had been unlawful. Their argument rested on two facts. First, volunteers were state troops, subject to their own officers, and could not be dismissed from service by a federal authority. Second, the Articles of War stated that no officer or soldier could be dismissed from the service without first being subject to a legal proceeding. Walker presented the letter to Secretary of War William Marcy, who then passed it on to Polk. Thus the Mississippians likely had a role in shaping the president's decision to order the court of inquiry.[11]

Although Wool objected to what he believed was Polk's meddling in military affairs, he ordered an inquiry into the incident. The men of the 2nd Mississippi Rifles received a fair share of the blame for their actions in the disturbances. Witnesses testified that "a number of men of the Virginia and Mississippi volunteers" were passing through the camp of the North Carolina regiment before the disturbance. One witnesses contended that several Mississippians had threatened to shoot Paine if an opportunity presented itself. One Mississippian was even heard boasting that he had "snapped a cap" at the colonel but his rifle had failed to discharge. Had it gone off, he said, "he would have blown the old devil's brains out." More testimony at the inquiry further implicated the Mississippians when a North Carolina private testified, "The officer of the guard was a Mississippian. He said he bet fifty dollars that there would be a 'stampede,' or fuss of some kind, in the North Carolina camp that night before 10 o'clock." Another witness claimed that he overheard a volunteer in the Tar Heel camp declare, "We can go now, I have fixed things with the guard." The 2nd Mississippi Rifles' adjutant, John A. Wilcox, appeared before the court as a witness for Paine. In the end, the court cleared Colonel Paine of any wrongdoing on his part, determining that a mutiny had indeed occurred at Camp Taylor on August 15, 1847. The participation of Mississippians in the mutiny did nothing to add to the glory and honor they so desperately sought.[12]

Another court martial that involved the 2nd Mississippi Rifles centered on a brothel at a rancho known to the volunteers as the Alamo located only one mile from Camp Taylor. Men of the Mississippi regiment were among the brothel's customers. In September, an incident involving the rancho was one factor that led to the court martial of Lt. Fleming Amyx of the Union Greys.[13] Amyx's company came to his tent one night when he happened to be in command. Private Cornelius W. Mann asked for a pass granting permission for him and his friends to visit the rancho. Amyx said that headquarters would not approve it. The man persisted. In jest, Amyx scribbled a few quick lines and handed the man a note that stated, "Privates Ratliffle, Simpson, Shields, and Mann have permission to visit the rancho to buy some cunt." Intended as a bawdy joke among themselves, it did not stay that way as Mann carried the note to brigade headquarters to see their reaction. Unfortunately for the lieutenant, the officers on duty at brigade headquarters did not share his sense of humor when Private Mann showed up there asking to have the pass approved.[14]

Foul play at the rancho soon brought Lieutenant Amyx to the attention of his superiors once again. On or about the night of September 26, 1847, a party of men from the 2nd Mississippi Rifles found the bodies of two members of their regiment hidden in a cornfield. They observed two suspicious Mexican men hurriedly leaving the rancho upon the discovery of the corpses. Amyx, convinced that these men had committed the murders, resolved to slip out of camp that night to pursue and apprehend the two rancheros. A group of approximately fifteen enlisted men decided to accompany the lieutenant, who was a favorite of his regiment, on his unauthorized mission. Unable to catch up with the two rancheros, Amyx and the men returned to camp the next morning. A court martial found the popular officer guilty of being out of camp without permission as well as using "blackguard" language unbecoming an officer. Possibly to set an example for the other volunteers, the court stripped him of his rank and pay for three months. Possibly as an example of their own, the men of Amyx's company elected the popular officer their new captain upon completion of his court-imposed punishment.[15]

Trussell credited Amyx's conviction to the bias that regulars had against volunteers. He wrote, "they hate the Volunteers as they do the devil and there is no love lost for the Volunteers hate them."[16] He was wrong, however, because the court was composed mainly of officers detailed from the volunteer brigade in which the Mississippians served. Those serving on the court were (President) Col. Robert T. Paine (1st North Carolina), Lt. Col. John A. Fagg (1st North Carolina), Capt. Montgomery D. Corse (1st Virginia), Capt. Patrick M. Henry (1st North Carolina), and (Judge Advocate) Lt. John A. Brown (4th US Artillery). Amyx had objected to the presence of Col. John F. Hamtramck of the 1st Virginia on the court since he was serving as Brigade Officer of the Day on the night the pass was written and carried to headquarters. Hamtramck voluntarily removed himself from the court. The accused acted as his own defense.[17] Amyx's trial caused some discord among the members of the Mississippi regiment. Amyx's friends, including Trussell, harbored resentment toward Adjutant Wilcox, who testified as a witness for the prosecution at the trial. Amyx even challenged the adjutant to a duel. Wilcox declined because Amyx was still under arrest, and, although not entirely forgotten, the incident passed.[18]

Additional misconduct by the Mississippi regiment soon came to General Wool's attention. Reuben Davis had rejoined his regiment at Saltillo, but his health continued to deteriorate until those around him began to fear for his life. His resignation stated that "Ill health and the situation of my private affairs at home, demand that I should abandon the army." Leaving Mexico in July for a second and final time, he left instructions that his position should be considered vacant on September 1, 1847. Colonel Curtis had befriended Davis at Saltillo, noting in his diary on July 18, "I . . . became acquainted with Col. Davis of the 2nd Mississippi who is going home tired of the war." Jefferson Davis had been the Mississippians' first choice for replacement, and, in July, several officers from the 2nd Mississippi Rifles sent a letter to Colonel Davis on behalf of their men asking him to return to

Mexico and take command of their regiment. The former colonel of the 1st Mississippi Rifles declined on the grounds that he had already consented to fill the unexpired congressional term occasioned by the death of Mississippi Senator Jesse Speight. In addition, it is doubtful that Davis could have commanded a regiment in the field at that time, as he was on crutches recovering from the painful wound to his right foot received at Buena Vista and was still on them two years later.[19]

The 2nd Mississippi Rifles had to conduct two elections before the position could be filled. The first, held on the evening of September 19, 1847, was nullified by General Wool "owing to the disgraceful and drunken scenes of last night, as exhibited by members of the Mississippi Regiment the election of Colonel, as directed in Orders No. 404." He angrily chided, "No election obtained by such contemtable [sic] means can be considered valid" and postponed the election until further notice.[20] A month later, Wool relented and allowed the election to proceed. The men chose the captain of Company G, Charles Clark, as their new colonel. The recent resignation of Lieutenant Colonel Kilpatrick who—like Davis—had been suffering from acute dysentery, had created another vacancy among the field officers. Even though some opposed him over his role in Amyx's court martial, John A. Wilcox, the regiment's adjutant, was chosen to fill the vacant post. The elections caused hard feelings between some of the men whose candidates lost. Trussell wrote that Captain McWillie had been promised the support of some of the officers in his bid for lieutenant colonel but that they switched their votes to Wilcox after the adjutant was defeated in the election for colonel. Remarked Trussell, "I expected we would have some fighting but it has passed off so far. But I expect we will have some yet."[21] Reared in Jacksonian society, these men took their military elections as seriously as they did their civil elections back home.

Scott's army captured Mexico City in September 1847, and around Saltillo thoughts of peace replaced rumors of war. The conflict, though, would not officially end for nine more months. In the meantime, the volunteers at Camp Taylor provided escorts for the wagons and pack mules that carried mail and supplies to and from Saltillo. The threat of attack on these trains by bandits was ever present. Although no more major battles were fought, the danger of falling prey to guerrilla raids remained very real. Sergeant William Scott, leaving Mexico on a furlough to visit home, lost his life in one such attack when he accompanied a mail escort near

Monterrey.[22] The Comanche sometimes raided the area around Saltillo, but the volunteer infantry had little luck in catching the mounted Indians once a raid had taken place.[23]

Friendly relations generally existed between soldiers and inhabitants surrounding Saltillo. Troops supported the local market and pumped money into the Saltillo economy with their purchases. The Americans also provided better protection against bandits and Comanches than the Mexican government had been able to before the war. Homesick volunteers frequently attended fandangos and danced until the early hours of the morning.[24] It appears from the soldiers' letters and journals that the women of Mexico were well thought of by the Americans. According to Samuel Chamberlain, though, on at least one occasion members of the 2nd Mississippi Rifles were guilty of an attack on the women of a local family. In his flamboyant fashion, the young dragoon recorded that he singlehandedly drove off the attackers and rescued the fair damsels.[25]

Evidently, not all the Mississippians matched Chamberlain's negative characterization. The father of Benjamin F. Workman replied to his son's account of speaking up against an execution of Mexican suspects. Wrote Joseph Workman, "the taking of the two Mexicans their trial & Execution has Interested me very much, and the part you acted has my Warmest approbation your protecting the poor crimenals and not desiring to Shoot them Contrasts in my Opinion with the character of the Hero which the Dastardly Conduct of those who Strove to abuse and even kill them to me is evident marks of Cowardice, the Hero is always brave where there is danger the Coward where there is none a Hero will treat the Vanquished with Linety a Coward will treat them with harshness and cruelty."[26]

Life continued uneventfully throughout the fall of 1847. David Cameron explained to his brother back in Mississippi why he had not written him sooner: "My delay in answering your gracious last note was in some degree influenced, in the hope of collecting somthing of interse to write; but in that I have in great measure been disappointed as the news of a general character is of little importance; and having nothing of private nature interesting."[27] Zachary Taylor's return to the United States resulted in General Wool's move to Monterrey in order to assume overall command of the army in northern Mexico. Colonel John F. Hamtramck, 1st Virginia Infantry, took command of the post at Saltillo. The volunteers, who were glad to see Wool go, did not like Hamtramck much better.[28] The mail came and went, carrying the latest rumors from Saltillo homeward on its return trip. One tale that reached home told of a woman who had enlisted in the regiment and had remained undetected in the ranks until her uniform grew tight and she ultimately gave birth to a child. Although both good health and high spirits prevailed in the camp of the 2nd Mississippi Rifles, the men longed to go home. Some wondered if Mississippi would have any unmarried girls left for them when the army finally let them go home.[29]

As 1847 drew to a close, the Mississippians had the opportunity to witness the ultimate in military punishment—an execution by firing squad. The condemned man, Bugler Victor Galbraith of the Arkansas Cavalry, had brought a woman into camp. She and Galbraith became intoxicated and disrupted the quiet of the camp with their revelries. Captain Gaston Meares went to Galbraith and ordered him to take the woman out of camp. Galbraith refused to obey, picked up a carbine, and said to his commander, "I am going to blow your God-Damn heart out." Comrades restrained Galbraith and prevented him from carrying out the deed. For several days following the incident, Galbraith continued to taunt Meares and threaten to kill him. A military court found Galbraith guilty of threatening the life of his superior officer and sentenced him to "death by musketry." The troops at Saltillo, including the Mississippians, formed a square with one side open. Because they were armed with rifles, not muskets as called for in the order, the Mississippi regiment was not required to provide a detail for Galbraith's firing squad and were there only to watch. At the execution, only two of the fifteen rounds of the firing squad's volley struck the prisoner. An examination of Galbraith determined that neither of the two wounds was serious enough to produce death. Bugler Galbraith was given a drink of water and then another detail came forward to finish the job. Wrote Trussell who witnessed the event, "They had to shoot him twice before they killed him."[30]

The new year ushered in the first anniversary of the 2nd Mississippi Rifles' enlistment, yet peace still seemed far away. While pondering their own future, some Mississippians wondered about the fate of Mexico as well. American troops generally believed that the people of Mexico were at least 200 years behind in development as compared to the United States and could not handle the responsibilities associated with republican government. The governor of Coahuila openly advocated the annexation of his state by the United States, but the Mississippians disapproved of his plan, unsure what status the inhabitants would have in the American political system. Would Mexicans be allowed to vote? Would they be made slaves? Or would they occupy some middle ground with something less than full citizenship? Musing over these political and ethical questions occupied the time of the waiting men.

Members of the regiment continued to hope for the chance to fight at least one battle against the Mexicans before returning home. Exclaimed Lieutenant Trussell, "the boys are all in good spirits [and] they are anxious for a fight." Writing in February 1848, the lieutenant described why engaging in battle was important. In a letter penned at Buena Vista, Trussell told his brother of an upcoming move to Mazapil. "If we do not get a fight there, . . ." wrote Trussell, "we will never have one in this country. . . . I want to have one fight. If we could get in one hard battle and I could come out safe, we could then return home with some honor." He continued, "But if we should never get into a battle in one year, after we get home it never will be known that we have been here in Mexico. I came here for a fight and I want it before I leave the country."[31] He and the other volunteers in his brigade were to be disappointed, because the time for battle had passed.

Even though the war was essentially over, danger still existed. Noted Josiah Gregg in a January 19, 1847, diary entry, "A few days ago three discharged volunteers of the Mississippi regiment, were massacred—horribly butchered [and] cut up—by some villains, on the road between [Saltillo] and Monterey, some 15 miles from here." The suspected culprits were caught with "many articles" belonging to the murdered Mississippians in their possession, leaving no doubt of their involvement in the deed. A quick inquiry cleared the way for the guilty men's execution.[32]

In February, the regiment sent another recruiting party back to the United States. Lieutenant Trussell, offered the opportunity to visit home as one of the recruiting officers, turned the job down. He wrote his brother explaining that there were three reasons for staying in Mexico. First, Trussell doubted the success of the venture and he could not bear to face the men of the regiment should he fail to bring back new recruits. Second, he was still optimistic that the Mississippians would see action. And third, his loyalty to his regiment would not allow him to leave. He summed up his feelings by saying, "If my Regt & Company gets into a fight I want to be there for them." Captain Alexander M. Jackson also felt compelled to stay, although his family asked him to resign and come home. The captain told them that he could not abandon the men of his company who had joined because of his recruiting efforts. He explained to his fiancée, "There are some, mere boys, to whose parents I am under the most solemn of pledges to remain with and protect. To leave them, therefore, unless from absolute necessity, would be a most infamous breach of promises."[33]

In May 1848, the 2nd Mississippi Rifles made one more move, this time 100 miles southwest to the town of Cedras. From there the regiment made one short excursion to nearby Mazapil. Far from their supply line, the Mississippians suffered from the lack of replacement items for their worn-out clothing. Under these circumstances, the government paid each member of the regiment $12. This amount allowed the volunteers $3 apiece for the four months they had to buy their own clothing from local merchants while at Cedras and Mazapil.[34]

Life at Cedras seemed even duller than it had been at camp at Buena Vista. Unlike Saltillo, the inhabitants of this region in Mexico were unfriendly and unwilling to fraternize with the Mississippians. "The fools here are afraid of us," exclaimed Lieutenant Trussell. Others probably shared his feelings when he wrote, "If we could be in active service, I would not care for staying here one of two years longer. But to be here in garrison [with] nothing to do but drill and about every eight or ten [days?] may have guard duty to do. I am tired of this."[35]

Not many details are known about the regiment's last few months in Mexico. Americans were weary of reading war news and wanted a change. Even the generals had abandoned the battlefields of Mexico for the more promising political arena in the United States. The men of the 2nd Mississippi Rifles must have been delighted when they received their orders to march home. Its services no longer needed, the regiment prepared to make its way northward to the Rio Grande. The charge of "rowdyism" arose once again before they left Mexico. Josiah Gregg contended that Colonel Hamtramack, in a hurry to rush home, left his brigade without a strong hand to keep its members in hand. Before leaving, the colonel placed the Mississippians and the Texans in rear of the column. Before evacuating Saltillo, Colonel Clark dismissed the 2nd Mississippi in the center of the town. Wrote Gregg, "Here Col. Clarke, commanding the Mississippians, did anything but credit to himself, in dismissing the regiment in town, thus permitting them to do as they pleased; so that half of them were drunk in an hour. Such a scene I never witnessed—500 drunk men in the square—yelling, swearing, outraging every Mexican they could see. . . . On one occasion a mob of soldiers collect[ed] at the *calabozo*, and forced out an American, who had been imprisoned for some outrage." Most residents had shut themselves up in their houses, but the disturbance by Mississippians left one townsman dead and several others wounded. Concluded Gregg, "I myself did not fail to feel the effects of their outrages. A Mississippian seeing my little servant boy with my favorite pony, dismounted him and galloped away with the horse; but I was so fortunate as to recover him again."[36]

The 2nd Mississippi Rifles made it to the mouth of the Rio Grande several weeks later. They boarded the steamers that carried them to the United States, expecting recognition for the hard service in Mexico. The citizens of New Orleans, however, tired of the thousands of volunteers who had treaded their streets, staged no parade for the 2nd Mississippi Rifles as they had their famous sister regiment. The *New Orleans Picayune* mentioned the regiment's arrival in a laundry list of other units coming home from Mexico. The 2nd Mississippi Rifles mustered out at Vicksburg late in July 1848.[37] Eager to resume their normal life, its members quickly rejoined the ranks of Mississippi's citizens. Those lucky enough to be home had survived a seventeen-month ordeal that veterans of the ill-fated regiment were unlikely to forget but few others would remember.

July 21, 1848, The *New Orleans Picayune* finally carried an article on the 2nd Mississippi Rifles. Unlike those that had lauded the 1st Mississippi Rifles, the short piece titled "Mortality in the Second Regiment of Mississippi Volunteers" summed up the worst period of the regiment's sad history and sounded more like an obituary than a news story: "The July number of the Medical and Surgical Review contains a communication of melancholy interest from the pen of the surgeon of the 2nd Mississippi Volunteers, Dr. Thomas N. Love. We find embodied in this article the appalling fact that within six months after the regiment had entered the service of the United States, it sustained a loss of one hundred and sixty by death, by disease. Eighty of these died in New Orleans, twenty-eight in the Gulf, and fifty-nine in Mexico. The malady which proved so fatal to the regiment is said to be closely allied to 'typhoid pneumonia,' but the surgeon thinks it should be denominated the 'cold plague.' Besides the deaths during the time mentioned, there were one hundred and thirty-four discharges, fifty transfers and desertions, and the regiment, which originally numbered eight hundred and eighty-five, contained but five hundred and thirty-four at the date of the surgeon's communication."[38] This scorecard of the 2nd Mississippi's sufferings, while notable at the time, failed to elevate the regiment to the levels of fame achieved by its sister regiment.

13
Evaluating the Role of the Mississippi Volunteers

The Mississippi riflemen, under Colonel Davis, were highly conspicuous for their gallantry and steadiness, and sustained throughout the engagement the reputation of veteran troops.

—Gen. Zachary Taylor's After Action Report, March 6, 1847

MOST WRITERS HAVE GENERALLY been harsh when evaluating the role of American volunteers in the Mexican War. There are good reasons for much of this criticism. Volunteers in Mexico drank, gambled, pillaged, raped, murdered, and even deserted the battlefield. The vast majority of volunteers accepted into the US service, like the 2nd Mississippi Rifles, saw little or no action against the enemy.[1] Thus, in the mass of American volunteers who went to Mexico, Jefferson Davis and the 1st Mississippi Rifles stand apart. The regiment, although not composed of men with perfect characters, managed to achieve lasting fame and glory while most other volunteer regiments faded into obscurity.

The two regiments of Mississippi Rifles provide a unique opportunity to study some of the volunteers in the Mexican War. The men of both regiments came from the same region of the United States. Their members essentially had the same backgrounds.[2] Why, then, did one regiment excel while the other did not? Comparing the two regiments gives some answers.

One reason is opportunity. The 1st Mississippi Rifles arrived in Mexico with the important factors of time and place in their favor. Northern Mexico was the scene of major fighting between the US forces and Mexico when the 1st Mississippi Rifles arrived on the Rio Grande. Through Davis's connections with Taylor, an influential benefactor the remainder of the general's life, his regiment was selected to make the advance deep into Mexican territory when other volunteer regiments that had arrived before the 1st Mississippi Rifles were left behind to guard the army's supply lines. This preference gave Davis and his regiment the opportunity to see action in the battle at Monterrey. The 1st Mississippi Rifles stayed with Taylor during the redistribution of American troops in Mexico needed for Scott's impending campaign against Vera Cruz. Although it did not seem fortuitous for the regiment at the time, Taylor's decision enabled the 1st Mississippi Rifles to be by the general's side at Buena Vista. Hence, Davis's regiment had the opportunity to participate in two of the war's major battles. The result was that reports of their exemplary behavior gave them the respect of the army and the adulation of the public. Jefferson Davis and the 1st Mississippi Rifles found the glory they sought.

The 2nd Mississippi Rifles, in contrast, never found the opportunity to prove themselves in battle. A rough gulf crossing took the regiment at Lobos Island where its officers and men expected to be incorporated into the force gathering for the Scott's campaign in central Mexico. But that was not to be. A change in orders sent the regiment to the Rio Grande to reinforce Taylor. The delays in reaching northern Mexico prevented any possible chance for the 2nd Mississippi Rifles to join Taylor at Buena Vista. Finally at Saltillo, the bulk of the fighting shifted away from them to Scott's army in Central Mexico. Thus, unlike the 1st Mississippi Rifles, the regiment did not have the chance to find glory.[3]

Regardless of examples of favoritism that helped shape the career of the 1st Mississippi Rifles, Jefferson Davis possessed real leadership ability that contributed to his regiment's success. Davis's experience in the regular army brought discipline to his rough volunteers. His political connections enabled the regiment to be armed with one of the most modern weapons of his time, the Model 1841 percussion rifle. Under his direction, the 1st Mississippi Rifles achieved a level of respect reserved for the most veteran troops. He provided the discipline needed to make volunteers into an effective fighting force. Regular officers with whom he served praised Davis, who was really one of their own.[4]

Reuben Davis lacked the qualities and commitment needed to manage the 2nd Mississippi Rifles. His militia experience had not prepared him for the task of commanding a regiment of volunteers in wartime. Although both poor health and the rampant illness suffered by his regiment hampered and challenged his effectiveness as a leader, unlike Jefferson Davis, who eagerly accepted his position as colonel of the 1st Mississippi Rifles, Rueben Davis reluctantly agreed to serve as the colonel of the 2nd Mississippi Rifles. Not a strong commander to begin with, his resignation due to his declining health and desire to return home to tend to business interests left the 2nd Mississippi Rifles without a firm guiding hand.[5]

Unfortunately Jefferson Davis possessed personality traits that sometimes hampered his relationship with his superiors and peers. [6] According to his biographer, William C. Davis, Jefferson Davis believed himself to be right in all matters, small and large. He rarely admitted mistakes or changed his mind once he had fixed his opinion. Surrounded by other strong-willed individuals—politicians, military officers, and statesmen—Davis often found himself in private and public disputes that became very personnel to him. He often appeared to others to be cool and aloof. He valued loyalty to the point where it clouded his judgment of friends and enemies. Like other Southerners of his class, Davis tended to guard jealously his reputation and, by extension, that of his regiment. The best example can be seen in his handling of the affair at the Tannery during the battle of Monterrey. Unwilling to share the glory of the fort's capture with any other unit, Davis chose to carry on a campaign of words against Col. William B. Campbell and the 1st Tennessee. He tried unsuccessfully to involve others, including General Quitman, in his dispute with the Tennessee regiment. It is possible that Taylor selected the 1st Mississippi Rifles to escort him to Saltillo as a means to remove Davis from Quitman's brigade, thereby defusing an unpleasant situation. It is conjecture, but perhaps Davis's adamant claim to the capture of the Tannery stemmed from complaints levied at the strict discipline he imposed on the regiment while camped at the mouth of the Rio Grande in August 1846. By cloaking his regiment in glory, he hoped to win the support of his men and justify his previous actions. Davis's popularity with his men did rise sharply after Monterrey. "[T]here is not a man in his [Davis's] regiment who would not sacrifice his life to obey him, so much has his gallant conduct raised him in their estimation." These words appeared in an October 13, 1846, letter written by Davis's brother-in-law, Pvt. Joseph D. Howell. While this source might be biased, it can also be noted that Mississippi newspapers no longer carried stories critical of Davis's management of his regiment after the Battle of Monterrey.[7]

Bickering between the officers within each regiment occurred, but the in-fighting had less harmful effects on the 1st Mississippi Rifles than on its sister regiment. Captain William R. Rogers complained incessantly about the character and efficiency of his regiment's other officers and its enlisted volunteers. The captain continually expressed a dislike and distrust of Jefferson Davis and Alexander K. McClung. Davis was aware of Rogers' ill feeling toward him and on the eve of the battle of Buena Vista asked him to set their differences aside for the good of the regiment. This Captain Rogers did. Thus opportunity for battle allowed the 1st Mississippi Rifles to pull together in order to fight the common foe.[8]

In the 2nd Mississippi Rifles, the lack of opportunity to engage the enemy resulted in a regiment with less cohesion. Rueben Davis's old political rival, Capt. Benjamin C. Buckley, openly opposed the colonel's authority while the regiment was at Matamoros, and Davis had to resort to the threat of force to restore order. Lieutenant Colonel Kilpatrick, who could have provided stability for the 2nd Mississippi Rifles, drifted out of the regiment's life when he became ill. Major Ezra Price, the hero of Monterrey and the field officer who remained with the regiment the longest, was not elected to fill either of the posts left vacant by Davis's and Kilpatrick's resignations. The company officers divided into factions centered on such prominent regimental figures as Lt. Fleming Amyx and Adj. John A. Wilcox. Amyx's court martial as well Clark's and Wilcox's election provided further cause for dissension. William Faulkner and Thomas C. Hindman carried their feud back to Mississippi with them. Incidents such as these led to a breakdown in discipline in the ranks of the 2nd Mississippi Rifles.

The character of the men of the two regiments was essentially the same—a mixture of good and bad. Several Mississippians observed that volunteers were unfit to fight an offensive war in Mexico. Captain Rogers believed that volunteers, whom he considered to be too wild and independent, did not make good invaders. Rueben Davis accurately summed up the volunteers' nature: he concluded that once a recruit had taken the oath of allegiance to the United States and had been mustered into the service of his country, a drastic change came over the man. The volunteer felt absolved from any obligation to God or man and, as a consequence, considered himself free to disregard every law of honesty with the exception of fidelity to the flag and his own personal courage. Hence many volunteers felt free to commit reprehensible acts in Mexico that at home would have been unthinkable to these same men.

Some contemporary and modern writers have described the men of the Mississippi Rifles using such terms as "young planters" and "professional gentlemen."[9] In many cases their actions do not fit these flowery descriptions. The men of both regiments cursed, drank, fornicated, and bickered. Samuel Chamberlain claimed that the first wave of volunteers to arrive in Mexico were superior to those who came later. If this were true, then it would follow that the men of the 2nd Mississippi Rifles were inferior to Jefferson Davis's regiment.[10] This is an unfair assessment. Given strong leadership and the opportunity to fight, there is no reason to believe that the 2nd Mississippi Rifles could not have proven themselves equal to their more famous sister regiment.

Several motives drew the men of the Mississippi Rifles to Mexico. The volunteers hoped to serve their country in what they perceived to be its time of need. Mexico had challenged the honor of the United States, and they eagerly went south, as one Mississippian put it, "to fight for the rights of [our] country." Once in Mexico, most volunteers expressed sympathy for the common Mexican citizen and actually believed that the American presence south of the border would benefit Mexico by exposing that "backward" country to true republican ideals. Some sought to parley fame won in Mexico into successful postwar political careers. Finally, not a few volunteers enlisted just for the chance to experience adventure in another part of the world.[11]

The Mississippi volunteers were a crosscut of American life at the time of the war. The remarks in the diaries and letters are amazingly similar to those of volunteers from other regions of the United States who participated in the conflict. Some were rough; some were refined. Some were illiterate; others were well educated. While most were unknown, a few had already achieved a fair amount of notoriety before the commencement of the war. Surprisingly little sectional animosity, so prevalent in the 1850s, appeared between the Mississippi volunteers and the volunteers from the northern and western states. The American volunteers of the Mexican War showed a unified purpose—defeating Mexico—and the division of spoils was not yet an issue with these comrades-in-arms.[12]

The Mississippi volunteers had a definite impact on the American war effort in northern Mexico. Although the careers of the two regiments were vastly different, both were equally important in their own way. The 1st Mississippi Rifles helped Taylor achieve victory at Monterrey. A few months later the regiment's heroic stand at Buena Vista prevented the Americans from suffering a crushing defeat at the hands of Santa Anna's soldiers. Although they did not participate in a single battle, the 2nd Mississippi Rifles helped the war effort by holding Taylor's gains in northern Mexico, thereby allowing Scott's campaign against Vera Cruz and Mexico City to proceed. Thus the role of the 1st Mississippi Rifles was to conquer territory while that of the 2nd Mississippi Rifles was to secure it. In any war, both roles are necessary for victory.[13]

What happened to these Mississippi volunteers after the Mexican War? Most faded into obscurity. Other former Mississippi volunteers, though, continued to fight new battles—both political and literal. Many of the officers of the 1st Mississippi Rifles sought political and military service in other conflicts. Lieutenant Amos B. Corwine tried his hand in the gold fields of California and served for a short time in a battalion of California Rangers attempting to track down marauding Mariposa Indians. Many others again saw action on the battlefields of 1861–1865. Most famous of these, of course, was Jefferson Davis, who reluctantly agreed to serve as president of the Confederate States of America. But others also obtained high positions of responsibility in the fledgling government and its army. Captain Douglas Cooper started the war as the colonel of the 1st Choctaw and Chickasaw Mounted Rifles and was later appointed overall commander of Confederate Indians in the Tran-Mississippi Department. Lieutenant Carnot Posey was colonel of the 16th Mississippi Infantry before being promoted to the rank of brigadier general. The regiment's adjutant, Richard Griffith, also rose to the rank of brigadier general after serving as colonel of the 12th Mississippi Infantry. Lieutenants Seaborne Mosses Phillips, Daniel R. Russell, William W. Brown, Samuel B. Thomas, and Christopher Mott served as colonels of the 10th 20th, 12th, and 19th Mississippi Infantry, respectively. Sergeant Horace H. Miller was elected lieutenant colonel of the 20th Mississippi Infantry and later led his own cavalry regiment. The major of the 2nd Mississippi Battalion of Minute Men was former lieutenant Henry Cook. Private James Z. George rose to the rank of brigadier general of Mississippi State troops during the war. Another private, Elkanah Greer, was elected colonel of the 3rd Texas Cavalry. Lesser posts were filled by other former members of the 1st Mississippi Rifles who served as company officers: Capt. John M. Sharp (Company I, 3rd Mississippi Infantry), Capt. William Delay (Company H, 9th Mississippi Infantry), Capt. Thomas Kyle (Company G, 3rd Mississippi Battalion of Minute Men), and Lt. W. W. Redding (Company I, 34th Mississippi Infantry). Following the Mexican War, the prudish and moody Capt. William P. Rogers moved to Texas after serving a short term as American consul in Vera Cruz, Mexico. In mid-1862 Rogers assumed command of the 2nd Texas Infantry and died on the earthen walls of Battery Robinette in the unsuccessful Confederate attempt to recapture Corinth, Mississippi. His death came before he could learn that Jefferson Davis planned to promote him to the rank of brigadier general. Thus the alumni of the 1st Mississippi Rifles provided one president, four generals, five colonels, one major, and four company officers to the Confederate cause.[14] It is most likely that the list is incomplete.

Many members of the 2nd Mississippi Rifles, unable to prove themselves in the Mexican War, found other opportunities for the glory that had eluded them in Mexico. Lieutenant Fleming Amyx moved to California and became a state legislator for Tuolume County. Unable to win political office in his home state, Lt. Andrew Jackson Trussell served as a Texas Ranger until he was lured to Nicaragua in support of William Walker, the famous filibuster. His health ruined by his stay in Central America, Trussell returned to Mississippi where he died before the start of the Civil War. Rueben Davis became a successful trial lawyer and major general of state troops. Charles Clark, the regiment's second colonel, returned to the battlefield, rising to the rank of major general in the Confederate Army. Wounded in the fighting at both Shiloh and Baton Rouge, Clark served out the war as the governor of Mississippi. Another former member of the 2nd Mississippi Rifles, William McWillie, had occupied the governor's mansion before the outbreak of the Civil War. John A. Wilcox, the regiment's adjutant and second lieutenant colonel, went to Richmond to represent Texas in the Confederate Congress. Lieutenant Thomas C. Hindman served as the colonel of the 2nd Arkansas Infantry before being promoted to brigadier general. William Barksdale, the regiment's quartermaster, rose to the rank of brigadier general in the Confederate Army and fell while leading his brigade at Gettysburg. Captain John B. Deason served as colonel of the 3rd Mississippi Infantry. Captain Andrew K. Blythe, colonel of the 44th Mississippi Infantry, was killed at Shiloh at the head of his regiment. Another alumni of the 2nd Mississippi Rifles, Surgeon D. A. Kinchloe, served in the same capacity in Blythe's 44th Mississippi Infantry. Lieutenant William C. Falkner served for a time as the colonel of the 2nd Mississippi Infantry before becoming colonel of his own cavalry regiment. Captain Frank Liddell, the lieutenant colonel of the 11th Mississippi Infantry, saw action at Manassas and Gaines Mill before his death at Sharpsburg. Lieutenant Beverly Matthews commanded Company G, 19th Mississippi Cavalry Battalion. Captain Adam McWillie fell at Manassas at the head of Company G, 18th Mississippi Infantry. Lieutenant Eli G. Henry was elected the captain of Company C, 18th Mississippi Infantry, and was acting lieutenant colonel for his regiment when he was killed at Malvern Hill. Captain Chesley S. Coffey resigned his position as the commander of Company D, 11th Mississippi Infantry after he was wounded at Williamsburg. Captain William M. Estelle commanded Company H, 38th Mississippi Infantry. Lieutenant James M. Jackson served in his old rank in Company A, 37th Mississippi Infantry. Lieutenant Edward B. Shelton served as a lieutenant in Company B, Ballentine's Cavalry Regiment.[15] The Civil War finally provided the 2nd Mississippi Rifles the opportunity to prove their mettle. The regiment provided two Mississippi governors, four generals, three colonels, one lieutenant colonel, one surgeon, and seven company officers. Doubtlessly, many enlisted men of the Mississippi Rifles made use of their military experience and represented their state in the Confederate Army as well. Unfortunately, their deeds have been lost with the passage of time.

One nagging myth continues to persist concerning Jefferson Davis and the 1st Mississippi Rifles at Buena Vista. This is the tale of Davis and his invincible "V." Most accounts of the battle tell of Colonel Davis slyly forming his regiment in the midst of battle in the unconventional V-shaped formation. Davis did little to dispel this idea that promoted his military prowess. The focus of attention on this one act of the battle diminishes and overshadows the important engagement earlier in the morning when the Mississippians singlehandedly held back the Mexico Army on the left flank and saved the Americans from a crushing defeat. This version of the battle also fails to give appropriate credit to the men of the 2nd and 3rd Indiana Infantry and Sherman's battery, who also helped to break up the later Mexican attack. More important, the post-battle reports do not always support what we have come to take as fact. The angle formed by these units was more a matter of chance than design. Davis was not the only field officer present during this incident; Col. James H. Lane maintained command of the 3rd Indiana. Moreover, Gen. Joseph Lane, brigadier of the Indian Brigade, was also there. Nevertheless, Taylor's widely published account of Davis's "V" in his official report of the battle permanently imprinted the episode on the minds of the American public and, until later events intervened, made Jefferson Davis a national hero in the United States.[16]

The significance of Jefferson Davis's Mississippi Rifles at Buena Vista has been overlooked by both his contemporaries and historians. The much applauded "V" formation did not smash the Mexican attack—soldiers armed with rifles standing in line of battle did. The Mississippi Rifles were a new phenomenon on the American military scene. Other rifle regiments existed, but their slow-loading weapons had relegated them to the task of sharpshooters or skirmishers. The riflemen of previous American wars performed their duties as Morgan's Riflemen at Saratoga, the Minute Men of Lexington and Concord, or Jackson's Kentuckians at New Orleans.[17] Jefferson Davis took riflemen out from behind the cover of rocks, trees, and cotton bales and placed them shoulder to shoulder on the battlefield with the rest of the troops. Armed with modern percussion rifles, the Mississippi volunteers performed the same battalion maneuvers as did the traditionally trained and equipped infantry. In addition, they had the advantage of being able to deliver a more accurate and deadly fire against the enemy. The weapon and Davis's training gave the Mississippians the confidence they needed to defy conventional logic and stand in the open as a superior force of Mexican cavalry thundered down upon them and coolly blast the enemy to a complete halt.

Much has been written concerning the impact that the Mexican War had on the Civil War that followed thirteen short years later. The most common facet pointed to by these writers is that many of the regular army's junior grade officers went on to become leaders in that bloody conflict. The connection between volunteers who participated in the conflict in Mexico has not received equal study. Perhaps it should, as the case of the Mississippi volunteers shows that many members of the 1st and 2nd Mississippi Rifles played important political and military roles in the Civil War as well. In addition to Mississippi's contribution to the leadership pool of the state and the Confederacy, the Mississippi Rifles were the prototype for the thousands of volunteer regiments—both North and South—of the Civil War. A little over a decade after the war with Mexico, similarly armed and trained volunteer regiments would face each other on American battlefields where the devastating firepower of the 1st Mississippi Rifles at Buena Vista would be repeated time and time again with the same bloody result—devastation for the attacker. The development of the rifleman from sniper into battlefield bulwark was the true legacy of Jefferson Davis and the Mississippi volunteers, a legacy evident on battlefields in the not-too-distant future.

Jefferson Davis returned to the United States a national hero. He quickly returned to Congress, this time as a senator appointed to fill the seat left vacant by the death of Jesse Speight. His military background and accomplishments in Mexico landed him the chairmanship of the Senate's Committee on Military Affairs. He left Congress in 1851 at the request of his state's Democratic political leaders to carry the party's banner in a troubled campaign for the Mississippi governorship. His loss did nothing to diminish his popularity. Incoming President Franklin Pierce asked Davis to serve in his cabinet as Secretary of War, a position he held from 1853 to 1857. The first West Point alumni to hold the office, Davis came to the post with a working knowledge of the army establishment from having served in the field during peace and war. His time at West Point and active service on the frontier and in Mexico gave him a personal knowledge of many of its officers. During his four-year tenure as Secretary of War, Davis dedicated himself to modernizing a military establishment he believed was outdated and in danger of falling behind the armies of other nations engaged in the Crimean War.

The former commander of the 1st Mississippi Rifles took a special interest in the development of small arms. Davis addressed his concern in his 1854 annual report to Congress, in which he wrote, "Though our arms have heretofore been considered the best in use, recent inventions in Europe have produced changes in small arms which are now being used in war, with such important results as have caused them to be noticed among the remarkable incidents of battles, and indicate that material modifications will be made in the future armament of troops." These changes made it possible to load a ball into a rifled or "grooved" barrel much easier than in the past. The Minié ball and rifled muskets were revolutionizing European battlefields, and Davis recognized this important fact. He told Congress, "My attention being drawn to the subject, I directed experiments to be made by the Ordnance Department, both as to the proper shape of the ball and the best method of grooving the barrel." The result of these tests showed "that the new weapon, while it can be loaded as readily as the ordinary musket, is at least equally effective at three times the distance. The foreign experiments indicate a still greater superiority of the new arms. These results render it almost certain that smooth-bored arms will be superseded as a military weapon." Davis further informed Congress that the Ordnance Department was currently developing new weapons that incorporated advances in loading. The result would be the M1855 Rifle, the M1855 Rifled Musket, and the M1861 Rifled Musket; all used on Civil War battlefields.[18]

Davis's experience told him that more was needed in this area. He wrote, "In anticipation of an increase, if not exclusive use of rifle arms by the regular Army, and because of the belief that the rifle or light infantry system of instruction, is best suited to the foot militia, I have caused inquiries to be instituted into the systems used by the light troops of other countries, that complete light infantry or tactics might be introduced into the service with such improvements as the experience of other armies has shown to be valuable." He had not remained idle as "A work on this subject is now in the course of preparation, and it is expected will be, in a short time, submitted to you for such actions as it may be deemed worthy to receive." This manual, adopted by Congress in 1855, was the work of a board of officers headed by Col. William J. Hardee. As historians and students of the Civil War know, what resulted from the Davis's direction was the board's adaptation of a French tactical system titled *Rifle and Light Infantry Tactics; For the Exercise and Maneuvers of Troops When Acting as Light Infantry or Riflemen.* Commonly known as *Hardee's Tactics*, the two-volume manual would train both the Northern and Southern armies in the coming conflict brought on by a growing rift between sections of the Union.[19] Just as he shaped the 1st Mississippi Rifles in his image, Jefferson Davis shaped the armies of 1861–1865, which went off to war in their own search for glory.

APPENDIX I

THE MODEL 1841 RIFLE

In the hands of the Mississippi Volunteers, the M1841 Rifle became one of the US Army's most famous weapons. It is sometimes called the "Windsor Rifle" or the "Whitney Rifle." In addition to Robbins, Kendall & Lawrence, and Eli Whitney, other manufacturers included Harpers Ferry Tryon, Robbins & Lawrence, Palmetto Armory, and Remington. Nevertheless, so closely are connected the Mississippians and the M1841 Rifle that it is best known to gun collectors and military historians as the "Mississippi Rifle."[1]

Putting rifles in the hands of American soldiers was not a new idea during the Mexican War. The War Department had experimented before with arming an entire regiment with rifles, but the experiment proved to be short. On the eve of the conflict with Mexico, the idea reemerged. The US Mounted Rifles, initially raised for service on the Oregon Trail, were slated to receive the M1841 Rifle. Both they and the US Regiment of Voltigeuers carried this weapon to Mexico. It was Jefferson Davis, however, who used his influence to see that his volunteer regiment from Mississippi received the M1841 Rifle.

Winfield Scott objected to arming Davis's entire regiment with rifles. According to period manuals, including the several authored by Scott and then in use by the US Army, only the two flank companies at most should be armed with rifles. The common smoothbore musket was thought to be the proper arm for an infantryman. Davis remained persistent, and all of his companies were finally armed with the M1841 Rifle.

The M1841 Rifle was not the first rifle adopted by the US Army. Others included the M1803 and M1817 Common Rifles. Both of these models used the flintlock ignition system for firing the weapon. Another flintlock rifle adopted by the US Army was the breach loading M1819 Halls Rifle, a truly revolutionary weapon for its time. Unlike other US military rifles, the Halls was equipped with a bayonet. The M1841 Rifle was intended to supersede these other models.

The M1841 Rifle had superior capabilities to the common flintlock musket. The effective range of the musket ended at roughly 100 yards. The range of the M1841 Rifle extended beyond 200 yards, twice as far as a musket. The M1841 Rifle also had the advantage of utilizing the new weatherproof percussion system for firing the weapon.

Observers thought the M1841 to be an attractive weapon. Fitted with a walnut stock, the overall length came to 48.8 inches. Brass barrel bands and patch box enhanced the looks of the rifle. Treated metal finishes included an acid browned barrel and case-hardened hammer and lockplate. Weighing roughly

9.5 pounds, the.54 caliber rifle used a 70-grain powder charge to fire a round ball. The actual diameter of the ball was .525, sized slightly smaller than the bore in order to facilitate loading the piece. No plan for attaching a bayonet to the rifle existed at the time of the Mexican War. Each weapon cost the government nearly $13.

Although the earlier military rifles required the users to load the piece from a pouch of loose shot and a powder flask, the Mississippians were equipped with cartridge boxes for their M1841 Rifles. The black leather boxes carried 40 rounds of prerolled ammunition and were supported on a 2-inch-wide white buff belt worn around the soldier's waist. The belt fastened with an oval-shaped brass belt plate bearing the letters "US." A small version of the plate was fixed to the front flap of the box. A smaller black leather cap box, filled with percussion caps needed to fire the weapon, was worn on the belt.[2]

The weapon was relatively new, a fact that caused some confusion. The Ordnance Department at first neglected to issue percussion caps to Davis's regiment. It was only after he called their attention to the omission that the needed percussion caps were sent. Davis had written, "The caps are indispensable and we have none."[3]

Although the weapon was new, Davis, as some writers have claimed, did not have to invent a drill for the rifle to teach his soldiers. The War Department had been experimenting with percussion rifles and muskets since the early 1830s and had been soliciting ideas for a drill manual from officers familiar with the use of percussion arms. Scott's 1829 *Abstract of Infantry Tactics; Including Exercising and Manoeuvres of Light Infantry and Riflemen; For the Use of the Militia of the United States* described the steps in loading the military rifle. The process started with the command "Load by eight commands."

> **1.** LOAD. One Motion. Carry back the right foot, making a half-face to the right, turning on the left heel; let fall the firelock, seizing it with the left hand at the swell, the elbow resting against the left side; the right hand quits its hold placing the thumb against the top of the hammer.
>
> **2.** Open-PAN. One Motion. The pan is pushed open with the right thumb; the right hand seizes the cartridge with the first three fingers, carries it to the mouth, which tears off the end, where it is brought close to the pan.
>
> **3.** PRIME. One Motion. The priming is shaken into the pan; the pan is shut by the third and little finger; the right hand then slides behind the cock, and hold the small of the stock between the third and little finger and the ball of the hand.
>
> **4.** Cast-ABOUT. First Motion. The soldier fronts, bringing the right foot to its original position; the rifle is brought, with the barrel outwards (sliding it with great care through the left hand) to the ground, the butt placed between the heels, the barrel between the knees, which must be sufficiently bent for that purpose; the left hand takes hold near the muzzle, the thumb stretched along the stock. Second Motion. The cartridge is put into the barrel, and the ramrod seized with the fore-finger and thumb of the right hand.

5. Draw-RAMROD. The ramrod is drawn by the right hand; the left quits the rifles and grasps the rod, the breadth of a hand from the bottom, which is sunk one inch into the barrel.

6. Ram-CARTRIDGE. One Motion. The cartridge is forced down by both hands; the left seizes the rifle near the tail-pipe; the soldier stands upright, and seizes, with the thumb and fore-finger, the small end of the rod.

7. Return-RAMROD. One Motion. The rod is drawn out, and returned by the right hand, which remains with the ball resting on the head of the ramrod—elbow square.

8. Shoulder-ARMS. First Motion. The left hand carries the rifle to the right shoulder, turning the guard outwards, the right receiving it in the proper position of the small. Second Motion. The left hand is carried quickly to the left thigh.[4]

However, this procedure was for flintlock rifles. In 1844 the US War Department issued General Order No. 44, which modified the loading process to accommodate weapons with percussion locks. The ten steps were (1) LOAD, (2) Handle-CARTRIDGE, (3) Tear-CARTRIDGE, (4) Charge-CARTRIDGE, (5) Draw-RAMMER, (6) Ram-CARTRIDGE, (7) Return-RAMMER, (8) Cast-ABOUT, (9) PRIME, and (10) Shoulder-ARMS.[5]

Many of the rifles used by Mississippians in the Mexican War went home with the veterans. Jefferson Davis believed that the rifles symbolized his regiment's accomplishments and wanted his men to retain their rifles as valuable keepsakes. An arrangement between the Mississippi and the War Department allowed the rifles to be counted against the state's militia allotment.[6] In 1861 M1841 rifles in private hands and the state's arsenal were put back into service in the hands of Mississippi volunteers, this time to be used against the United States.

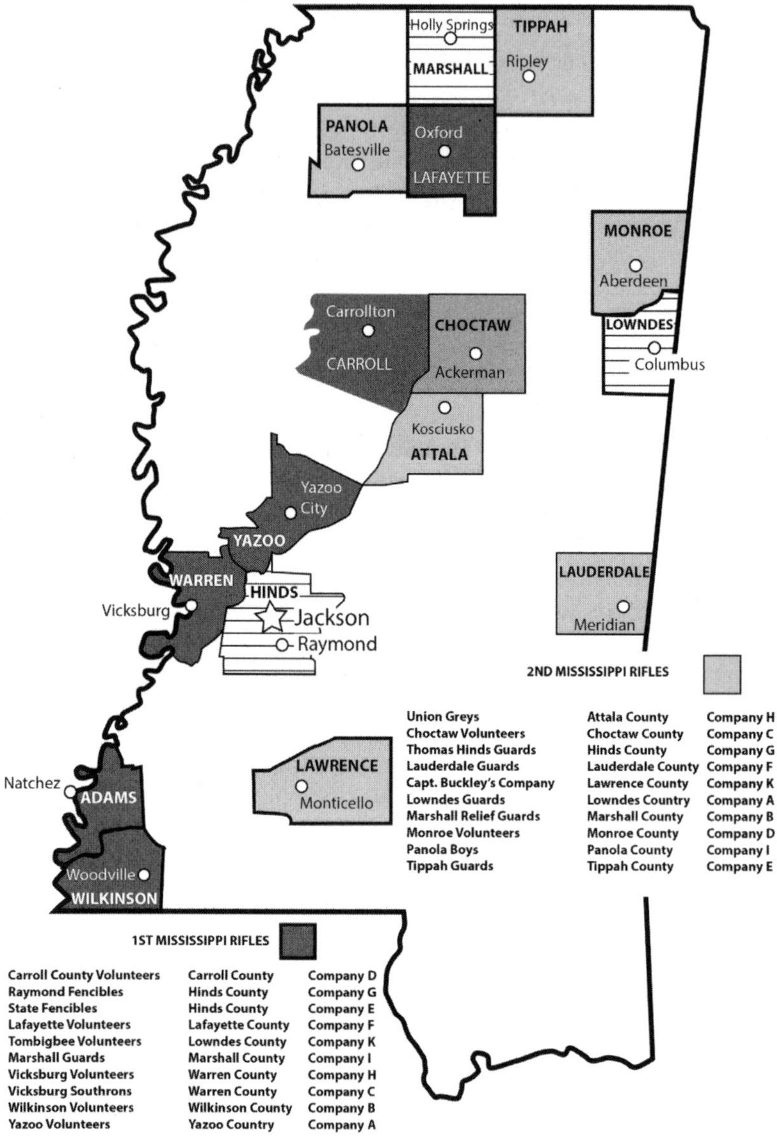
Holly Springs
MARSHALL
TIPPAH
Ripley
PANOLA
Batesville
Oxford
LAFAYETTE
MONROE
Aberdeen
LOWNDES
Columbus
Carrollton
CARROLL
CHOCTAW
Ackerman
Kosciusko
ATTALA
Yazoo City
YAZOO
WARREN
Vicksburg
HINDS
Jackson
Raymond
LAUDERDALE
Meridian
2ND MISSISSIPPI RIFLES
Union Greys | Attala County | Company H
Choctaw Volunteers | Choctaw County | Company C
Thomas Hinds Guards | Hinds County | Company G
Lauderdale Guards | Lauderdale County | Company F
Capt. Buckley's Company | Lawrence County | Company K
Lowndes Guards | Lowndes Country | Company A
Marshall Relief Guards | Marshall County | Company B
Monroe Volunteers | Monroe County | Company D
Panola Boys | Panola County | Company I
Tippah Guards | Tippah County | Company E
LAWRENCE
Monticello
Natchez
ADAMS
Woodville
WILKINSON
1ST MISSISSIPPI RIFLES
Carroll County Volunteers | Carroll County | Company D
Raymond Fencibles | Hinds County | Company G
State Fencibles | Hinds County | Company E
Lafayette Volunteers | Lafayette County | Company F
Tombigbee Volunteers | Lowndes County | Company K
Marshall Guards | Marshall County | Company I
Vicksburg Volunteers | Warren County | Company H
Vicksburg Southrons | Warren County | Company C
Wilkinson Volunteers | Wilkinson County | Company B
Yazoo Volunteers | Yazoo Country | Company A

APPENDIX 2

COUNTY OF ORIGIN BY REGIMENT

Union Greys	Attala County	2nd Miss. Rifles, Company H
Carroll County Volunteers	Carroll County	1st Miss. Rifles, Company D
Choctaw Volunteers	Choctaw County	2nd Miss. Rifles, Company C
Raymond Fencibles	Hinds County	1st Miss. Rifles, Company G
State Fencibles	Hinds County	1st Miss. Rifles, Company E
Thomas Hinds Guards	Hinds County	2nd Miss. Rifles, Company G
Lauderdale Guards	Lauderdale County	2nd Miss. Rifles, Company F
Lafayette Volunteers	Lafayette County	1st Miss. Rifles, Company F
Capt. Buckley's Company	Lawrence County	2nd Miss. Rifles, Company K
Tombigbee Volunteers	Lowndes County	1st Miss. Rifles, Company K
Lowndes Guards	Lowndes Country	2nd Miss. Rifles, Company A
Marshall Guards	Marshall County	1st Miss. Rifles, Company I
Marshall Relief Guards	Marshall County	2nd Miss. Rifles, Company B
Monroe Volunteers	Monroe County	2nd Miss. Rifles, Company D
Panola Boys	Panola County	2nd Miss. Rifles, Company I
Tippah Guards	Tippah County	2nd Miss. Rifles, Company E
Vicksburg Volunteers	Warren County	1st Miss. Rifles, Company H
Vicksburg Southrons	Warren County	1st Miss. Rifles, Company C
Wilkinson Volunteers	Wilkinson County	1st Miss. Rifles, Company B
Yazoo Volunteers	Yazoo Country	1st Miss. Rifles, Company A

APPENDIX 3

COUNTY OF ORIGIN BY REGIMENT POPULATION

County	*Country Seat*	*White Pop. (1840)*	*Slaves* (1840)*
Adams (1799)	Natchez	4,910	14,241
Attala (1833)	Kosciusko	2,955	1,082
Carroll (1833)	Carrollton	5,236	5,344
Choctaw (1833)	Ackerman	4,443	1,564
Hinds (1821)	Raymond (JACKSON)	6,778	12,275
Lafayette (1836)	Oxford	3,676	2,842
Lauderdale (1833)	Meridian	3,992	1,353
Lawrence (1814)	Monticello	3,648	2,272
Lowndes (1830)	Columbus	5,730	8,771
Marshall (1836)	Holly Springs	9,258	8,260
Monroe (1821)	Aberdeen	5,146	4,083
Panola (1836)	Batesville	2,237	2,415
Tippah (1836)	Ripley	7,309	2,134
Warren (1809)	Vicksburg	5,223	10,493
Wilkinson (1802)	Woodville	3,269	10,894
Yazoo (1823)	Yazoo City	3,116	7,339

*Although recent biographers of Jefferson Davis point out that the Mississippian tended to treat his slaves as members of his extended family, his endorsement of a pamphlet entitled *Negroes and Negro Slavery: The First, An Inferior Race—The Latter, Its Normal Condition* shows his attitude toward the discussion of race that was then unfolding: "Dear Sir, I have read the enclosed pages with great interest, and not as a Southern man merely, but as an American, I thank you for your able and manly exposure of a fallacy which more than any or all other causes has disturbed the tranquility of our people and endangered the perpetuity of our constitutional union. With high regard I am your obedient servant, Jeffe'n Davis." J. H. Van Evrie, M.D., *Negroes and Negro Slavery: The First, An Inferior Race—The Latter, Its Normal Condition*. (Baltimore: John D. Toy, Printer, 1853), inside cover.

Lieutenant Chesley Sheldon Coffey, whose slaves assisted him in making shoes, sent this admonition to his brother back home: "I want you to feed the Negros well and Clothe them well at all hazards." In another letter, we instructed "tell the Negros that I am well and would Like to see how well they have Done Since I Lefte." In a third letter Coffey writes, "Give my Respects to Melissa . . . tell hir that I am thinkfull to hir for I ntrust She takes Care of the Little Negros." Mary Ellen Rowe, ed., "The Mexican War Diary of Chesley Sheldon Coffey," *The Journal of Mississippi History* 44, No. 3 (August 1982): 248, 250, 252.

APPENDIX 4

THE 1ST AND 2ND REGIMENTS OF MISSISSIPPI RIFLES

COMPARISON OF STATISTICS

Description of force	Foot	Foot
Number of regiment	1st	2nd
Number of companies	10	10
Term of service	12 months	For the war
Date mustered in	June 1846	January 1847
Place mustered in	Vicksburg	Vicksburg
Strength when mustered in		
Commissioned officers	35	44
NCOs and privates	903	822
Aggregate	938	866
Recruited since muster	3	171
Joined since muster	3	158
Aggregate number of volunteers	941	1,037
Discharged		
Officers resigned	2	20
Disability	348	178
By civil authority	–	–
By order	37	9
Deaths		
Ordinary	63	186
Killed in action	54	–
Died of wounds	4	–
Accidental	–	1
Wounded		
In action	108	–
Accidental	–	–
Desertions	5	37
Strength when mustered out		
Commissioned officers	45	41
NCOs and privates	381	565
Aggregate	426	606
Date mustered out	June 1847	July 1848
Place mustered out	New Orleans	Vicksburg

Note: The War Department's figures for the volunteer and regular forces raised for the Mexican War contain many discrepancies. This is true for the 1st and 2nd Mississippi Rifles. Subtracting the aggregate figure mustered out from the aggregate number mustered in leaves a number of volunteers unaccounted. For the 1st Mississippi Rifles the number of unaccounted number of volunteers is 96 while for the 2nd Mississippi Rifles the number of unaccounted volunteers rises to 175. One source of the poor record keeping was blamed on volunteer officers' lack of familiarity with filling out army forms. Another problem was that officers sometimes failed to turn in required reports.

NOTES

Preface

1. Richard Bruce Winders, *Mr. Polk's Army: The American Military Experience in the Mexican War* (College Station: Texas A&M University Press, 1997), 147; Mary Ellen Rowe, ed., "The Mexican War Diary of Chesley Sheldon Coffey," *The Journal of Mississippi History* 44.3 (August 1982): 238. While the 2nd Mississippi Rifles ranked fifth in the number of overall losses of any volunteer regiment, no other regiment was visited by two deadly epidemics while in service. By Rowe's reckoning, the 2nd Mississippi Rifles had lost 26 percent of its personnel to sickness before ever reaching Mexico.

Introduction

1. Samuel Augustus Mitchell, *An Accompaniment to Mitchell's Reference and Distance Map of the United States* (Philadelphia: Mitchell and Hinman, 1834), 281; John Ray Skates, *Mississippi: A Bicentennial History* (New York: Norton; Nashville: American Association for State and Local History, 1979), 81–82.
2. Samuel Augustus Mitchell, *Mitchell's Geographical Reader: A System of Modern Geography Comprising a Description of the World* (Philadelphia: Thomas, Cowperthwait and Company, 1845), 135; Mitchell, *Accompaniment to Reference and Distance Map*, 83. Mississippi had sixty-eight counties at the time of the Mexican War and ranked seventeenth in order of population according to the 1840 census.
3. Mitchell, *Geographical Reader*, 135–36; Skates, *Bicentennial History*, 83.
4. Mitchell, *Accompaniment to Reference and Distance Map*, 281; Mitchell, *Geographical Reader*, 135.
5. Skates, *Bicentennial History*, 84, 85, 87; Richard Aubrey McLemore, *A History of Mississippi* (2 vols.; Jackson: University and College Press of Mississippi, 1973), 1:298.
6. James E. Winston, "Mississippi and the Independence of Texas," *Southwestern Historical Quarterly* 21.4 (July 1917): 37.
7. Winston, "Mississippi and the Independence of Texas," 38, 43–48, 51–53; Robert A. May, *John Anthony Quitman: Old South Crusader* (Baton Rouge: Louisiana State Press, 1985), 76–89; William Fairfax Gray, *From Virginia to Texas, 1835* (Houston: Gray, Dillaye, and Company, 1909; reprint ed., Houston: Fletcher Young, 1965), 31–32. A speculator in western lands, Gray traveled from Virginia to Texas, stopping for some time to inspect lands in Mississippi. There he met John A. Quitman,

captain of the Natchez Fencibles. Gray considered him to be "a man of firmness, and a gentleman, but not a good drill officer; voice and manner both bad." Quitman rose to the rank of major general of volunteers in the Mexican War.

8. McLemore, *History of Mississippi*, 1:299.

9. Richard B. Morris, ed., *Encyclopedia of American History*, revised and enlarged ed. (New York: Harper & Brothers, 1961), 177, 189.

10. McLemore, *History of Mississippi*, 1:299.

11. Morris, ed., *Encyclopedia*, 191–92.

12. Ibid., 194–95. In November 1845, Polk sent John Slidell of Louisiana on a secret mission to Mexico with an offer to pay $5 million for New Mexico and $5 million for California. In return, the Mexican government was asked to recognize the independence of Texas, but the administration of Jose Herrera refused to accept Slidell's credentials. Mariano Paredes, Herrera's successor as president after a December coup, still refused to meet with the American emissary. Slidell requested his passport and left Mexico in March 1846.

13. Robert A. Brent, "Mississippi and the Mexican War," *The Journal of Mississippi History* 31.3 (August 1969): 204.

14. Justin Smith, *The War with Mexico* (2 vols.; Gloucester, MA: Peter Smith, 1963), 1:181; George C. Furber, *The Twelve Months Volunteer* (Cincinnati: J.A. and U.P. James, 1848), 40–41; *Congressional Globe*, 29th Cong., 1st Sess., December 1, 1845–August 10, 1846, 788–95; Lawrence F. Kennedy, ed., *The Biographical Dictionary of the American Congress* (Washington, DC: US Government Printing Office, 1971). The 29th US Congress was in session from March 4, 1845, to March 3, 1847. The first session met from December 1, 1845, to August 10, 1846. The second session met from December 7, 1846, to March 3, 1847. One special session of the Senate was held from March 4, 1845, to March 20, 1845. Members of the House of Representatives from Mississippi were Stephen Adams of Aberdeen (absent during the vote on the war measure), Jefferson Davis of Warrenton, Robert W. Roberts of Hillsboro, and Jacob Thompson of Oxford. Jesse Speight of Plymouth was the only Mississippi Senator present at the time of the vote, as Robert J. Walker had resigned his seat in March to become the Secretary of the Treasury. His replacement, Joseph W. Chalmer of Holly Springs, was absent.

15. Brent, "Mississippi and the Mexican War," 205.

16. US House of Representatives, *Adjutant General's Report of the Forces Employed in the Mexican War*, 31st Cong., lst Sess., 1850, Ex. Doc. No. 24, 22c. These figures were compiled by the author using this document that lists the number and origin troops in the Mexican War.

Chapter 1

1. *The Southron*, April 15 and June 3, 1846; James T. McIntosh, ed., *The Papers of Jefferson Davis* (5 vols.; Baton Rouge: Louisiana State University Press, 1974), 2:610 and 608.

2. Dunbar Rowland, *Military History of Mississippi, 1803–1898* (Spartanburg, SC: Reprint Company, 1978), 18–31; McIntosh, ed., *Davis Papers*, 2:610, note

6; *New Orleans Times Picayune*, May 22, 1846; *The Mississippian*, July 10, 1846; Robert Lorry and William H. McCradle, *A History of Mississippi* (Jackson, MS: R.H. Henry and Company, 1891), 305–6.

3. Rowland, *Military History of Mississippi*, 14–15.
4. Rowland, *Military History of Mississippi*, 15; *The Mississippian*, May 27, 1846.
5. *The Southron*, May 27 and June 3, 1846.
6. *The Mississippian*, May 27, 1846; *The Southron*, June 3, 1846.
7. *The Southron*, June 3, 1846.
8. *The Mississippian*, May 20, 1846.
9. *The Southron*, May 27, 1846.
10. *The Mississippi Democrat*, May 20 and 27 and June 10, 1846; *The Mississippian*, May 20, 1846. *The Mississippi Democrat* of May 20 and June 10, 1846, listed the names of the men enrolled in the Carroll Country Volunteers.
11. *The Southron*, June 3, 1846.
12. Robert A. Brent, "Mississippi and the Mexican War," *The Journal of Mississippi History* 31.3 (August 1969): 207; McIntosh, ed., *Davis Papers*, 2:608–9, 644–48.
13. *The Mississippi Democrat*, June 10, 1846.
14. *The Woodville Republican*, June 20, 1846; *The Mississippi Democrat*, June 17, 1846.
15. *The Mississippian*, June 3, 1846.
16. *The Mississippian Democrat*, June 17, 1846.
17. *The Woodville Republican*, June 20, 1846; *The Southron*, June 24 and July 1, 1846.
18. McIntosh, ed., *Davis Papers*, 3:9–10; Dunbar Rowland, *The Military History of Mississippi, 1803–1898* (Spartanburg, SC: Reprint Company, 1978), 20–21; Lorry and McCradle, *A History of Mississippi*, 306–7.
19. US Congress, House of Representatives, *Military Forces Employed in the Mexican War: Letters from the Secretary of War Transmitting Information in Answer to a Resolution of the House, of July 31, 1847, Relative to the Military Forces Employed in the Late War with Mexico*. 31st Cong., 1st Sess., 1850, Exec. Doc. No. 24, 2c; McIntosh, ed., *Davis Papers*, 2:672; *The Mississippi Democrat*, June 17, 1846; *The Mississippian*, June 17, 1846; Rowland, *Military History of Mississippi*, 15–18.
20. *The Southron*, June 10, 1846. "We do not mean to say that the manual of military exercises should not be taught carefully, and does not assist greatly all warlike operations. We acknowledge its utility, but deny its indispensability. Volunteers have gone to the frontier to fight, and fight they can if allowed. They have not gone there to be kept back from honorable stations, shut up in close quarters, and put under petty formalists and drill officers under pretense that they cannot be trusted on the field until all the etiquette to the trimming of a whisker and the button of a coat has been perfectly acquired."
21. *The Mississippi Democrat*, July 8, 1846; *The Woodville Republican*, June 27, 1846.
22. *The Mississippi Democrat*, July 8, 1846.
23. *The Southron*, May 17, 1846; *The Mississippi Democrat*, May 20 and 27, 1846.
24. *The Woodville Republican*, June 20, 1846.

25. Rowland, *Military History of Mississippi*, 21; *The Southron*, June 24, 1846.

26. McIntosh, ed., *Davis Papers*, 2:675; Lynda Jane Lasswell, "The First Regiment of Mississippi Infantry in the Mexican War and Letters of Jefferson Davis Concerning the War" (MA thesis, Rice University, May 1969), 66.

27. Joseph E. Chance, *The Second Texas Infantry: From Shiloh to Vicksburg* (Austin: Eakin Press, 1984), 14. During the Civil War, Rogers rose to the rank of colonel in command of the 2nd Texas Infantry and was killed on October 4, 1862, at Corinth, Mississippi. His behavior in the attack on Battery Robinett was praised by both Confederates and Unionists alike.

28. Rowland, *Military History of Mississippi*, 21; *The Southron*, June 2, 1846; "Volunteer Officer, Alexander Keith McClung," *Southern Literary Messenger* 21.1 (January 1855): 2–3.

29. *The Republican*, June 27, 1846.

30. Rueben Davis, *Recollections of Mississippi and Mississippians* (Boston: Houghton Mifflin, 1889), 212–14.

31. McIntosh, ed., *Davis Papers*, 2:677–79; Lasswell, "The First Regiment of Mississippi Infantry," 69–71; *The Mississippi Democrat*, July 15, 1846.

32. Jefferson Davis, "Autobiography of Jefferson Davis," *Bedford's Magazine* (January 1890): 255; McIntosh, ed., *Davis Papers*, 2:694, note 5, and 700; Dunbar Rowland, *Mississippi* (2 vols.; Spartanburg, SC: Reprint Company, 1976), 1:260. Henry T. Ellett, elected to fill the vacancy left by Davis' resignation, took his seat on January 26, 1847.

33. McIntosh, ed., *Davis Papers*, 2: 617–18.

34. McIntosh, ed., *Davis Papers*, 3:187–88. Grady McWhiney, "Jefferson Davis and the Art of War," *Civil War History* 2.2 (June 1978): 103. Although Davis attended the US Military Institute, McWhiney found little evidence to show that his philosophy of war was shaped by either reference in his writings to either West Point instructor Dennis Hart Mahon or Jomini's *The Art of War*.

Chapter 2

1. Hudson Strode, *Jefferson Davis: Private Letters, 1823–1889* (New York: Harcourt, Brace, & World, 1966), 38–39; James T. McIntosh, ed., *The Papers of Jefferson Davis* (5 vols.; Baton Rouge: Louisiana State University Press, 1974), 2:693–94; Lynda Jane Lasswell, "The First Regiment of Mississippi Infantry in the Mexican War and Letters of Jefferson Davis Concerning the War" (MA thesis, Rice University, May 1969), 77, 81–84.

2. Justin Smith, *The War with Mexico* (2 vols.; Gloucester, MA: Peter Smith, 1963), 2:195.

3. McIntosh, ed., *Davis Papers*, 2:693–94.

4. Erna Risch, *Quartermaster Support of the Army: History of the Corps, 1775–1939* (Washington, DC: Office of the Quartermaster General, 1962), 251–53; *The Mississippi Democrat*, July 15, 1846.

5. *The Mississippian*, May 20, 1846; *The Woodville Republican*, January 9 and June 19, 1847. The ladies of Wilkinson County made a flag for their county's volunteers.

Accidentally left in the knapsack of a sick volunteer at Cerralvo, the flag was not used at Monterrey. During the Battle of Buena Vista, the flag was worn on the back of one of the Mississippians, as none could be spared to carry it. The Wilkinson County Volunteers carried the flag back to Mississippi where it was flown at a barbecue celebrating their return.

6. George Winston Smith and Charles Judah, *Chronicles of the Gringos* (Albuquerque: University of New Mexico Press, 1968), 30–32; Samuel E. Chamberlain, *My Confession: The Recollections of a Rouge* (Lincoln: University of Nebraska Press, 1987), 32; *The Republican*, June 27, 1846.

7. *The Southron*, April 15, 1846; *The Mississippian*, May 27, 1846.

8. Chamberlain, *My Confession*, 122; *The Woodville Republican*, May 1, 1847.

9. *The Mississippi Democrat*, July 15 and 22, 1846; *The Daily Picayune*, July 14 and 15, 1846.

10. *The Mississippi Democrat*, July 29, 1846; McIntosh, ed., *Davis Papers*, 3:16–17.

11. *The Daily Picayune*, July 15 and 17, 1846.

12. McIntosh, ed., *Davis Papers*, 3:xxxi and 11; Lasswell, "First Regiment of Mississippi," 88–89, 94; *The Mississippi Democrat*, July 27, 1846.

13. US Congress, House of Representatives, *Military Forces Employed in the Mexican War: Letters from the Secretary of War Transmitting Information in Answer to a Resolution of the House, of July 31, 1847, Relative to the Military Forces Employed in the Late War with Mexico*. 31st Cong., 1st Sess., 1850, Exec. Doc. No. 24, 22c.

14. McIntosh, ed., *Davis Papers*, 3:xxxi and 11–12; Lasswell, "First Regiment of Mississippi Infantry," 92; *The Southron*, September 23, 1846; *The Woodville Republican*, August 22, 1846.

15. Chance Franklin Smith, the Mexican War Diary of Captain Franklin Smith, Mississippi Department of Archives and History, Archives and Library Division, Record Number Z 618, October 21, 1846 (hereafter Franklin Smith Diary); *The Mississippi Democrat*, August 9, 1846; *The Southron*; December 17, 1846; Joseph E. Chance, ed., *The Mexican War Journal of Captain Franklin Smith* (Jackson: University of Mississippi Press, 1991), 73.

16. Smith, *The War with Mexico*, 1:206; Erna Risch, *Quartermaster Support of the Army: History of the Corps, 1775–1939* (Washington, DC: Office of the Quartermaster General, 1962), 259–63.

17. John Disturnell, *A Correct Map of the Seat of War in Mexico: Being a Copy of General Aristas Map, Taken at Resaca de la Palma* (New York: John Disturnell, 1847).

18. McIntosh, ed., *Davis Papers*, 3:xxxi and 14–15; *The Woodville Republican*, August 22, 1846; *The Southron*, September 23, 1846; *The Mississippi Democrat*, September 9, 1846; K. Jack Bauer, *Zachary Taylor: Soldier, Planter, Statesman of the Old Southwest* (Baton Rouge: Louisiana State University Press, 1985), 113–14; Strode, *Private Letters*, 41.

19. Smith, *The War with Mexico*, 1:225–26; Luther Giddings, *Sketches of a Campaign in Northern Mexico* (New York: G.P. Putnam, 1853), 47.

20. Disturnell, *Correct Map of the Seat of War*.

21. *The Southron*, September 23, 1846.

22. *The Southron*, September 23, 1846, Hudson Strode, *Jefferson Davis: American Patriot, 1808–1861* (New York: Harcourt Brace, 1955), 162; James C. Browning Diary, Mississippi Department of Archives and History; Eleanor Damon Pace, ed., "The Diary of William P. Rogers, 1846–1862," *The Southwestern Historical Quarterly* 32.4 (April 1929): 261. According to Strode, Davis angrily lectured the men of the regiment on the rights of private property when he learned some of them had raided a nearby cornfield, and then he sent money to the owner to pay for the stolen corn.

23. *The Mississippi Democrat*, September 30, 1846.

24. Mary Ellen Rowe, ed., "The Mexican War Diary of Chesley Sheldon Coffey, "*The Journal of Mississippi History* 44.3 (August 1982): 250; *The Southron*, September 23, 1846. Coffey, an officer in the 2nd Mississippi Rifles, promised to try to send his sister a "Baild Dog."

25. University of Texas, Center for American History, "Howard Morris, 1st Mississippi Rifles, to Mrs. Pamela Pinkhise, August 18, 1846"; *The Mississippi Democrat*, September 8, 1846.

26. Ibid.

27. Pace, ed., "Rogers Diary;" Lasswell, "First Regiment of Mississippi Infantry," 98–99; Franklin Smith Diary; Louis C. Duncan, "A Medical History of General Zachary Taylor's Army of Occupation in Texas and Mexico, 1845–1846," *The Military Surgeon: Journal of the Association of Military Surgeons of the United States* 40 (July 1921): 82; *The Southron*, September 23, 1846; US War Department, *General Regulations for the Army of the United States, 1841* (Washington, DC: J. and G.E. Gideon, 1841), 261. The official army ration called for ¾ pound of pork or bacon or 1¼ pound of fresh or salt beef, 18 oz. of bread or flour or 12 oz. of hard bread, 1¼ pounds of candles, 2 quarts of salt, 4 quarts of vinegar, 8 quarts of peas or beans or (in lieu thereof) 10 pounds of rice, 6 pounds of coffee, and 12 pounds of sugar to the hundred rations. On campaign the ration of bread was raised to 1 pound.

28. James C. Browning Diary, Mississippi Archives.

29. *The Southron*, September 23, 1846; Smith and Judah, *The Chronicles of the Gringos*, 287–89; John Reese Kenly, *Memoirs of a Maryland Volunteer* (Philadelphia: J.B. Lippincott & Co., 1873), 47–50; Benjamin Franklin Scribner, *A Campaign in Mexico* (Philadelphia: J. Gihon, 1850), 27; Amy S. Greenberg, *A Wicked War: Polk, Clay, Lincoln, and the 1846 Invasion of Mexico* (New York: Alfred Knopf, 2012), 117. On the night of September 7, 1846, a riot occurred near Camargo on board the steamer *Corvett* when two companies of the 1st Georgia Infantry battled each other over a choice spot on the ship's upper deck. Colonel Edward Baker arrived with twenty to twenty-five men from his regiment, the 4th Illinois Infantry. Baker was wounded in the attempt to quell the disturbance. Several of the Georgians were injured and at least one killed before the fighting ended. Captain Kenly reported that a conflict over ownership of a catfish between the 1st Ohio Infantry and the Baltimore and DC Battalion was narrowly avoided without bloodshed. This event occurred at the volunteer camp near the mouth of the Rio Grande. Although Greenberg does not mention this episode, she does give important background information on Col. Edward D. Baker, who was wounded in quelling a disturbance that broke out among Georgia Volunteers.

30. *The Mississippi Democrat*, September 30, 1846; Smith. *The War with Mexico*, 1:108.

31. Chance, ed. *Mexican War Journal of Captain Franklin Smith*, 9; Pace, ed., "Rogers Diary," 261; Lasswell, "First Regiment of Mississippi Infantry," 100–5; McIntosh, ed., *Davis Papers*, 3:16–17 and 19, note 1; James C. Browning Diary, Mississippi Archives.

32. James C. Browning Diary, Mississippi Archives.

33. US Congress, House, *Military Forces Employed in the Mexican War Letters from the Secretary of War Transmitting Information in Answer to a Resolution of the House, of July 31, 1847, Relative to the Military Forces Employed in the Late War with Mexico*, 31st Cong., 1st Sess., 1850, Exec. Doc. No. 24, 1–2; Smith, *War with Mexico*, 1:196, 205, and 476, note 25; *The Woodville Republican*, August 22, 1846.

34. Rowland, *Military History of Mississippi*, 19; Lasswell, "First Regiment of Mississippi," 131.

35. Rowland, *Military History of Mississippi*, 28–29; Franklin Smith Diary, October 9–10, 1846; Lasswell, "First Regiment of Mississippi Infantry," 100–5. A complete muster roll of Captain Shivors's Company can be found in Charles D. Spurlin, *Texas Veterans in the Mexican War: Muster Rolls of Texas Military Units* (St. Louis, MO: Ingmire), 206–8. The company numbered sixty-three: three officers, eight noncommissioned officers, and fifty-two privates.

36. Nathaniel C. Brooks, *A Complete History of the Mexican War: its Causes, Conduct, and Consequences* (Philadelphia: Grigg, Elliot, and Company; Baltimore: Hutchison and Seebold, 1849; reprint ed., Chicago: Rio Grande Press, 1965), 165–66.

37. Francis Hamtramack Claiborne, *Life and Correspondence of John A. Quitman* (2 vols.; New York: Harper & Brothers, 1860), 1:227, 1:236–40.

38. Brooks, *Complete History*, 166.

39. *The Southron*, September 23, 1846.

Chapter 3

1. James T. McIntosh, ed., *The Papers of Jefferson Davis* (5 vols.; Baton Rouge: Louisiana State University Press, 1974), 3:19, from note 1; Joseph E. Chance, ed. *The Mexican War Journal of Captain Franklin Smith* (Jackson: University of Mississippi Press, 1991), 10; Eleanor Damon Pace, ed., "The Diary of William P. Rogers, 1846–1862," *The Southwestern Historical Quarterly* 32.4 (April 1929): 261; *The Southron*, September 23, 1846.

2. Franklin Smith Diary, August 26, 1846.

3. Chance, ed., *Mexican War Journal of Captain Franklin Smith*, 12–13; James C. Browning Diary, Mississippi Archives.

4. Chance, ed., *Mexican War Journal of Captain Franklin Smith*, 13; *The Mississippi Democrat*, September 30, 1846; McIntosh, ed., *Davis Papers*, 3:xxxi; Pace, ed., "Rogers Diary," 262.

5. McIntosh, ed., *Davis Papers*, 3:19, from note 9; *The Southron*, September 23, 1846; *The Woodville Republican*, October 10 and 16, 1846; *The Mississippi Democrat*, September 30, 1846.

6. *The Woodville Republican*, October 16, 1846; John Reese Kenly, *Memoirs of a Mary-*

land Volunteer (Philadelphia: J.B. Lippincott & Co., 1873), 54. Kenly recalled the Mexican markets along the Rio Grande where soldiers purchased items to supplement their diets. Common foodstuffs included milk (sold by the cupful from crocks), eggs (sold in piles of three), red peppers, peaches, various types of melons, unknown varieties of vegetables, and fresh meat (as good as any that could be purchased at US markets). Horses, cattle, hay, and corn could be purchased alongside the fruit, vegetables, and meat.

7. Chance, ed., *Mexican War Journal of Captain Franklin Smith*, 14–17. Patton became ill himself and was discharged from the service.

8. Nathaniel C. Brooks, *A Complete History of the Mexican War: Its Causes, Conduct, and Consequences* (Philadelphia: Grigg, Elliot, and Company; Baltimore: Hutchison and Seebold, 1849; reprint ed., Chicago: Rio Grande Press, 1965), 166–68; *The Southron*, November 4 and 11, 1846; Erna Risch, *Quartermaster Support of the Army: History of the Corps, 1775–1939* (Washington, DC: Office of the Quartermaster General, 1962), 263–73; Justin Smith, *The War with Mexico* (2 vols.; Gloucester, MA: Peter Smith, 1963), 1:482–83, from note 13. Justin Smith claimed that Taylor's transportation problems stemmed from his own inability to plan his troop movements effectively and was not due to inefficiency on the part of the Quartermaster Department. *The Southron* reported the following numbers of troops left behind by Taylor: Camargo, 2,100; Matamoros, 1,000; between Matamoros and the mouth of the river, 4,550; and Point Isabel, 120. The army's sick list included approximately 700 at Camargo with the same number at Matamoros.

9. *The Mississippi Democrat*, September 30, 1846; McIntosh, ed., *Davis Papers*, 3:xxxi.

10. McIntosh, ed., *Davis Papers*, 3: 80.

11. Winfield Scott, *An Abstract of Infantry: Including Exercises and Manueuvres of Light-Infantry and Riflemen for the Use of the Militia of the United States* (Boston: Hilliard, Gray, Little, and Wilkins, 1830), 107–35.

12. Chance, ed., *Mexican War Journal of Captain Franklin Smith*, 23–24; Luther Giddings, *Sketches of a Campaign in Northern Mexico* (New York: G.P. Putnam, 1853), 98–100. Taylor's General Order No. 108, Camargo, August 28, 1846, set the amount of baggage that was to be carried: to each division and brigade headquarters, one wagon; to each regimental field and staff, four pack mules; to the officers of each company, two pack mules; and to every eight noncommissioned officers, musicians, and privates, one pack mule. Two James Boyds are listed on the regiment's roster: one in Company F (Lafayette Volunteers) and one in Company G (State Fencibles). This was most likely Boyd of the State Fencibiles, who was raised in Hinds County.

13. Chance, ed., *Mexican War Journal of Captain Franklin Smith*, 24; James C. Browning Diary, Mississippi Archives.

14. *The Nashville Union*, September 17, 1846; Pace, ed., "Rogers Diary," 262; War Department, *General Regulations for the Army of the United States, 1841* (Washington, DC: J. and G.E. Gideon, 1841), 35–36. Sutlers were appointed by the Secretary of War at the rate of one per regiment. It was their role to sell extra items such as ink, paper, pies, buttons, shirts, and so on to the soldiers under their jurisdiction.

Although the sutler could offer credit, written permission form the soldier's company commander had to be provided in cases where credit exceeded half the soldier's monthly pay. The sutler stood at the pay table to collect the money due him by each soldiers on payday.

15. *The Nashville Union*, September 17, 1846; S. Compton Smith, *Chile Con Carne: or, The Camp and the Field* (New York: Miller & Curtis, 1857), 58–60; Smith, *The War with Mexico*, 1:236.

16. *The Southron*, December 17, 1846. Private Marcellus Foute, son of Col. Jacob Foute of Mississippi, remained unconscious for four hours after he fell through an open hatchway. He never fully recovered and was left behind at Cerralvo when the regiment marched to Monterrey. The injured volunteer followed but arrived several days after the battle. Foute then returned to Mississippi, traveling in the company of Jefferson Davis, who was on furlough. Capt. Franklin Smith said of Foute, "if this young man lives he will be an ornament to his family and country."

17. *The Southron*, October 25, 1846.

18. James C. Browning Diary, Mississippi Archives; Smith, *Chile Con Carne*, 66–67, 69–76.

19. *The Nashville Union*, September 17, 1846; *The Woodville Republican*, January 2, 1847; Giddings, *Sketches of a Campaign*, 120; George C. Furber, *The Twelve Months Volunteer*. (Cincinnati: J.A. and U.P. James, 1848), 123.

20. *The Woodville Republican*, October 16, 1846.

21. *The Woodville Republican*, October 16, 1846; McIntosh, ed., *Davis Papers*, 3:xxxii; Pace, ed., "Rogers Diary," 262–63.

22. Brooks, *Complete History*, 169–70; Smith, *The War with Mexico*, 2:226, 236, and 495, from note 21.

23. Brooks, *Complete History*, 170–71; Pace, ed., "Rogers Diary," 263.

24. McIntosh, ed., *Davis Papers*, 3:xxxii, Pace, ed., "Rogers Diary," 263; *Complete History of the Mexican War*, 170–72; *The Southron*, October 25, 1846; Francis Hamtramack Claiborne, *Life and Correspondence of John A. Quitman* (2 vols.; New York: Harper & Brothers, 1860), 1:244.

25. *The Woodville Republican*, October 16, 1846.

26. *The Mississippi Democrat*, November 4, 1846; Dunbar Rowland, *Military History of Mississippi, 1803–1898* (Spartanburg, SC: Reprint Company, 1978), 19.

Chapter 4

1. *The Mississippi Democrat*, January 6, 1847.

2. Nathaniel C. Brooks, *A Complete History of the Mexican War: Its Causes, Conduct, and Consequences* (Philadelphia: Grigg, Elliot, and Company; Baltimore: Hutchison and Seebold, 1849; reprint ed., Chicago: Rio Grande Press, 1965), 182–84.

3. Ibid., 165, 176–77.

4. Brooks, *Complete History*, 182–84; Justin Smith, *The War with Mexico* (2 vols.; Gloucester, MA: Peter Smith, 1963), 1:243–46.

5. John Reese Kenly. *Memoirs of a Maryland Volunteer* (Philadelphia: J.B. Lippincott & Co., 1873), 119.

6. Brooks, *Complete History*, 165, 177; Smith, *The War with Mexico*, 1:248–251.
7. Brooks, *Complete History*, 176–79; Smith, *The War with Mexico*, 1:251–52; George Winston Smith and Charles Judah, *Chronicles of the Gringos* (Albuquerque: University of New Mexico Press, 1968), 79–82.
8. James T. McIntosh, ed., *The Papers of Jefferson Davis* (5 vols.; Baton Rouge: Louisiana State University Press, 1974), 3:101; *The Mississippi Democrat*, January 6, 1847.
9. *The Mississippi Democrat*, January 6, 1847.
10. McIntosh, ed., *Davis Papers*, 3:101; William B. Campbell, "Mexican War Letters of William Bowen Campbell, of Tennessee, Written to Governor David Campbell, of Virginia, 1846–1847," *Tennessee Historical Magazine* 1 (June 1915): 143–44.
11. McIntosh, ed., *Davis Papers*, 3:47–52 and 102.
12. Winfield Scott, *An Abstract of Infantry: Including Exercises and Manueuvres of Light-Infantry and Riflemen for the Use of the Militia of the United States* (Boston: Hilliard, Gray, Little, and Wilkins, 1830), 107–35. The following article seems to correspond to the descriptions of Davis's movements at both Monterrey and Buena Vista, once the regiment was commanded to "Advance Firing": "Article1745. 1st. At the command (or signal) for the whole line to *fire advancing*, the men of each file will keep together, preserving their distances, and align themselves as accurately as may be, in the direction from which the command is given, loading and firing as rapidly as is consistent with order and execution; the moment the man in front has fired, he will commence loading, and the other man of his file will pass to the front by the right."
13. Joseph Davis Howell, Mississippi Department of Archives and History; William C. Davis, *Jefferson Davis: The Man and the Hour, A Biography* (New York: HarperCollins, 1991), 140. Davis contends in his biography that Jefferson Davis went into battle that day on foot, having left his horse, Tartar, in camp under the care of Jim Green, the slave who accompanied him to Mexico as his personal servant. Davis also states that Davis was still wearing civilian clothing at the time of the battle.
14. "Volunteer Officer, Alexander Keith McClung," *Southern Literary Messenger* 11.1 (January 1855): 2–3, 9–11; McIntosh, ed., *Davis Papers*, 3:25–29, 44–45, 47–52, and 100–5; Joseph Davis Howell, Mississippi Archives.
15. "Sketches of Our Volunteer Officers," 9–11; McIntosh, ed., *Davis Papers*, 3:67–68 and 71–73.
16. McIntosh, ed., *Davis Papers*, 3:25–29, 63, 71–73, and 100–5; *The Mississippi Democrat*, November 11, 1846. *The Mississippi Democrat* contains a letter describing the battle from a writer identified as J.E.S. Howell; Joseph Davis Howell, Mississippi Archives.

17. William Estes, "The Battle of Monterey," *Fort Worth Gazette*, January 5, 1885.
18. McIntosh, ed., *Davis Papers*, 3:72–105.
19. McIntosh, ed., *Davis Papers*, 3:27 and 73; Louis C. Duncan, "A Medical History of General Zachary Taylor's Army of Occupation in Texas and Mexico, 1845–1846," *The Military Surgeon: Journal of the Association of Military Surgeons of the*

United States 40 (July 1921): 92–93. According to Duncan, Dr. Nathan S. Jarvis narrowly missed being killed by lancers about this time. Jarvis was tending to some wounded in a four- to five-foot-deep quarry pit on the city's north side. The surgeon had already performed one amputation and was beginning another when "three fugitives rushed into the pit saying that a large body of lancers was approaching. I [Jarvis] never raised my eyes to observe them The lancers were soon after repulsed by a regiment of Ohio and Mississippi Volunteers." Jarvis said had he raised up to look at the lancers, he and the others in the pit would have been killed, as were several soldiers and an officer in an adjacent pit.

20. McIntosh, ed., *Davis Papers*, 3:73.
21. Smith, *War with Mexico*, 1:255; Joseph Davis Howell, Mississippi Archives.
22. "Sketches of Our Volunteer Officers," 9–11; McIntosh, ed., *Davis Papers*, 3:28–29.
23. Brooks, *Complete History*, 185–86; Smith, *War with Mexico*, 1:246–48.
24. Smith, *War with Mexico*, 1:255; McIntosh, ed., *Davis Papers*, 3:37–38 and 41.
25. Brooks, *Complete History*, 187; McIntosh, ed., *Davis Papers*, 3:35; Pace, ed., "Rogers Diary," 267.
26. McIntosh, ed., *Davis Papers*, 3:35–38 and 64–64.
27. McIntosh, ed., *Davis Papers*, 3:36; James K. Holland, "Diary of a Texan Volunteer in the Mexican War," *Southwestern Historical Quarterly* 30.1 (July 1926): 26; Smith and Judah, *Chronicles of the Gringos*, 89.
28. Joseph Davis Howell, Mississippi Archives.
29. Smith and Judah, *Chronicles of the Gringos*, 84–85.
30. Estes, "Battle of Monterey."
31. Estes, "Battle of Monterey"; Davis, "Autobiography of Jefferson Davis," 256–57.
32. Smith and Judah, *Chronicles of the Gringos*, 85; Joseph Davis Howell, Mississippi Archives.
33. Smith and Judah, *Chronicles of the Gringos* 85, 89.

Chapter 5

1. Nathaniel C. Brooks, *A Complete History of the Mexican War: Its Causes, Conduct, and Consequences* (Philadelphia: Grigg, Elliot, and Company; Baltimore: Hutchison and Seebold, 1849; reprint ed., Chicago: Rio Grande Press, 1965), 188.
2. Ibid., 188–89.
3. Ibid., 192–95.
4. William Estes, "The Battle of Monterey," *Fort Worth Gazette*, January 5, 1885; Brooks, *Complete History*, 190–91; Robert Ryal Miller, *Shamrock and Sword* (Norman: University of Oklahoma Press, 1989), 47.
5. Justin Smith, *The War with Mexico* (2 vols.; Gloucester, MA: Peter Smith, 1963), 1:505–6; Brooks, *Complete History*, 108 in appendix; Louis C. Duncan, "A Medical History of General Zachary Taylor's Army of Occupation in Texas and Mexico, 1845–1846," *The Military Surgeon: Journal of the Association of Military Surgeons of the United States* 40 (July 1921): 93–94, 102–3; *The Woodville Republican*, October 10, 1846.

6. James T. McIntosh, ed., *The Papers of Jefferson Davis* (5 vols.; Baton Rouge: Louisiana State University Press, 1974), 3:24.

7. Eleanor Damon Pace, ed., "The Diary of William P. Rogers, 1846–1862," *The Southwestern Historical Quarterly* 32. 4 (April 1929):263.

8. Hudson Strode, ed., *Jefferson Davis: Private Letters, 1823–1889* (New York: Harcourt, Brace & World, 1966), 42; *The Mississippi Democrat*, October 21, 1846.

9. *The Mississippi Democrat*, November 4, 1846; Joseph Davis Howell, Mississippi Archives; James C. Browning Diary, Mississippi Archives; Joseph E. Chance, ed., *My Life in the Old Army: The Reminiscences of Abner Doubleday* (Fort Worth: Texas Christian University Press, 1998), 167–68. Chance raises interesting questions about Howell's character and believes he was an unreliable, unprincipled scoundrel. Doubleday discusses Howell's misconduct as secretary of a commission sent to Mexico in the mid-1850s to investigate a fraud perpetrated on the US government known as the Gardner Mine Claim. Doubleday refers to Howell as Davis's "wild brother-in-law" and contends that Davis, then the Secretary of War, had recommended him for the post. Says Doubleday of Howell, "He was utterly useless as a secretary for his education had been very much neglected." In addition, Howell often drank and even caused an incident that put the commission's safety at risk. His Mexican War letters certainly were written with a goal to praise his influential brother-in-law to his family back home in Mississippi.

10. Francis Hamtramack Claiborne, *Life and Correspondence of John A. Quitman* (2 vols.; New York: Harper & Brothers, 1860), 1:271; Pace, ed., "Rogers Diary," 263–65; Strode, ed., *Jefferson Davis: Private Letters*, 42; Brooks, *Complete History*, 192; Robert Seth Henry, *The Story of the Mexican War* (Indianapolis: Bobbs-Merrill, 1950), 162–63; Smith, *War with Mexico*, 1:263.

11. McIntosh, ed., *Davis Papers*, 3:24.

12. George Winston Smith and Charles Judah, *Chronicles of the Gringos* (Albuquerque: University of New Mexico Press, 1968), 79–82.

13. William B. Campbell, "Mexican War Letters of William Bowen Campbell, of Tennessee, Written to Governor David Campbell, of Virginia, 1846–1847," *Tennessee Historical Magazine* 1 (June 1915): 144; John Blount Robertson, *Reminiscences of a Campaign in Mexico; By a Member of "The Bloody First"* (Nashville: John York and Company, 1849), 167–74.

14. McIntosh, ed., 3:113–17; Robert A. May, *John Anthony Quitman: Old South Crusader* (Baton Rouge: Louisiana State Press, 1985), 170–71. According to McIntosh, Quitman resented the fact that Davis did not call on the general's family while he was in Mississippi. He further states that Quitman believed Davis to be jealous of his reputation. According to May, however, Davis did visit home and returned to Mexico with letters and a scarf from Eliza, Quitman's wife. May states that Davis was cool toward the general and failed to call on Quitman socially while at Victoria, further alienating the two former friends.

15. *The Nashville Union*, November 11, 17, and 19, 1846; *The Republican*, October 10 and 23, November 21, and December 5, 1846; *The Mississippi Democrat*, October 14 and November 11, 1846.

16. Pace, ed., "Rogers Diary," 266–67; William C. Davis, *Jefferson Davis: The Man and the Hour, A Biography* (New York: HarperCollins, 1991), 146–47.
17. Ibid., 264–65.
18. *Compiled Service Records of the Mississippi Volunteers in the Mexican War*, National Archives Microfilm, M863, Roll #2, Records of George W. Hise.
19. Joseph Davis Howell, Mississippi Archives.
20. Ibid.
21. Franklin Smith Diary, October 12, 21, and 26, 1846.
22. McIntosh, ed., *Davis Papers*, 3:xxxii.
23. *New Orleans Picayune*, November 13, 1847.
24. Strode, *Private Letters*, 44.
25. *The Mississippi Democrat*, October 14 and October 21, 1846.
26. *The Southron*, November 26, 1846.
27. John Reese Kenly, *Memoirs of a Maryland Volunteer* (Philadelphia: J.B. Lippincott & Co., 1873), 171.
28. Joseph E. Chance, ed., *The Mexican War Journal of Captain Franklin Smith* (Jackson: University of Mississippi Press, 1991), 125; Richard B. Winders, *Mr. Polk's Army: The American Military Experience in the Mexican War* (College Station: Texas A&M University Press, 1997), 161.
29. Smith, *War with Mexico*, 1:262–64.
30. Ibid., 1:264.
31. Pace, ed., "Rogers Diary," 268–69.

Chapter 6

1. Eleanor Damon Pace, ed., "The Diary of William P. Rogers, 1846–1862," *The Southwestern Historical Quarterly* 32.4 (April 1929): 271.
2. Justin Smith, *The War with Mexico* (2 vols.; Gloucester, MA: Peter Smith, 1963), 1:349–51; Marcus Cunliffe, *Soldiers & Civilians: The Martial Sprit in America, 1776–1865* (Boston: Little, Brown, 1968), 310–17. Cunliffe's work contains an excellent account of Polk's struggle to find a general suitable to his taste and needs.
3. Smith, *War with Mexico*, 1:351–56.
4. Richard Bruce Winders, *Mr. Polk's Army: The American Military Experience in the Mexican War* (College Station: Texas A&M University Press, 1997), 70–71.
5. Smith, *War with Mexico* 1:355.
6. Smith, *War with Mexico*, 1:366–67; John Reese Kenly, *Memoirs of a Maryland Volunteer* (Philadelphia: J.B. Lippincott & Co., 1873), 174; James C. Browning Diary, Mississippi Archives; Francis Hamtramack Claiborne, *Life and Correspondence of John A. Quitman* (2 vols.; New York: Harper & Brothers, 1860), 1:277.
7. Kenly, *Maryland Volunteer*, 176–77, 184; Pace, ed., "Rogers Diary," 270–71.
8. Claiborne, *Life and Correspondence of John A. Quitman*, 1:284.
9. Smith, *War with Mexico*, 1:359; Pace, ed., "Rogers Diary," 269.

10. Pace, ed., "Rogers Diary," 269; *The Woodville Republican*, February 6, 1847, Claiborne, *Life and Correspondence of Quitman*, 1:287.
11. Kenly, *Maryland Volunteer*, 191; Smith, *War with Mexico*, 1:542, from note 22. The Mexican forces at Victoria numbered about 1,000 cavalry of whom only 200 were regulars. Governor Valencia wanted to fight the Americans, but Santa Anna ordered that no battle should take place. The Mexican forces left the city before Quitman's Brigade arrived.
12. Smith, *War with Mexico*, 1:358.
13. George Winston Smith and Charles Judah, *Chronicles of the Gringos* (Albuquerque: University of New Mexico Press, 1968), 93.
14. Smith, *War with Mexico*, 1:357–58. Alexander Doniphan and his regiment, the 1st Missouri Mounted Volunteers, left Fort Leavenworth in June 1846 as a part of Col. Stephen Kearny's Army of the West. After claiming New Mexico for the United States, Kearny took 300 dragoons and proceeded on to California. Doniphan left Santa Fe to fulfill the main purpose of his mission, the capture and occupation of Chihuahua. Winning battles at El Brazito (fought on December 25, 1846 near El Paso) and Sacramento (fought on February 28, 1847, near Chihuahua), Doniphan and his Missourians entered Chihuahua. After finally making contact with General Wool, Doniphan was instructed by Taylor to bring his regiment to Saltillo. Once there, the Missourians were ordered to the mouth of the Rio Grande where they were mustered out of service as their 12-month enlistment was nearly finished.
15. *The Woodville Republican*, February 6, 1847; James C. Browning Diary, Mississippi Archives.
16. Joseph E. Chance, ed., *The Mexican War Journal of Captain Franklin Smith*. (Jackson: University Press of Mississippi, 1991), 142–43, 209–10.
17. Smith, *War with Mexico*, 1:356; John S.D. Eisenhower, *So Far from God: The US War with Mexico, 1846–1848* (New York: Doubleday; originally published by Random House, 1889), 170 and 173–175. Scott sent his message to Taylor by two separate couriers. The letter, carried by Lt. Alexander Richey, 4th US Infantry, fell into the hands of the Mexicans when the officer was murdered after going into the Villa Gran to purchase provisions. The dispatches Richey carried were taken to Santa Anna and the Mexican leader was informed of Scott's latest plan. Taylor stopped at Villa Gran with his escort on his return to Monterrey and demanded that Richey's killers be turned over to him, but the guilty parties could not be located.
18. Smith, *War with Mexico*, 1:362; Eisenhower, *So Far from God*, 172–73.
19. Smith, *War with Mexico*, 1:363; Pace, ed., "Rogers Diary," 272; James T. McIntosh, ed., *The Papers of Jefferson Davis* (5 vols.; Baton Rouge: Louisiana State University Press, 1974), 3:114; Franklin Smith Diary, January 3, 1847.
20. *The Woodville Republican*, February 6, 1847; Kenly, *Maryland Volunteer*, 192–93.
21. Pace, ed., "Rogers Diary," 271.
22. *The Mississippi Democrat*, December 30, 1846.
23. *The Mississippi Democrat*, December 30, 1846; *The Woodville Republican*, January 2, 847.

24. McIntosh, ed., *Davis Papers*, 3:xxxiii and 112.
25. Smith, *War with Mexico*, 1:362.
26. Kenly, *Maryland Volunteer*, 209–10.
27. Smith, *War with Mexico*, 1:368; McIntosh, ed., *Davis Papers*, 3:114.
28. McIntosh, ed., *Davis Papers*, 3:115; Pace, ed., *Davis Papers*, 271–72; Robert A. May, *John Anthony Quitman: Old South Crusader* (Baton Rouge: Louisiana State Press, 1985), 170–71.
29. Pace, ed., "Rogers Diary," 272. Captain Rogers made a New Year's resolution to stop drinking, but he noted on February 4, 1847, that he had been unable to keep his pledge.
30. Ibid.

Chapter 7

1. Nathaniel C. Brooks, *A Complete History of the Mexican War: Its Causes, Conduct, and Consequences* (Philadelphia: Grigg, Elliot, and Company; Baltimore: Hutchison and Seebold, 1849; reprint ed., Chicago: Rio Grande Press, 1965), 202.
2. Brooks, *Complete History*, 203; Samuel E. Chamberlain, *My Confession: The Recollections of a Rouge* (Lincoln: University of Nebraska Press, 1987), 93–97; Justin Smith, *The War with Mexico* (2 vols.; Gloucester, MA: Peter Smith, 1963), 1:370–71 and 562. Taylor hoped to gain the release of these prisoners after his success at Buena Vista, but they were not set free until after Scott captured Mexico City in September 1847.
3. Chamberlain, *My Confession*, 89–92; Samuel G. French, *Two Wars: An Autobiography* (Nashville: The Confederate Veteran, 1901), 76.
4. Brooks, *Complete History*, 90; Chamberlain, *My Confession*, 106–11.
5. Brooks, *Complete History*, 90; Chamberlain, *My Confession*, 111–12.
6. US War Department, *Report of the Secretary of War for 1847* (Washington, DC: Wendell and Van Benthuysen, 1847), 112–13.
7. Smith, *War with Mexico*, 1:380–81; James Henry Carleton, *Battle of Buena Vista* (New York: Harper & Brothers, 1848), 229–34; *Report of the Secretary of War for 1847*, 111. Captain Carleton, 2nd US Dragoons, participated in the fighting at Buena Vista and afterward wrote a history of the battle. He estimated the Mexican Army to number 6,500 cavalry and 17,000 infantry, artillery, sappers, and engineers for a total of 23,500. It is interesting to note that Santa Anna had made a similar forced march 11 years earlier, arriving unexpectedly at San Antonio on February 23, 1836. Once there, he defeated the rebel forces that had taken refuge in the old mission known as the Alamo.
8. Smith, *War with Mexico*, 1:386 and 388; John S.D. Eisenhower, *So Far from God: The US War with Mexico, 1846–1848* (New York: Random House, 1989), 183.
9. Smith, *War with Mexico*, 1:374.
10. Carleton, *Battle of Buena Vista*, 229–35; Eisenhower, *So Far from God*, 183.
11. James C. Browning Diary, Mississippi Archives.
12. Brooks, *Complete History*, 90–91.

13. Smith, *War with Mexico*, 1:384. The American right flank rested on the valley's east wall, while the left flank rested on the west wall.

14. *Report of the Secretary of War of 1847*, 91.

15. Brooks, *Complete History*, 91. For a detailed account of the Kentucky and Indiana regiments at Buena Vista see Richard V. Sailbury, "Kentuckians at Buena Vista," *The Filson Club Quarterly* 61.1 (January 1987):34–53; James A. Ramage, "John Hunt Morgan and the Kentucky Cavalry Volunteers in the Mexican War," *The Register of the Kentucky Historical Society* 81.4 (Autumn 1983): 343–65; R.C. Burley, "Indiana in the Mexican War: The Indiana Volunteers," *Indiana Magazine of History* 15 (September 1919): 260–92; R.C. Burley, "Indiana in the Mexican War: The Buena Vista Campaign," *Indiana Magazine of History* 15.4 (December 1919): 293–326; R.C. Burley, "Indiana in the Mexican War: The Buena Vista Controversy," *The Indiana Magazine of History* 15 (March 1920): 46–68. For an excellent account from the viewpoint of a young Illinois officer, see Otto B. Engleman, ed. and trans., "The Second Illinois in the Mexican War: Mexican War Letters of Adolph Engleman," *Journal of the Illinois State Historical Society* 26 (January 1934): 357–452.

16. [By an] Eye-Witness, *Complete History of the Late War with Mexico* (New York: F. J. Dow and Company, 1850), 60. This work appears as an appendix in the Rio Grande Press edition of Brooks, *Complete History*.

17. James T. McIntosh, ed., *The Papers of Jefferson Davis* (5 vols.; Baton Rouge: Louisiana State University Press, 1974), 3:144 and 159; Eleanor Damon Pace, ed., "The Diary of William P. Rogers, 1846–1862," *The Southwestern Historical Quarterly* 32.4 (April 1929): 274; *The Woodville Republican*, April 10, 1847.

18. Brooks, *Complete History*, 91.

19. Ibid., 92.

Chapter 8

1. *Report of the Secretary of War, which Accompanied the Annual Message of the President of the United States to Both Houses of the Thirtieth Congress* (Washington, DC: Wendall and Van Benthuysen, 1847), 141; Clara Ehinger, ed., "Augustus Ehinger: Diary of His Travels from Illinois to Mexico, and During His Services as a Member of Company H, 2nd Regiment Illinois Volunteers, During the Mexican War," Typed Manuscript, Property of Mrs. W.C. Preston, Fort Worth Public Library, Genealogy, Local History and Archives, 44 and 51. In defense of the 2nd Indiana Volunteers, Gen. Joseph Lane contented that the regiment had fired twenty rounds (per man) before the regiment broke from its position. At the prescribed rate of fire of three rounds per minute, this would mean that the regiment at a minimum was engaged somewhere around 10 minutes against an estimated 3,000 to 4,000 of the enemy before its rearward movement.

2. James T. McIntosh, ed., *The Papers of Jefferson Davis* (5 vols.; Baton Rouge: Louisiana State University Press, 1974), 3:123, 132, 134, 140, 152, 157, and 162; H. Montgomery, *The Life of Major General Zachary Taylor, 12th President of the United States*, (Auburn, NY: Derby & Miller, 1854), 335; R.C. Burley, "Indiana in the Mexican War: The Buena Vista Controversy," *The Indiana Magazine of History*

15 (March 1920): 46–68; Benjamin Franklin Scribner, *A Campaign in Mexico* (Philadelphia: J. Gihon, 1850), 63; Lew Wallace, *An Autobiography* (2 vols.; New York: Harper & Brothers, 1904), 1:192. In his autobiography, Wallace refuted the notion that the 2nd Indiana fled the field. He accounted for the men of the regiment with the following figures: killed and wounded, 90; caring for casualties, 40; rallied by Colonel Bowles, 25, rallied at the ranch, 15; rallied by General Lane and others, 190, for a total of 360. This was close to the number of men that the regiment took into the battle. According to Scribner, a third of the men of the Indiana regiment joined other regiments, while the remainder continued to serve under Lt. Colonel William R. Haddon and formed a distinct regimental front during the rest of the battle. Nevertheless, the fact remained that a significant number of Indiana Volunteers fled the battlefield, an embarrassment to their state that was only laid to rest by the Civil War.

3. McIntosh, ed., *Davis Papers*, 3:124, 132, 135, 141, 146, 152, 157, 158, and 162; Grady McWhiney and Sue McWhiney, eds., *To Mexico with Taylor and Scott, 1845–1847* (Waltham, MA: Blaisdell, 1969), 90.
4. Ibid., 3:143–44.
5. Ibid., 3:132 and 146.
6. Ibid., 3:124 and 142.
7. Ibid., 3:3:142.
8. *Report of the Secretary of War, which Accompanied the Annual Message of the President of the United States to Both Houses of the Thirtieth Congress* (Washington, DC: Wendall and Van Benthuysen, 1847), 145. Colonel James H. Lane, who commanded the 3rd Indiana Volunteers, described the incident from his perspective in his official after action report. According to Lane, he estimated the strength of the 1st Mississippi Rifles at about 200, also saying that that was the approximate strength of the 2nd Indiana Volunteers who had taken up position on Davis's right flank. He estimated the strength of his own regiment at about 500. He reported that his movement to his place in the line had inverted his regiment and that he had to order his men to "Face to the Rear" in order to fire at the enemy. He reported that "Our fire was then delivered, and the enemy's column immediately broke and fled in the utmost confusion." The reports of Davis and Lane fail to state who, if anyone, was in overall command during the incident, as each described his regiment's action without clarifying the command situation.
9. *Report of the Secretary of War for 1847*, 92.
10. *Report of the Secretary of War for 1847*, 93; McIntosh, ed., *Davis Papers*, 3:143.
11. *Report of the Secretary of War for 1847*, 94, 106–7.
12. Ibid., 164.
13. McIntosh, ed., *Davis Papers*, 3:159.
14. *Report of the Secretary of War for 1847*, 146–67; McIntosh, ed., *Davis Papers*, 3:159–60.
15. *Report of the Secretary of War for 1847*, 94; Henry W. Benham, "Recollection of Mexico and the Battle of Buena Vista" (unpublished copy for *Old and New Magazine*, 1871), 22.

16. *Report of the Secretary of War for1847*, 118–19. All of O'Brian's cannoneers had been disabled or killed during his stand after the departure of the 2nd Indiana. He returned to Captain Washington, his battery commander, and was given two more 6-pound guns. In his second desperate stand of the day, all of O'Brian's new cannoneers, many of whom were recruits, were also killed or disabled. O'Brian had two horses shot from under him and a third wounded during the day. The officer was wounded in the leg yet he stayed on the field.

17. *Report of the Secretary of War* for *1847*, 160; Benham, "Battle of Buena Vista," 23. According to Benham, Bragg brought his battery up but said to Taylor, "I have no support; They will take my pieces." Taylor answered, "They will take them anyway, fire away," later adding, "Give 'em hell, Bragg."

18. *Report of the Secretary of War for 1847*, 94–95; McIntosh, ed., *Davis Papers*, 3:143; James C. Browning Diary, Mississippi Archives.

19. Eleanor Damon Pace, ed., "The Diary of William P. Rogers, 1846–1862," *The Southwestern Historical Quarterly* 32.4 (April 1929): 274–75; *Report of the Secretary of War for 1847*, 95.

20. *Report of the Secretary of War for 1847*, 57.

Chapter 9

1. Justin Smith, *The War with Mexico* (2 vols.; Gloucester, MA: Peter Smith, 1963), 1:396 and 561; US War Department, *Report of the Secretary of War for 1847* (Washington, DC: Wendell and Van Benthuysen, 1847), 57; Louis C. Duncan, "A Medical History of General Zachary Taylor's Army of Occupation in Texas and Mexico, 1845–1846," *The Military Surgeon: Journal of the Association of Military Surgeons of the United States* 40 (July 1921): 98–102; James Henry Carleton, *Battle of Buena Vista* (New York: Harper & Brothers, 1848), 212. According to Duncan, American casualties were 267 killed, 456 wounded, and 23 missing. These are higher figures than those given by Justin Smith. Troops engaged included General Staff, 41; 1st Dragoon, A and E, 133; 2nd Dragoons, E, 76; 3rd Artillery, C and B, 150; 4th Artillery, B, 117; Arkansas Cavalry, 479; Kentucky Cavalry, 330; Mississippi Rifles, 368; 2nd Indiana 107; 3rd Indiana, 65; 1st Illinois, 580; 2nd Illinois, 573; Texas Volunteers, 61; and McCullough's Spy Company, 27. Carleton said that "the Mississippi regiment lost more heavily than any other—one out of 3.75 men." Smith stated that Santa Anna had withdrawn to open ground where his cavalry could be of more use.

2. *The Woodville Republican*, April 3, 1847; James T. McIntosh, ed., *The Papers of Jefferson Davis* (5 vols.; Baton Rouge: Louisiana State University Press, 1974), 3:144 and 149; *The Mississippi Democrat*, April 14, 1847.

3. Eleanor Damon Pace, ed., "The Diary of William P. Rogers, 1846–1862," *The Southwestern Historical Quarterly* 32.4 (April 1929): 274–75; Nathanial C. Brooks, *A Complete History of the Mexican War: Its Causes, Conduct, and Consequences* (Philadelphia: Grigg, Elliot, and Company; Baltimore: Hutchison and Seebold, 1849; reprint ed., Chicago: Rio Grande Press, 1965), 95.

4. *Report of the Secretary of War, which Accompanied the Annual Message of the Presi-*

dent of the United States to Both Houses of the Thirtieth Congress (Washington, DC: Wendall and Van Benthuysen, 1847), 97, 108, 141 152, 159, 163.

5. Oran Perry, *Indiana in the Mexican War* (Indianapolis: W.B. Burford, 1908), 300–21. Perry's report on the Indiana Volunteers in the Mexican War has a section on the controversy, including a transcript of Bowles' hearing.

6. "Joseph D. Howell to His Father," March 2, 1847, Mississippi Department of Archives and History; Pace, ed., "Rogers Diary," 276–78; *The Mississippi Democrat*, April 14, 1847. Howell, who was now working for the Quarter Master Department, had to travel on to Point Isabel because the head of the depot at Camargo said that he did not have enough clothing on hand for a requisition submitted by Taylor. Away on this errand, Howell missed participating in the Battle of Buena Vista.

7. Pace, ed., "Rogers Diary," 279.

8. Pace, ed., "Rogers Diary," 279–80; Smith, *War with Mexico*, 1:400, 562; Luther Giddings, *Sketches of a Campaign in Northern Mexico* (New York: G.P. Putnam, 1853), 291–94; Robert Seth Henry, *The Story of the Mexican War* (Indianapolis: Bobbs-Merrill, 1950), 254; S. Compton Smith, *Chile Con Carne: or, The Camp and the Field* (New York: Miller & Curtis, 1857), 150–72; James C. Browning Diary, Mississippi Archives. The guerrilla forces under José Urrea harassed Taylor's supply line from Camargo to Monterrey. These raids had been planned to coincide with Santa Anna's advance on Saltillo. Guerrilla raids on trains destroyed wagons and supplies, killed escorts and teamsters, and for a time blocked all passage. The threat hastened troop shipment to Mexico and even diverted some men meant for Scott.

9. Pace, ed., "Rogers Diary," 280, 282–83; Samuel E. Chamberlain, *My Confession: The Recollections of a Rouge* (Lincoln: University of Nebraska Press, 1987), 201–2.

10. Pace, ed., "Rogers Diary," 283–84.

11. Ibid., 284.

12. *Compiled Service Records of the Mississippi Volunteers in the Mexican War*, Microfilm Roll #3, Letter from Colonel Alexander Mitchell in the records of William H.H. Patterson; Pace, ed., "Rogers Diary," 284; *The Mississippian*, June 18, 1847. In June, Patterson was reported to be in Mississippi and recovering in the Jackson home of General Jack Bradford.

13. McIntosh, ed., *Davis Papers*, 3:166–67; *The Mississippi Democrat*, April 14, 1847; Lew Wallace, *An Autobiography* (2 vols.; New York: Harper & Brothers, 1904), 1:178. Wallace claimed that Davis presented Bowles with a rifle as a token of his esteem after the battle. The Indiana troops were offended by the favors Bowles received from Taylor, Davis, and the 1st Mississippi Rifles.

14. John Porter Bloom, "With the American Army in Mexico" (PhD dissertation, Emory University, 1955; Ann Arbor, MI: University Microfilms International), 145.

15. Pace, ed., "Rogers Diary," 284–85; Joseph E. Chance, *Jefferson Davis's Mexican War Regiment* (Jackson: University Press of Mississippi, 1991), 199–200; Joseph E. Chance, *The Second Texas Infantry: From Shiloh to Vicksburg*. (Austin: Eakin Press, 1984), 15. Rogers and Simons would later serve together once more as colonel and lieutenant in the 2nd Texas Infantry during the Civil War.

16. Lynda Jane Lasswell, "The First Regiment of Mississippi Infantry in the Mexican War and Letters of Jefferson Davis Concerning the War" (MA thesis, Rice University, May 1969), 208–9, 211; McIntosh, ed., *Davis Papers*, 3:xxxiv and 177–79.
17. *New Orleans Picayune*, June 5, 1847.
18. *New Orleans Picayune*, June 10, 1847.
19. *New Orleans Times Picayune*, June 10 and 11, 1847; *The Mississippian*, June 18 and 25, 1847; McIntosh, ed., *Davis Papers*, 3:181; Dunbar Rowland, *Military History of Mississippi, 1803–1898* (Spartanburg, SC: Reprint Company, 1978), 28. Captain Douglas H. Cooper, as the senior officer present, commanded the 250 Mississippi volunteers who took part in the parade. Companies participating in the event were A, Lt. Amos B. Corwin; B, Lt. James Colhoun; C, Capt. John Willis; E, Capt. John L. McManus; F, Capt. William Delay; H, Capt. John S. Clendenin; and K, Capt. William P. Rogers. Perhaps the omission of Company I was an oversight on the part of the reporter covering the event, but Companies D and G were not present as their ship had not yet arrived at New Orleans. The volunteers were "Clothed in . . . civilian garb."
20. McIntosh, ed., *Davis Papers*, 3:182.
21. *New Orleans Picayune*, June 11, 1847.
22. *The Woodville Republican*, August 14, 1847.
23. Lasswell, "The First Mississippi Infantry," 221.
24. McIntosh, ed., *Davis Papers*, 3:184.
25. *The Woodville Republican*, June 19, 1847; *The Mississippian*, June 7 and 25, 1847; *The Southron*, June 5 and 25, 1847.
26. *The Mississippian*, June 25, July 2 and 9, 1847. In his absence, Jefferson Davis had a representative read a letter to the crowd to explain his reasons for not attending the celebration.
27. *The Mississippian*, June 25, July 9, August 6 and 13, 1847.
28. *The Mississippian*, July 30, August 6 and November 11, 1847; *Compiled Service Records of the Mississippi Volunteers in the Mexican War*, M863, Roll #2, Records of Captain John L. McManus. Several members of the regiment wished to continue their military service in the Mexican War. The War Department issued a third call for Mississippi volunteers in July 1847. Philip Muldoon, a veteran of the 1st Mississippi, helped raise a company for the newly authorized Battalion of Mississippi Riflemen. In November, former members of the Marshall Guards were reported to be raising a company for the battalion. Other former members wished to form a company of mounted volunteers for service in Mexico. Captain John L. McManus even offered to have the men of such a mounted company purchase their own mounts, if the government could not provide them with the animals. They were unsuccessful in their endeavors, even with an influential ally such as Jefferson Davis on their side.
29. McIntosh, ed., *Davis Papers*, 3:185–86, 193–94, 207, 215–16; *New Orleans Picayune*, June 4, 1847.
30. *The Woodville Republican*, May 1, 1847.

Chapter 10

1. Dunbar Rowland, *Military History of Mississippi, 1803–1898* (Spartanburg, SC: Reprint Company, 1978), 29.

2. *The Republican*, December 5, 1846. "The regiment will consist of: [Field and Staff] 1 colonel, 1 lieutenant colonel, 1 major, 1 adjutant, a lieutenant to be selected from one of the companies, but not in addition, [Non Commissioned Staff] 1 sergeant major, I first lieutenant, 2 principal musicians, and 10 Companies, each of which will consist of 1 captain, 1 first lieutenant, 2 second lieutenants, 4 sergeants, 4 corporals, and 80 privates. Should the number of privates not fall below 64 on being mustered, they will be received." The companies were allowed to have fewer privates than the 1st Mississippi Rifles.

3. *The Southron*, December 10, 1846.

4. *The Mississippi Democrat*, December 16, 1846.

5. *The Southron*, December 10, 1846; *The Mississippi Democrat*, December 16, 1846; Robert Lorry, Robert and William H. McCradle. *A History of Mississippi* (Jackson, MS: R.H. Henry and Company, 1891), 315–16.

6. *The Southron*, January 1, 1847; Rowland, *Military History of Mississippi*, 29; George Winston Smith and Charles Judah, *Chronicles of the Gringos* (Albuquerque: University of New Mexico Press, 1968), 38–39; *The Mississippi Democrat*, December 30, 1846.

7. H. Grady Howell Jr., ed., *A Southern Lacrimosa: The Mexican War Journal of Dr. Thomas Neely Love, Surgeon, Second Regiment Mississippi Volunteer Infantry, USA* (Madison, MS: Chickasaw Bayou Press, 1995), 1–3.

8. Ibid., 4–9.

9. Ibid., 10–13.

10. Ibid., 14–18.

11. Thomas N. Love, M.D., "Remarks on the Diseases of the 2d Mississippi Rifles," *The New Orleans Medical and Surgical Journal* (July 1848): 4. Portions of Love's article appear in *Chronicles of the Gringos*, 49–53; *The Mississippi Democrat*, December 16, 1846. The camp had been named for Alexander K. McClung, who as lieutenant colonel of the 1st Mississippi Rifles was grievously wounded in his regiment's attack on the Tannery complex at Monterrey, September 21, 1846. *The Mississippi Democrat* reported that the "citizens of Columbus have sent for a splendid sword to be presented to Col. McClung."

12. *The Mississippi Democrat*, January 13, 1847; *The Daily Picayune*, January 8, 1847; Howell, ed., *A Southern Lacrimosa*, 18–19.

13. *The Southron*, December 10, 1846.

14. *The Mississippi Democrat*, December 20, 1846; Howell, ed., *A Southern Lacrimosa*, 21–22; Reuben Davis, *Recollections of Mississippi and Mississippians* (Boston: Houghton Mifflin, 1890), 221–22.

15. *The Republican*, January 23, 1847; Rowland, *Military History of Mississippi*, 30. The following election results were reprinted from *The Vicksburg Whig*. Major: Ezra R. Price, 154; J.W. Winston, 145; E. Downing, 133; W.D. Laird, 95; A.A. Over-

ton, 72; H. Amyx, 58; and A.L. Hamilton, 54. Lieutenant Colonel (1st ballot): George Clark, 305; J.H. Kilpatrick, 254; E.G. Henry, 233 (Clark refused the office unless he had a clear majority, thus a second ballot was held), Kilpatrick, 422; and Clark, 322. From Rowland comes the tally for colonel: Reuben Davis, 485; and B.C. Buckley, 312.

16. *The Mississippi Democrat*, November 4, 1846; Rowland, *Military History of Mississippi*, 19. Price did not wait for his state to call up its volunteers but instead crossed into Louisiana with a company from Mississippi called the Sparrow Volunteers. This company became company E, 4th Louisiana Regiment of Volunteers, and Price was elected one of the company's lieutenants. Enlisted for only three months, the regiment mustered out in August. Price traveled to Monterrey on foot in order to take part in the battle at Monterrey. Illness forced him to leave the 2nd Mississippi, and he returned to the United States for treatment. Price died at Lexington, Kentucky, in July 1848.
17. Davis, *Recollections of Mississippi and Mississippians*, 222.
18. Ibid., 224–25, 228–29.
19. *The Southron*, October 25, 1846.
20. Davis, *Recollections of Mississippi and Mississippians*, 223.
21. *The Mississippian*, July 7, 1847; Davis, *Recollections of Mississippi and Mississippians*, 222. Davis gave a short account of his service with the 2nd Mississippi Rifles in his autobiography that was published the same year of his death.
22. Thomas N. Love, M.D., "Remarks on the Diseases of the 2d Mississippi Rifles," *The New Orleans Medical and Surgical Journal* (July 1848): 4; Howell, ed., *A Southern Lacrimosa*, 24–25.
23. Love, "Diseases of the 2d Mississippi," 4, 7, 8; Howell, ed., *A Southern Lacrimosa*, 26.The symptoms Love describes for the "cold plague" are similar to meningitis, outbreaks of which can occur in camp-like situations.
24. *The Daily Picayune*, January 10 and 20, 1847; *The Courier*, January 15, 1847; *The New Orleans Commercial Bulletin*, January 15 and 18, 1847; Love, "Diseases of the 2d Mississippi," 4; Howell, ed., *A Southern Lacrimosa*, 26.
25. Howell, ed., *A Southern Lacrimosa*, 29.
26. *New Orleans Picayune*, January 21, 1848.
27. J. Jacob Oswandel, *Notes on the Mexican War, 1846–1848* (Philadelphia: n.p., 1885), 40.
28. Davis, *Recollections of Mississippi and Mississippians*, 230.
29. *New Orleans Picayune*, January 24 and January 27, 1848.
30. Howell, ed., *A Southern Lacrimosa*, 34–36.
31. *New Orleans Picayune*, January 27, 1848.
32. *New Orleans Picayune*, January 29, 1848.
33. Davis, *Recollections of Mississippi and Mississippians*, 230; Love, "Diseases of the 2d Mississippi," 5; *The Mississippian*, July 9, 1847; Howell, ed., *A Southern Lacrimosa*, 33–35; *The Daily Picayune*, January 20, 24, and 29, 1847; *The Southron*, Febru-

ary 5, 1847; John Duffy, ed., *The Rudolph Matas History of Medicine in Louisiana* (2 vols.; Baton Rouge: Louisiana State University Press, 1958), 2:216 and 229.

34. Howell, ed., *A Southern Lacrimosa*, 32.

35. *The Mississippian*, July 9, 1847.

36. *The Southron*, February 5, 1847; *The Courier*, January 29, 1847; *The Daily Picayune*, January 24 and 27, 1847.

37. US Congress, House of Representatives, "Relative to the Conditions of the Second Mississippi Rifles and the Mississippi Battalion in New Orleans," 30th Cong., 1st Sess., Misc. Doc. No. 66 1848, Jenkins Garrett Collection, University of Texas at Arlington; *The Mississippian*, January 25, 1848; *The Southron*, February 5, 1847. This resolution was passed by the Mississippi legislature on March 24, 1848, over a year after the regiment was in New Orleans. A third Mississippi unit, a battalion of riflemen, also suffered in the city at another time. Two months earlier, the Mississippi legislature voted to provide $3,000 and $2,000, respectively, for the relief of the 2nd Mississippi Rifles and the Battalion of Mississippi Riflemen, still in the field.

38. *New Orleans Picayune*, January 22 and 30, 1848.

39. *New Orleans Picayune*, January 30, 1847; *The Southron*, February 5, 1847.

40. Oswandel, *Notes*, 30, 32–35, 37–40.

41. *The Daily Picayune*, January 1 and February 3, 1847; and Love, "Diseases of the 2d Mississippi," 5.

42. Oswandel, *Notes*, 30, 32–35, 37–40; *The Daily Picayune*, January 22, 30, and 31, 1847; *The Courier*, January 27, 28, 29 and February 1, 1847; *The New Orleans Commercial Bulletin*, January 6, 8, 26, 28, 30 and February 1, 1847; and Smith and Judah, *Chronicles of the Gringos*, 46–47.

43. Howell, ed., *A Southern Lacrimosa*, 42.

44. Howell, ed., *A Southern Lacrimosa*, 38–39, 45.

45. Love, "Diseases of the 2d Mississippi," 5, 6, 13; Howell, ed., *A Southern Lacrimosa*, 43; *The Woodville Republican*, March 20, 1847; *The Mississippian*, July 9, 1847.

46. Davis, Recollections, 230–31; *The Mississippian*, July 9 and 10, 1847; *The Woodville Republican*, March 20, 1847; Compiled Service Records of the Mississippi Volunteers in the Mexican War, Roll #4; K. Jack Bauer, *Surfboats and Horse Marines* (Annapolis: United States Naval Institute, 1969), 72. From the Compiled Service Records, the regiment landed at Lobos on February 14 and February 19, 1847. It re-embarked on the 24th of the month and landed at Brazos Island on February 28 and March 3. According to Bauer, Scott intended to use the 1st and 2nd Pennsylvania, the New York volunteers, and the Louisiana volunteers as part of his force. The South Carolina regiment had also arrived at Lobos Island by mistake, but it was allowed by Scott to stay. The 2nd Mississippi Rifles, however, were sent back to the mouth of the Rio Grande, and their transports then picked up some of Worth's regulars for the trip to Lobos Island.

47. Howell, ed., *A Southern Lacrimosa*, 56–57, 62.

48. Davis, *Recollection*, 232–33; Howell, ed., *A Southern Lacrimosa*, 62; *The Mississippian*, July 30, 1847.

Chapter 11

1. H. Grady Howell Jr., ed., *A Southern Lacrimosa: The Mexican War Journal of Dr. Thomas Neely Love, Surgeon, Second Regiment Mississippi Volunteer Infantry, USA* (Madison, MS: Chickasaw Bayou Press, 1995), 66–67.
2. Ibid., 69.
3. Rueben Davis, *Recollections of Mississippi and Mississippians* (Boston: Houghton Mifflin, 1889), 231–32. Davis recalled arriving at Brazos Santiago on February 23, 1847, the day of the Battle of Buena Vista. He contended that he had the regiment unloaded and moving up the river the next day. This is not true.
4. Davis, *Recollections*, 233–35; Howell, ed., *A Southern Lacrimosa*, 79–80.
5. Davis, *Recollections*, 232–33, 240–43; Howell, ed., *A Southern Lacrimosa*, 81–85, 87, 90. In his memoirs, Davis claims that it was he that recognized the disease as smallpox and that Love refused to believe it. Once the regiment reached Monterrey, Love collected statements from the regiment's officers to show that he had warned the colonel that the men had smallpox and that Davis had brought the sick men forward against his recommendations.
6. Davis, *Recollections*, 232–33, 240–43.
7. Howell, ed., *A Southern Lacrimosa*, 47–51, 86, 90–91.
8. Graham A. Barringer, ed., "The Mexican War Journal of Henry S. Lane," *Indiana Magazine of History* 53 (1957): 418; Wallace, Lew. *An Autobiography* (2 vols.; New York: Harper & Brothers, 1904), 1:123 and 136; R.C. Burley, "Indiana in the Mexican War: The Indiana Volunteers," *Indiana Magazine of History* 15 (September 1919): 283–85. Barringer confused the two Mississippi regiments and identified the Mississippians at Matamoros on March 5, 1847, as Col. Jefferson Davis' regiment when in fact it was Col. Reuben Davis, 2nd Mississippi Rifles. The 1st Mississippi Rifles were still at Saltillo on the date mentioned by Lane. The 1st Indiana had been left behind while the 2nd and 3rd Indiana were allowed to accompany Taylor. Feeling neglected, the men of the 1st Indiana resented this treatment by Taylor and were eager to move ahead. Wallace said that the 1st Indiana had taken over the camp from the 1st Mississippi and the 2nd Mississippi took the camp over from the 1st Indiana.
9. Davis, *Recollections*, 232; and Andrew Jackson Trussell, "Letter to James Madison Trussell," October 28, 1847, GA66–3, Trussell Family Papers, Jenkins Garrett Collection, University of Texas at Arlington (hereafter Trussell Papers). Davis incorrectly claimed that Buckley resigned soon after the incident. Buckley was in command of the regiment for a time during the summer of 1847. However, he did resign from the service in October later that year.
10. Davis, *Recollections*, 235, 239.
11. Trussell Papers, "Letter to James Madison Trussell," March 19, 1847, GA66–3.
12. Davis, *Recollections*, 240–43.
13. Ibid.
14. Ibid., 243–54. Taylor had sent Lt. Col. Thomas T. Fauntleroy with 500 troopers of the 2nd US Dragoons and Col. James P. Drake and the 1st Indiana Infantry to Caidereta [Cadereyta] to support the train in case it was attacked.

15. *The Mississippian*, June 11, 1847.
16. Howell, ed., *A Southern Lacrimosa*, 89–90.
17. Ibid., 89–99.
18. Davis, *Recollections*, 246–48; Howell, ed., *A Southern Lacrimosa*, 106–8.
19. Eleanor Damon Pace, ed., "The Diary of William P. Rogers, 1846–1862," *The Southwestern Historical Quarterly* 32.4 (April 1929): 284. According to Pace, Reuben Davis later married Rogers' sister-in-law. Rogers and Davis had been friends before the war.
20. Ibid.
21. Barringer, ed., "The Mexican War Journal of Henry S. Lane," 423, 429. Lane attributed some of the illness suffered by the 2nd Mississippi to their frequent "sprees."
22. *Compiled Service Records of the Mississippi Volunteers in the Mexican War*, National Archives Microfilm, M863, Roll 4; Howell, ed., *A Southern Lacrimosa*, 113.
23. Ibid., 125.
24. Ibid., 118.
25. Ibid., 108–9.
26. Ibid., 113, 118, 120–25.
27. Ibid., 113–14, 119.
28. Ibid., 116–17.
29. Andrew Brown, *History of Tippah County, Mississippi: The First Century* (Ripley, MS: Tippah County Historical and Genealogy Society, n.d.), 80–84; Marcus Cunliffe, *Soldiers & Civilians: The Martial Sprit in America, 1776–1865* (Boston: Little, Brown, 1968), 405. Lieutenant Hindman's claim of Falkner's unauthorized visit to Aguas Calientes may have been forgiven by Falkner except that Hindman and his father tried to block Falkner's 1849 attempt to qualify for a government pension because of his wounds. Falkner stabbed Robert Holt Hindman to death after the latter's gun misfired as he tried to shoot Falkner. Another victim of the feud, Erasmus W. Morris, was shot dead by Falkner in 1851. During the Civil War, Hindman rose to the rank of major general in the Confederate Army. Falkner—the grandfather of the American author William Faulkner—wrote several pieces of literature, including two epic poems based on the Mexican War: *The Spanish Heroine* and *The Siege of Monterey*. Faulkner was shot and killed by a former business partner on November 5, 1889.
30. Richmond, ed., "Andrew Trussell in the Mexican War," 86; Trussell Papers, "Letter to James Madison Trussell," June 27, 1847, GA66–3; *The Mississippian*, June 21 and August 8, 1847.
31. Ibid.
32. Love, "Diseases of the 2d Mississippi," 13.
33. Joseph E. Chance, ed. *Mexico Under Fire: Being the Diary of Samuel Ryan Curtis, 3rd Ohio Volunteer Regiment, During the American Military Occupation of Northern Mexico, 1846–1847* (Fort Worth: Texas Christian University Press, 1994), 193–94; Clara Ehinger, ed., "Augustus Ehinger: Diary of His Travels from Illinois to Mexico, and During His Services as a Member of Company H, Second Regiment

Illinois Volunteers, During the Mexican War," Typed Manuscript, Property of Mrs. W.C. Preston, Fort Worth Public Library, Genealogy, Local History and Archives, 60 and 62.

34. Richmond, ed., "Andrew Trussell in Mexico," 88; Trussell Papers, "Letter to James M. Trussell," June 6, 1847, GA66–3.

35. Justin Smith, *The War with Mexico* (2 vols.; Gloucester, MA: Peter Smith, 1963), 1:417; *The Mississippian*, July 30, 1847.

36. Jefferson Davis, "Autobiography of Jefferson Davis," *Bedford's Magazine* (January 1890), 260; *The Mississippian*, August 6, 1847; John Porter Bloom, "With the American Army in Mexico" (PhD dissertation, Emory University, Ann Arbor, MI: University Microfilms International, 1955), 63. Offered the rank of brigadier general by President Polk, Jefferson Davis turned it down, explaining, "I declined on the grounds that volunteers are militia, and that the Constitution reserved to the State the appointment of all militia officers."

37. Trussell Papers, "Letter to E.M. Eubanks," July 10, 1847, GA66–3.

38. Mary Ellen Rowe, ed., "The Mexican War Diary of Chesley Sheldon Coffey," *The Journal of Mississippi History* 44.3 (August 1982): 250.

39. Trussell Papers, "Letter to James M. Trussell," June 27, 1847, GA66–3; "Letter to E. M. Eubanks," July 10, 1847, GA66–3; *The Mississippian*, July 16, 1847.

40. Miguel E. Soto, "Andrew Jackson Trussell in Mexico," in *Essays on the Mexican War*, edited by Wayne Culter, John S. Eisenhower, Miguel Soto, and Douglas Richmond (College Station: Texas A&M University Press, 1986), 88; Stella M. Drumm, ed., *Down the Santa Fe Trail and into Mexico: The Diary of Susan Shelby Magoffin, 1846–1848* (Lincoln: University of Nebraska Press, 1982), 362; Lew Wallace, *An Autobiography* (2 vols.; New York: Harper & Brothers, 1904), 1:192. Brigadier General John Ellis Wool had distinguished himself at the Battle of Plattsburg during the War of 1812. He was unpopular with the volunteers, some of whom thought the general wore his sword even while he ate and slept.

41. Rowe, "Mexican War Letters of Chesley Sheldon Coffey," 246.

42. US Congress, House of Representatives, *Forces Employed in the Mexican War: Letters from the Secretary of War Transmitting Information in Answer to a Resolution of the House, of July 31, 1847, Relative to the Military Forces Employed in the Late War with Mexico.* 31st Cong., 1st Sess., 1850, Exec. Doc. No. 24, 22c; Bloom, "With the American Army in Mexico,"173. Bloom stated that a high percentage of desertion among volunteers occurred in the United States on route to embarkation to Mexico.

Chapter 12

1. H. Grady Howell Jr., ed., *A Southern Lacrimosa: The Mexican War Journal of Dr. Thomas Neely Love, Surgeon, Second Regiment Mississippi Volunteer Infantry, USA* (Madison, MS: Chickasaw Bayou Press, 1995), 208.

2. Ibid., 208.

3. *The Mississippian*, July 9, 1847. It was reported that Carleton R. Munford had killed Lt. Washington S. Mahan. Mahan died at China on June 1, 1847.

4. William S. Hoffman, *North Carolina in the Mexican War* (Raleigh: State Department of Archives and History, 2nd printing, 1963), 20; Samuel E. Chamberlain, *My Confession: The Recollections of a Rouge* (Lincoln: University of Nebraska Press, 1987), 168–72. The uninvited guest who started the brawl was Samuel Chamberlain. He provides a colorful account of the affair in *My Confession*.
5. Douglas Richmond, "Andrew Jackson Trussell in Mexico," in *Essays on the Mexican War*, edited by Wayne Culter, John S. Eisenhower, Miguel Soto, and Douglas Richmond (College Station: Texas A&M University Press, 1986), 94.
6. Mary Ellen Rowe, ed., "The Mexican War Diary of Chesley Sheldon Coffey, "*The Journal of Mississippi History* 44.3 (August 1982): 29. Coffey wrote of the lodge saying "we got a Lodge with us we have a Greate Eal [sic] of work to Do as much as Could be Expected Agadent Wilcox is the master I my Self am the S.W. & Capt Daniels is J.W. Henry J. Davis has taken one Degree I told the master that I had presented his patition to Tho-hinds Lodge and it was with Drew but from mis Conduct Since he has bin her is verry Good and I Could not vote a Ganst him myself I think that he will make a pretty good mason."
7. Chamberlain, *Confessions of a Rouge*, 144–45.
8. US Congress, Senate, *Message from the President of the United States in Answer to a Resolution of the Senate, Calling for the Proceedings of the Court of Inquiry Convened at Saltillo, Mexico, January 12, 1848, for the Purpose of Obtaining Full Information Relative to an Alleged Mutiny at Buena Vista, about 15th August, 1847*. 30th, 1st Sess., Senate Exec. Doc. No. 62; Richard B. Winders, "Will the Regiment Stand It?" in Richard V. Francaviglia and Douglas W. Richmond, eds., *Dueling Eagles: Reinterpreting the US-Mexican War, 1846–1848* (Fort Worth: Texas Christian University Press, 2000), 68–90.
9. US Congress, House of Representatives, 30th Cong., 1st Sess., Ex. Doc. No. 78, 4, 14.
10. Ibid., 1–3, 5–5.
11. Ibid., 8–9.
12. William S. Hoffman, *North Carolina in the Mexican War* (Raleigh: State Department of Archives and History, 2nd printing, 1963), 20–21; George Winston Smith and Charles Judah, *Chronicles of the Gringos* (Albuquerque: University of New Mexico Press, 1968), 424–31; US Congress, Senate, 30th Cong., 1st Sess., Senate Exec. Doc. No. 62, 6, 67, 96, 114, 115, 116, 161, 172, 187, 204.
13. US War Department, Office of Adjutant General, *Court Martial Records of Lieutenant Flemish Amyx, 2nd Mississippi Rifles*, September 28, 1847, EE553, National Archives, Washington, DC.
14. US War Department, *Court Martial Records*; Trussell Papers, "Letter to James Madison Trussell," October 26, 1847. GA66–3.
15. US War Department, *Court Martial Records*; Trussell Papers, "Letter to James Madison Trussell," October 26, 1847, GA66–3; William Hughs Robarts, *Mexican War Veterans: A Complete Roster of the Regular and Volunteers Troops in the War Between the United States and Mexico, From 1846–1848* (Washington, DC: Brentano's, 1887), 9. Robarts compiled a catalog of the various volunteer units with

a list of officers, but not enlisted men, from each unit. Trussell noted that one of the two Mexicans who killed the two Mississippians at the ranch was hanged on October 18, 1847—the same day the election to fill the post of lieutenant colonel was held.

16. Soto, "Andrew Trussell in Mexico," 91.
17. US War Department, *Court Martial Records.*
18. Soto, "Andrew Trussell in Mexico," 91.
19. *Compiled Service Records of the Mississippi Volunteers in the Mexican War*, National Archives Microfilm, M863, Roll 4; Jefferson Davis, "Autobiography of Jefferson Davis," *Bedford's Magazine* (January 1890): 260; Dunbar Rowland, *Military History of Mississippi, 1803–1898* (Spartanburg, SC: Reprint Company, 1978), 8; Joseph E. Chance, ed., *Mexico Under Fire: Being the Diary of Samuel Ryan Curtis, 3rd Ohio Volunteer Regiment, During the American Military Occupation of Northern Mexico, 1846–1847* (Fort Worth: Texas Christian University Press, 1994), 208; James T. McIntosh, ed., *The Papers of Jefferson Davis* (5 vols.; Baton Rouge: Louisiana State University Press, 1974), 3:194–95; Clement Eaton, *Jefferson Davis* (New York: The Free Press, 1977), 64.
20. US War Department, *Order No, 454, By Command of Brig. Gen. Wool, Head Quarters Buena Vista*, September 20, 1847, National Archives, Washington, DC.
21. Soto, "Andrew Trussell in Mexico," 90; Trussell Papers, "Letter to James Madison Trussell," October 26, 1847, GA66–3. (Note: The edited version of Trussell's October 26, 1847, letter omits details of the election.) Election of colonel: First ballot, October 15, 1847: Clarke, 166; Wilcox, 155; Buckley, 102; and Amyx, 67. As in the January 1847 election for colonel, Clark refused to take the office unless he received a majority. Second ballot, October 16, 1847: Buckley and Amyx withdrew; Clark, 246; and Wilcox, 227. Clark accepted the position and became the regiment's new colonel. Election for Lieutenant Colonel: October 18, 1847: Wilcox, 237; McWillie, 141; and Blythe, 98. Of the officers in Trussell's company, Daniels, Trussel, and [Edward B.] Shelton wanted Clark and McWillie, but [Jesse G.] Steele favored Wilcox.
22. *The Mississippian*, November 5, 1847.
23. Rowe, ed., "Letters of Chesley Shelton Coffey," 250–51; Bloom, "With the American Army in Mexico," 153.
24. Soto, "Andrew Trussell in Mexico," 95–96.
25. Chamberlain, *My Confession*, 145. For a review of the American relationship with Mexican women, see Bloom, "With the American Army in Mexico," 271–80, in his chapter, "Gringos and Greaser-itas.
26. Benjamin F. Workman Papers, Mississippi Department of Archives and History.
27. Mississippi Department of Archives and History, Special Collections Section, Manuscript Collection, Access No. 88.01, "David Cameron to Allan A. Cameron, November 21, 1847."
28. Soto, "Andrew Trussell in Mexico," 91, 93.
29. Trussell Papers, "Letter to James Madison Trussell," January 9, 1848, GA66–4. The story about the women in the ranks of the 2nd Mississippi Rifles appeared in

an article titled "Notes from Captain Tom Tobins" and was printed in *The Mississippian*, November 19, 1847.

30. US War Department, Office of the Adjutant General, *Court Martial Records of Bugler Victor Galbraith, Arkansas Cavalry*, Buena Vista, November 1, 1847, EE611, National Archives, Washington, DC; Soto, "Andrew Trussell in Mexico," 94; Robarts, *Mexican War Veterans*, 59–60; US Congress, House of Representatives, *Military Forces Employed in the Mexican War: Letters from the Secretary of War Transmitting Information in Answer to a Resolution of the House, of July 31, 1847, Relative to the Military Forces Employed in the Late War with Mexico*, 31st Cong., 1st Sess., 1850, Exec. Doc. No. 24, 22h. Also see Chamberlain, *My Confession*, 224–26, for a colorful account of the execution and his version of the events leading up to it. Captain Gaston Meares was allowed to raise a mounted company at Buena Vista out of volunteers mustered out of Colonel Yell's old 12-month regiment. Mearse's remustered mounted volunteers saw service in the area around Saltillo from May 1847 until June 1848. Mearse had served as a lieutenant and adjutant of Yell's regiment until the death of the colonel at Buena Vista. After Yell's death, Lt. Col. John Sheldon Roane was elected colonel and Mearse was elected lieutenant colonel of the Arkansas Cavalry.

31. Soto, "Andrew Trussell in Mexico," 94–96.

32. Josiah Gregg, *Diaries and Letter of Josiah Gregg* (2 vols.; Norman: University of Oklahoma Press, 1941), 2:218.

33. Soto, "Andrew Trussell in Mexico," 92, 95–96; Bloom, "With the American Army in Mexico," 9. According to *Compiled Service Records*, Roll #5, Jackson did resigned on March 5, 1848, but reenlisted in his old company 14 days later and was reelected captain on March 25, 1848.

34. Rowland, *Military History of Mississippi*, 31; Soto, "Andrew Trussell in Mexico," 95; *Compiled Service Records of the Mississippi Volunteers*, M863, Roll #4.

35. Soto, "Andrew Trussell in Mexico," 98–99.

36. Gregg, *Letters and Diaries of Josiah Gregg*, 2:218–19.

37. Rowland, *Military History of Mississippi*, 31. The citizens of Wilkinson County treated their returning volunteers to a barbecue at Fort Adams on August 3, 1848.

38. *New Orleans Picayune*, July 21, 1848.

Chapter 13

1. Justin Smith, *The War with Mexico* (2 vols. Gloucester, MA: Peter Smith, 1963), 1:207–8; K. Jack Bauer, *The Mexican War* (New York: Macmillan, 1974), 83. Smith claimed that the volunteers needed four to five months of strict training and discipline to make them good soldiers. They were naturally alien to the habits of real soldiers, and, in the absence of an enemy, the volunteers were prone to fight each other. Some of the officers, especially general officers of volunteers, were devoid of any qualifications necessary for their rank.

2. H. Grady Howell Jr., *Mississippi Rifles: A Muster of All Known Mississippi Soldiers, Sailors, and Marines Who Served in the Mexican War, 1846–1848* (Greenville, SC:

Southern Historical Press, 2005), 10. The 1st Mississippi was raised chiefly from the following counties: Carroll, Hinds, Lafayette, Warren, Wilkinson, and Yazoo. The 2nd Mississippi was raised mainly from the counties of: Tippah, Lauderdale, Jefferson, Panola, Attala, Lawrence, and Covington. Companies, or parts of companies, for both regiments came from Lowndes, Marshall, and Monroe counties.

3. Robert Lorwy and William H. McCradle. *A History of Mississippi* (Jackson, MI: R.H. Henry and Company, 1891), 315; Philip R.N. Katcher, *The Mexican-American War, 1846–1848* (London: Osprey, 1989), 5. Lowry and McCradle concluded that "If the opportunity had been afforded them [2nd Miss.] there can be no doubt that they would have shed additional luster upon American arms, and added new glory to the escutcheon of Mississippi." Katcher noted that fewer deaths by volunteers in battle resulted not from their unwillingness to fight but from the lack of opportunity to do so.

4. Jefferson Davis drew praise from his superiors and the regular officers with whom he worked. See comments concerning Davis after Buena Vista in chapter 9.

5. Rueben Davis, *Recollections of Mississippi and Mississippians* (Boston: Houghton Mifflin, 1889), 223, 252, 253; Andrew Brown, *History of Tippah County, Mississippi: The First Century* (Ripley, MS: Tippah County Historical and Genealogy Society, n.d.), 77. Although Rueben Davis had been a brigadier general in the Mississippi militia, he lacked the skill and desire to command a regiment in wartime. Davis acknowledged his shortcomings in his biography, writing that, even though he was not the best commander, he had always tried to discharge his duties as colonel faithfully.

6. Clement Eaton, *Jefferson Davis* (New York: The Free Press, A Division of McMillan Publishing Company, 1977), x; Cass Canfield, *The Iron Will of Jefferson Davis* (New York: Harcourt Brace Jovanovich, 1978), 51. According to Eaton, Davis was an extremely sensitive man who often presented a stoic front to those around him. Canfield used the works of two other writers, Samuel E. Morris and Allen Tate, to illustrate aspects of Davis's personality that sometimes caused trouble for him. Morris said that Davis could be very charming but that he lacked tact. Davis was unwilling to delegate authority and had the habit of antagonizing people around him. Tate states that Davis "could not manage men, and he was too great a character to let men manage him." In *Jefferson Davis: The Man and the Hour, A Biography* (New York: HarperCollins, 1991), William C. Davis weaves Davis's personality throughout his biography, explaining how his traits shaped his own life as well as the events in which he was involved.

7. Hudson Strode, *Jefferson Davis: Private Letters, 1823–1889* (Harcourt, Brace & World, 1966), 44; Grady McWhiney, "Jefferson Davis and the Art of War," *Civil War History* 2.2 (June 1978): 110.

8. Davis, *Recollections*, 236; Eleanor Damon Pace, ed., "The Diary of William P. Rogers, 1846–1862," *The Southwestern Historical Quarterly* 32.4 (April 1929): 265.

9. Lowry and McCradle, *History of Mississippi*, 311; *The Mississippi Democrat*, October 14, 1846. The notion that the members of the 1st Mississippi were "young planters and professional gentlemen" appeared during the war and has been carried forward by other writers. In their history of Mississippi, Lowry and McCra-

dle write that the men of the regiment came from the best families of Mississippi. This notion was very likely bravado and cannot be proved or disproved without an exhaustive effort to determine the economic background of these volunteers.

10. Samuel E. Chamberlain, *My Confession: The Recollections of a Rouge* (Lincoln: University of Nebraska Press, 1987), 144–45; Francis A. Lord, *They Fought for the Union* (New York: Bonanza Books, 1960), 3. In his work on federal soldiers in the Civil War, Lord claims that those soldiers who volunteered first were unreliable. He says of later volunteers, "He had not enlisted in the spring of 1861 because he was bound by domestic and economic ties that were not easily severed as were those less stable elements that were usually found to predominate in the militia units that responded to earlier calls." This view of volunteers differs from that advanced by Chamberlain who claimed the later volunteers were inferior to the 12-month volunteers.

11. Bloom, "With the American Army in Mexico," 14. Bloom attributed the willingness of the volunteers to go to Mexico to a desire to see the world, patriotism, ambition, combativeness, and pride.

12. For a collection of writings of various Mexican War soldiers representing different regions of the United States, see Bloom, "With the American Army in Mexico" and Judah and Smith, *Chronicles of the Gringos.*

13. R.C. Burley, "Indiana in the Mexican War: The Buena Vista Campaign," *Indiana Magazine of History* 15.4 (December 1919): 309. The 1st Indiana's career was similar to that of the 2nd Mississippi—it was kept in the rear and saw no action. At the end of the regiment's term of service, Taylor sent the following lines to Col. James Drake: "All must know who are in the slightest degree acquainted with military operations in carrying on a war in an enemy's country, over long lines from a base of operations, which has been our case, that a considerable portion of the troops employed must be engaged in guarding depots, keeping open lines of communication, escorting trains, etc., which are as important, arduous and dangerous as the duties of those engaged in battle, each depending upon the other to insure success, therefore equally honorable to all concerned."

14. Dunbar Rowlan, *Military History of Mississippi, 1803–1898* (Spartanburg, SC: Reprint Company, 1978), 35, 37–39, 58, 61, 64, 70, 73, 75, 78, 100, 102, 148, 208, 235, 237, 240, 308, 504, 561; Lowry and McCradle, *History of Mississippi*, 313–15. For Mississippi's involvement in the Confederacy during the Civil War, see General Clement A. Evans, ed., *Confederate Military History* (13 vols.; Confederate Publishing Company, 1899; The Blue & Grey Press, n.d.); Vol. 12, *Alabama and Mississippi*. 239–41, 247–49, 250–51, 256–58, and 265–66.

15. Rowland, *Military History of Mississippi*, 34, 38–39, 40, 45, 50, 53–55, 66, 89–90, 92–94, 99, 145, 147–48, 235, 239, 324, 330, 333, 354, 356–57, 375, 452, 500; Lowry and McCradle, *History of Mississippi*, 315–16.

16. Hudson Stode, *Jefferson Davis: American Patriot* (New York: Harcourt Brace, 1955), 194; Grady McWhiney and Perry D. Jamieson, *Attack and Die: Civil War Military Tactics and the Southern Heritage* (Tuscaloosa: University of Alabama Press, 1982), 27; Steven E. Woodward, *Jefferson Davis and His Generals: The Failure of Confederate Command in the West* (Lawrence: University Press of Kansas, 1990), 9–10.

Strode says that Davis emerged from the Mexican War as one of the nation's most lauded leaders. The numerous newspaper accounts that appeared throughout the United States describing the deeds of Davis and his regiment supports this statement. Strode thought that the "V" formation at Buena Vista was less important to the success of the battle than Davis's own courage and ability. Davis, though, continued to think that he and his regiment had played a vital role in the American victory in the war. On his return to the United States, Davis told the Mississippi legislature that his Mississippians had "in no small degree contributed to the triumph which finally perched upon the banner of the United States."

17. Marcus Cunliffe, *Soldiers & Civilians: The Martial Sprit in America, 1776–1865* (Boston: Little, Brown, 1968), 415. Up to this point the term "Riflemen" had conjured up images of independent woodsmen in the mind of the American public. The popular image of the "Hunters of Kentucky" beating back the British at New Orleans and sharp-eyed frontiersmen, such as David Crockett picking off Mexicans at the Alamo are still an important part of the American heritage.

18. *Appendix to the Congressional Globe*, 33rd Cong., 2nd Sess., December 4, 1854, 18.

19. *Appendix to the Congressional Globe*, 33rd Cong., 2nd Sess., December 4, 1854, 18; McWhiney and Jamieson, *Attack and Die*, 49–50; Nathaniel Cheairs Hughes Jr., *General William J. Hardee: Old Reliable* (Baton Rouge: Louisiana University State Press, 1992), 41–50. Originally published in 1965, Hughes' chapter on Hardee's role in developing the tactics manual that bears his name has come the closest to linking Davis in any significant way. The manual easily could have been called *Davis's Tactics* instead of *Hardee's Tactics*. Hughes contends that Davis, who had a good command of written French, worked with Hardee on the project on a "daily" basis.

Appendix 1

1. Frederick P. Todd, *American Military Equipage, 1851–1872* (3 vols.; (Providence, RI: Company of Military Historians, 1974), 1:118; Ralph E. Arnold, "US Model 1841 Rifle: The Famous 'Mississippi,'" *The Gun Report* 1.4 (September 1973): 14–21.

2. The type of accoutrements issued to the Mississippians was determined by examining the *Combined Service Records of the Mississippi Volunteers in the Mexican War*, Washington, DC, Microfilm Series M863, National Archives, Rolls 1–8.

3. George Winston Smith and Charles Judah, *Chronicles of the Gringos* (Albuquerque: University of New Mexico Press, 1968), 384.

4. Winfield Scott, *Abstract of Infantry Tactics; Including Exercising and Manoeuvres of Light Infantry and Riflemen; For the Use of the Militia of the United States* (Boston: Hilliard, Gray, Little, and Wilkins, 1830), 99–100.

5. Richard Bruce Winders, *Mr. Polk's Army: The American Military Experience in the Mexican War* (College Station: Texas A&M University Press, 1997), 96; Headquarters of the Army, Adjutant General's Office, Washington, [DC], General Order No. 44, October 30, 1844.

BIBLIOGRAPHY

Government Documents

Appendix to the Congressional Globe. 33rd Congress, 2nd Session, December 4, 1854, 18.

Compiled Service Records of the Mississippi Volunteers in the Mexican War. National Archives Microfilm, M863, 9 Rolls.

Congressional Globe. 29th Congress, 1st Session, December 1, 1845–August 10, 1846, 788–95.

US Congress, House of Representatives. 31st Congress, 1st Session, 1850. *Adjutant General's Report of the Forces Employed in the Mexican War*. Executive Document No. 24.

US Congress, House of Representatives. "Relative to the Conditions of the Second Mississippi Rifles and the Mississippi Battalion in New Orleans." 30th Congress, 1st Session, 1848, Misc. Document No. 66.

US Congress, Senate. 30th Congress, 1st Session, 1848. *Message of the President of the United States, in Answer to a Resolution of the Senate, Calling for Proceedings of the Court of Inquiry Convened at Saltillo, Mexico, January 12, 1848, for the Purpose of Obtaining Full Information Relative to an Alleged Mutiny at Buena Vista, about the 15th August 1847*. Senate Executive Document No. 62.

US War Department. *Order No, 454, By Command of Brig. Gen. Wool, Head Quarters Buena* Vista, September 20, 1847. National Archives, Washington, DC.

US War Department. *Report of the Secretary of War of 1847*. Washington, DC: Wendell and Van Benthuysen, 1847.

US War Department, Office of the Adjutant General. *Court Martial Records of Bugler Victor Galbraith, Arkansas Cavalry*, Buena Vista, November 1, 1847, EE611, National Archives, Washington, DC.

US War Department, Office of Adjutant General. *Court Martial Records of Lieutenant Flemish Amyx, 2nd Mississippi Rifles*. September 28, 1847, EE553, National Archives, Washington, DC.

Archives

Browning, James C. Diary. Mississippi Department of Archives and History, Jackson.

Ehinger, Clara, ed. "Augustus Ehinger: Diary of His Travels from Illinois to Mexico, and During His Services as a Member of Company H, Second Regiment Illinois Volunteers, During the Mexican War." Typed Manuscript, Property of Mrs. W.C. Preston, Fort Worth Public Library, Genealogy, Local History and Archives.

Howell, Joseph Davis. Mississippi Department of Archives and History, Jackson.

Smith, Chance Franklin. The Mexican War Diary of Captain Franklin Smith, Mississippi Department of Archives and History, Archives and Library Division, Record No. Z618.

Trussell Family Papers. Jenkins Garrett Collection, University of Texas at Arlington.

University of Texas, Center for American History. "Howard Morris, 1st Mississippi Rifles, to Mrs. Pamela Pinkhise, August 18, 1846."

Newspapers

The Courier (New Orleans).

The Daily Picayune (New Orleans).

The Mississippian (Jackson).

The Mississippi Democrat (Carrollton).

The Nashville Union.

The New Orleans Commercial Bulletin.

The New Orleans Times Picayune.

The Southron (Jackson).

The Vicksburg Whig.

The Woodville Republican (Woodville).

Articles

Arnold, Ralph E. "US Model 1841 Rifle: The Famous 'Mississippi.'" *The Gun Report* 19, no. 4 (September 1973): 14–21.

Barringer, Graham A., ed. "The Mexican War Journal of Henry S. Lane." *Indiana Journal of History* 52 (1957): 283–434.

Benham, Henry W. "Recollection of Mexico and the Battle of Buena Vista." Boston: Unpublished copy for *Old and New Magazine*, 1871.

Brent, Robert A. "Mississippi and the Mexican War." *The Journal of Mississippi History* 31, no. 3 (August 1969): 202–14.

Buchanan, A. Russell, ed. "George Washington Trahern: Texan Cowboy Soldier from Mier to Buena Vista." *Southwestern Historical Quarterly* 58 (July 1954): 60–90.

Burley, R.C. "Indiana in the Mexican War: The Buena Vista Campaign." *Indiana Magazine of History* 15, no. 4 (December 1919): 292–326.

Burley, R.C. "Indiana in the Mexican War: The Buena Vista Controversy." *The Indiana Magazine of History* 15 (March 1920): 46–68.

Burley, R.C. "Indiana in the Mexican War: The Indiana Volunteers." *Indiana Magazine of History* 15 (September 1919): 260–92.

Campbell, William B. "Mexican War Letters of William Bowen Campbell, of Tennessee, Written to Governor David Campbell, of Virginia, 1846–1847." *Tennessee Historical Magazine* 1 (June 1915): 129–67.

Davis, Jefferson. "Autobiography of Jefferson Davis." *Bedford's Magazine* (January 1890): 255–76.

Duncan, Louis C. "A Medical History of General Zachary Taylor's Army of Occupation in Texas and Mexico, 1845–1846." *The Military Surgeon: Journal of the Association of Military Surgeons of the United States* 40 (July 1921): 76–104.

Engleman, Otto B., ed. and trans. "The Second Illinois in the Mexican War: Mexican War Letters of Adolph Engleman." *Journal of the Illinois State Historical Society* 26 (January 1934): 257–452.

Estes, William. "The Battle of Monterey." *Fort Worth Gazette*, January 5, 1885.

Holland, James K. "Diary of a Texan Volunteer in the Mexican War." *Southwestern Historical Quarterly* 30 (July 1926): 1–33.

Love, Thomas N., M.D. "Remarks on the Diseases of the 2d Mississippi Rifles." *The New Orleans Medical and Surgical Journal* (July 1848): 1–13.

McWhiney, Grady. "Jefferson Davis and the Art of War." *Civil War History* 2.2 (June 1978): 101–12.

Pace, Eleanor Damon, ed. "The Diary of William P. Rogers, 1846–1862," *The Southwestern Historical Quarterly* 32.4 (April 1929): 259–99.

Ramage, James A. "John Hunt Morgan and the Kentucky Cavalry Volunteers in the Mexican War." *The Register of the Kentucky Historical Society* 81.4 (Autumn 1983): 343–65.

Rowe, Mary Ellen, ed. "The Mexican War Diary of Chesley Sheldon Coffey. "*The Journal of Mississippi History* 44.3 (August 1982): 235–52.

Sailbury, Richard V. "Kentuckians at Buena Vista." *The Filson Club Quarterly* 61.1 (January 1987): 34–53.

"Sketches of Our Volunteer Officer, Alexander Keith McClung." *Southern Literary Messenger* 21 (January 1855): 36–60.

Winston, James E. "Mississippi and the Independence of Texas." *Southwestern Historical Quarterly* 21.4 (July 1917): 36–60.

Maps

Disturnell, John. *A Correct Map of the Seat of the War in Mexico: Being a Copy of General Arista's Map, Taken at Rescaca de la Palma*. New York: John Disturnell, 1847.

Books

Bauer, K. Jack. *Surfboats and Horse Marines*. Annapolis: Macmillan, 1974.

Bauer, K. Jack. *Zachary Taylor: Soldier, Planter, Statesman of the Old Southwest*. Baton Rouge: Louisiana State University Press, 1985.

Brooks, Nathaniel C. *A Complete History of the Mexican War: Its Causes, Conduct, and Consequences*. Philadelphia: Grigg, Elliot, and Company; Baltimore: Hutchison and Seebold, 1849; reprint ed., Chicago: Rio Grande Press, 1965.

Brown, Andrew. *History of Tippah County, Mississippi: The First Century*. Ripley, MS: Tippah County Historical and Genealogy Society, n.d.

[By an] Eye-Witness. *Complete History of the Late War with Mexico*. New York: F.J. Dow and Company, 1850.

Carleton, James Henry. *Battle of Buena Vista*. New York: Harper & Brothers, 1848.

Canfield, Cass. *The Iron Will of Jefferson Davis*. New York and London: Harcourt Brace Jovanovich, 1978.

Chamberlain, Samuel E. *My Confession: The Recollections of a Rouge*. Lincoln: University of Nebraska Press, 1987.

Chance, Joseph E. *Jefferson Davis's Mexican War Regiment*. Jackson: University Press of Mississippi, 1991.

Chance, Joseph E. *The Second Texas Infantry: From Shiloh to Vicksburg*. Austin: Eakin Press, 1984.

Chance, Joseph E., ed. *Mexico under Fire: Being the Diary of Samuel Ryan Curtis, 3rd Ohio Volunteer Regiment, During the American Military Occupation of Northern Mexico, 1846–1847*. Fort Worth: Texas Christian University Press, 1994.

Chance, Joseph E., ed., *My Life in the Old Army: The Reminiscences of Abner Doubleday*. Fort Worth: Texas Christian University Press, 1998.

Chance, Joseph E., ed. *The Mexican War Journal of Captain Franklin Smith*. Jackson: University of Mississippi Press, 1991.

Claiborne, Francis Hamtramack. *Life and Correspondence of John A. Quitman*. 2 vols. New York: Harper & Brothers, 1860.

Cunliffe, Marcus. *Soldiers & Civilians: The Martial Sprit in America, 1776–1865*. Boston: Little, Brown, 1968.

Davis, Rueben. *Recollections of Mississippi and Mississippians*. Boston: Houghton Mifflin, 1889.

Davis, William C. *Jefferson Davis: The Man and the Hour, A Biography*. New York: HarperCollins, 1991.

Disturnell, John. *A Correct Map of the Seat of War in Mexico: Being a Copy of General Aristas Map, Taken at Resaca de la Palma*. New York: John Disturnell, 1847.

Drumm, Stella M., ed. *Down the Santa Fe Trail and into Mexico: The Diary of Susan Shelby Magoffin, 1846–1848*. Lincoln: University of Nebraska Press, 1982.

Duffy, John, ed. *The Rudolph Matas History of Medicine in Louisiana*. 2 vols. Baton Rouge: Louisiana State University Press, 1958.

Eaton, Clement. *Jefferson Davis*. New York: The Free Press, 1977.

Eisenhower, John S.D. *So Far from God: The US War with Mexico, 1846–1848*. New York: Random House, 1989.

Ferrell, Robert H. *Monterrey Is Ours! The Mexican War Letters of Lieutenant Dana, 1845–1847*. Lexington: University of Kentucky Press, 1990.

French, Samuel G. *Two Wars: An Autobiography*. Nashville: The Confederate Veteran, 1901.

Furber, George C. *The Twelve Months Volunteer*. Cincinnati: J.A. and U.P. James, 1848.

Giddings, Luther. *Sketches of a Campaign in Northern Mexico*. New York: G.P. Putnam, 1853.

Gray, William Fairfax. *From Virginia to Texas, 1835*. Houston: Gray, Dillaye, and Company, 1909; reprinted ed., Houston: Fletcher Young, 1965.

Greenberg, Amy S. *A Wicked War: Polk, Clay, Lincoln, and the 1846 US Invasion of Mexico.* New York: Knopf, 2012.

Gregg, Josiah. *Diary and Letters of Josiah Gregg, 1840–1850.* 2 vols. Edited by Maurice Fulton. Norman: University of Oklahoma Press, 1941–44.

Henry, Robert Seth. *The Story of the Mexican War*. Indianapolis: Bobbs-Merrill, 1950.

Hoffman, William S. *North Carolina in the Mexican War*. Raleigh: State Department of Archives and History, 2nd printing, 1963.

Howell, H. Grady Jr., ed. *A Southern Lacrimosa: The Mexican War Journal of Dr. Thomas Neely Love, Surgeon, Second Regiment Mississippi Volunteer Infantry, USA*. Madison, MS: Chickasaw Bayou Press, 1995.

Hughes, Nathaniel Cheairs Jr. *General William J. Hardee: Old Reliable*. Baton Rouge: Louisiana University State Press, 1992.

Huntington, R.T. *Accoutrements of the United States Infantry, Riflemen, and Dragoons: 1834–1839*. Alexandria Bay, NY: Museum Restoration Services, 1987.

Johannsen, Robert W. *To the Halls of the Montezumas: The Mexican War of the Imagination.* New York: Oxford University Press, 1985.

Kenly, John Reese. *Memoirs of a Maryland Volunteer*. Philadelphia: J.B. Lippincott & Co., 1873.

Kennedy, Lawrence F., ed. *The Biographical Dictionary of the American Congress*. Washington, DC: US Government Printing Office, 1971.

Lord, Francis A. *They Fought for the Union*. New York: Bonanza Books, 1960.

Lorwy, Robert, and William H. McCradle. *A History of Mississippi*. Jackson, MS: R.H. Henry and Company, 1891.

McIntosh, James T., ed. *The Papers of Jefferson Davis*. 5 vols. Baton Rouge: Louisiana State University Press, 1974.

McLemore, Richard Aubrey. *A History of Mississippi*. 2 vols. Jackson: University and College Press of Mississippi, 1973.

McWhiney, Grady, and Perry D. Jamieson. *Attack and Die: Civil War Military Tactics and the Southern Heritage*. Tuscaloosa: University of Alabama Press, 1982.

McWhiney, Grady, and Sue McWhiney, eds. *To Mexico with Taylor and Scott, 1845–1847*. Waltham: MA: Blaisdell, 1969.

May, Robert A. *John Anthony Quitman: Old South Crusader*. Baton Rouge: Louisiana State Press, 1985.

Miller, Robert Ryal. *Shamrock and Sword*. Norman: University of Oklahoma Press, 1989.

Mitchell, Samuel Augustus. *An Accompaniment to Mitchell's Reference and Distance Map of the United States*. Philadelphia: Mitchell and Hinman, 1834.

Mitchell, Samuel Augustus. *Mitchell's Geographical Reader: A System of Modern Geography Comprising a Description of the World*. Philadelphia: Thomas, Cowperthwait and Company, 1845.

Montgomery, H. *The Life of Major General Zachary Taylor, 12th President of the United States*. Auburn, NY: Derby & Miller, 1854.

Morris, Richard B., ed. *Encyclopedia of American History*. Revised and enlarged ed. New York: Harper & Brothers, 1961.

Oswandel, Jacob. *Notes on the Mexican War, 1846–1848.* Philadelphia: n.p., 1885.

Perry, Oran. *Indiana in the Mexican War.* Indianapolis: W. B. Burford, 1908.

Risch, Erna. *Quartermaster Support of the Army: History of the Corps, 1775–1939.* Washington, DC: Office of the Quartermaster General, 1962.

Robarts, William Hughs. *Mexican War Veterans: A Complete Roster of the Regular and Volunteers Troops in the War between the United States and Mexico, from 1846–1848.* Washington, DC: Brentano's, 1887.

Robertson, John Blount Robertson. *Reminiscences of a Campaign in Mexico; By a Member of "The Bloody First."* Nashville: John York and Company, 1849.

Rowland, Dunbar. *Military History of Mississippi, 1803–1898.* Spartanburg, SC: Reprint Company, 1978.

Rowland, Dunbar, *Mississippi*, 2 vols. Spartanburg, SC: Reprint Company, 1976.

Sandweiss, Martha A., Rick Stewart, and Ben Huseman, eds., *Eyewitness to War: Prints and Daguerreotypes of the Mexican War.* Fort Worth: Amon Carter Museum; Washington, DC: Smithsonian Institution Press, 1989.

Scott, Winfield. *An Abstract of Infantry: Including Exercises and Maneuvers of Light-Infantry and Riflemen for the Use of the Militia of the United States.* Boston: Hilliard, Gray, Little, and Wilkins, 1830.

Scott, Winfield. *Infantry Tactics.* 3 vols. New York: Harper & Brothers, 1840.

Scribner, Benjamin Franklin. *A Campaign in Mexico.* Philadelphia: J. Gihon, 1850.

Skates, John Ray. *Mississippi: A Bicentennial History.* New York: Norton; Nashville: American Association for State and Local History, 1979.

Smith, George Winston, and Charles Judah. *Chronicles of the Gringos.* Albuquerque: University of New Mexico Press, 1968.

Smith, Justin. *The War with Mexico.* 2 vols. Gloucester, MA: Peter Smith, 1963.

Smith, S. Compton. *Chile Con Carne: or, The Camp and the Field.* New York: Miller & Curtis, 1857.

Spurlin, Charles D. *Texas Veterans in the Mexican War: Muster Rolls of Texas Military Units.* St. Louis, MO: Ingmire, 1984.

Strode, Hudson. *Jefferson Davis: American Patriot, 1808–1861.* New York: Harcourt Brace, 1955.

Strode, Hudson, ed. *Jefferson Davis: Private Letters, 1823–1889.* New York; Harcourt Brace & World, 1966.

Thorpe, T.B. *Our Army at Monterey. Being a Correct Account of the Proceedings and Events which Occurred to the "Army of Occupation" Under the Command of Major General Taylor, From the Time of Leaving Matamoros to the Surrender of Monterey. With a Description of the Three Days' Battle and the Storming of Monterey.* Philadelphia: Carey and Hart, 1848.

Todd, Frederick P. *American Military Equipage, 1851–1872.* 3 vols. Providence, RI: Company of Military Historians, 1974.

Van Evrie, J.H., M.D. *Negroes and Negro Slavery: The First, An Inferior Race—The Latter, Its Normal Condition.* Baltimore: John D. Toy, 1853.

Wallace, Lew. *An Autobiography*. 2 vols. New York: Harper & Brothers, 1904.

US War Department. *General Regulations for the Army of the United States, 1841*. Washington, DC: J. and G. E. Gideon, 1841.

Woodward, Steven E. *Jefferson Davis and His Generals: The Failure of Confederate Command in the West*. Lawrence: University Press of Kansas, 1990.

Theses and Dissertations

Bloom, John Porter. "With the American Army in Mexico." PhD dissertation, Emory University. Ann Arbor, MI: University Microfilms International, 1955.

Honeycutt, Judy. "Mississippi in the Mexican War." Master's thesis, University of Southern Mississippi, 1970.

Lasswell, Lynda Jane. "The First Regiment of Mississippi Infantry in the Mexican War and Letters of Jefferson Davis Concerning the War." Master's thesis, Rice University, May, 1969.

INDEX